D0122304

GREEN HELL

GREEN HELL

HOW ENVIRONMENTALISTS PLAN TO CONTROL YOUR LIFE AND WHAT YOU CAN DO TO STOP THEM

STEVE MILLOY

Since 1947
REGNERY
PUBLISHING, INC.
An Eagle Publishing Company

Cataloging-in-Publication data on file with the Library of Congress

ISBN 978-1-59698-585-8

Published in the United States by
Regnery Publishing, Inc.
One Massachusetts Avenue, NW
Washington, DC 20001
www.regnery.com

Manufactured in the United States of America

10 9 8 7 6 5 4 3 2 1

Books are available in quantity for promotional or premium use. Write to Director of Special Sales, Regnery Publishing, Inc., One Massachusetts Avenue NW, Washington, DC 20001, for information on discounts and terms or call (202) 216-0600.

Distributed to the trade by:
Perseus Distribution
387 Park Avenue South
New York, NY 10016

To Goggy

CONTENTS

INTRODUCTION

Move over red, white, and blue—America is going green. Green energy. Green technology. Green homes. Green cars. Green jobs. Green commerce. Green living. Green government. We've just elected our first green president, Barack Obama, as well as numerous senators and local representatives who campaigned on promises of leading America to greener pastures. You can color our—your—future green.

The green vision goes something like this: we are going to live in a "sustainable" manner and be kind to the planet. We will shrink our carbon footprints, eventually becoming carbon neutral. Thinking globally and acting locally, we will stop climate change and protect wildlife and the wilderness from man's destructive ways. We will end our addiction to oil by repowering America with clean, renewable energy; nay, we will *reinvent* energy. Our goal is a healthy and just planet where people live in harmony with nature.

But perhaps, unlike others in a mad rush to start bicycling, recycling, and carbon de-cycling, you've been distracted from the greening of America by the many other crises and controversies our nation is facing: the global financial meltdown, the wars in Iraq and

Afghanistan, Islamic terrorism, volatile gasoline prices, spiraling health care costs, illegal immigration, and so on. They are, indeed, a formidable lot. That said, it's time you recognize that a great green tsunami is heading your way, threatening to wash away your standard of living and many of your liberties.

Like many Americans, your sense of the green movement may be that it simply advocates small lifestyle changes to benefit the environment. But the green agenda, in fact, is much more ambitious; it promotes countless new restrictions and regulations designed to reorder society from top to bottom.

And so the greens bombard us with an endless list of "dos" and "don'ts": Take colder showers. Turn the heat down. Use less air conditioning. Dry your clothes on a clothesline. Drive small, fuel efficient vehicles or stop driving altogether. Avoid imported or non-locally grown food. Bring your own bags to the supermarket. Buy energy efficient lightbulbs. Lose weight. (Fat people allegedly use more gasoline.) Buy expensive "green" electricity. Shun bottled water and drive-thru restaurants. Use cloth diapers. Clean your house with "natural" products. Use a non-motorized push lawnmower. Pay more for "fair trade" coffee. Don't use disposable cameras. Vacation closer to home.

All these admonitions have something in common—you living on a smaller, more inconvenient, more uncomfortable, more expensive, less enjoyable, and less hopeful scale. And the greens' moral hectoring is just the beginning. Green ideologues are bursting with an impatient zeal to begin dictating, through force of law, your mobility, diet, home energy usage, the size of your house, how far you can travel, and even—as we shall see—how many children you can have.

You may be tempted to dismiss all this as a gross exaggeration. But this is how the greens *themselves* describe their intentions, as this book shows. Their words alone reveal their true intent: to curtail, to ration, to force, to deny, to compel, and to squeeze.

Make no mistake: living green is really about someone else micro-regulating *you*—downsizing your dreams and plugging each one of us into a brand new social order for which we never bargained. It's about you living under the green thumb and having the boundaries of your life drawn by others.

The central concept of this book is that there is hardly any area of your life that the greens consider off-limits to intrusion. There is almost no personal behavior of yours that they consider too trivial or too sacrosanct to regulate.

Greens aim to bring about their brave new world through federal law or local ordinance. But where that's not practical, they'll settle for inducing artificial shortages, pricing you out of your "bad" habits by hiking taxes and surcharges, or simply trying to condition you, and those around you, to believe you are engaging in an act of severe personal transgression.

The greens justify all this as necessary to solve our alleged "planetary emergency." But they don't intend for you to live this downsized and penitent lifestyle for some finite period of time until the supposed crisis is over. It is to be a permanent restructuring of life as you know it. Throughout this book you will encounter, up close and personal, the myriad encroachments and invasive oversight mechanisms of your day-to-day life that are lurking behind that shiny, seductive label that reads "green."

A powerful network of individuals and organizations is propelling this agenda. Its adherents have sought for decades to transform our economy and our way of life based on various environmental pretexts—looming food shortages, deforestation, population growth, even global cooling. Manmade global warming is simply their latest—

and by far most successful—organized campaign to achieve this transformation. Green activists have now ensconced themselves throughout our federal, state, and local governments and regulatory
agencies—and in our courtrooms, boardrooms, and classrooms.
Though most work in relative anonymity and obscurity, many are
quite outspoken—Al Gore is, perhaps, the best known.

There is a vast and multilayered network of private organizations
working to advance green policy. From the Earth Liberation Front, an
FBI-labeled terrorist group, to "street theater" groups like Greenpeace
and the Rainforest Action Network, to suit-and-tie "mainstream"
activist organizations like the Natural Resources Defense Council and
Environmental Defense Fund, to "old money" private foundations
like the Rockefeller Foundation and the Pew Charitable Trusts, the
greens can muster an array of forces—protesters, lawyers, scientists,
journalists, and others—to get things done. Serious money makes it
all work. The ten largest green groups had revenues of more than
$1.36 billion in 2007 and net assets in excess of $7.1 billion.[1]

The green workhorses are the Natural Resources Defense Council,
boasting $88 million in annual revenue and $167 million in assets,
according to *Forbes*, and the Environmental Defense Fund, enjoying
$83 million in annual revenue and $108 million in assets. These two
groups are the core of the green army. They serve as brain trusts,
lawyers, lobbyists, organizational bridges between the limousine
greens and the street ruffians, and flypaper for eco-celebrities such as
Barbara Streisand (EDF), Robert Redford (NRDC), and Leonardo
DiCaprio (NRDC).

One of the most socially inequitable aspects of this movement is
that, as the ever-rising green establishment gains more power over
your life, its members are devising lots of nifty loopholes, exemptions,
and free passes for their rich and powerful friends and allies who have

helped them further their political agenda into the mainstream—so that they can escape *your* fate.

It seems that 200-plus years of the technological innovation, free market-driven prosperity, and individual freedoms that have defined America's unique place in the world—and have drawn countless generations of immigrants to our shores in search of a better life—have not impressed the greens. They plan to diminish the famous geographic, social, and economic mobility of Americans—the very things that have always made us feel that "anything is possible." They are keen to reverse our noble advancements in producing more goods and services at less cost. They rail against economic growth as a blight upon society and the planet. They applaud technological retrogression as a virtue and seek to resurrect windmills, zeppelins, clotheslines, and iceboxes.

But is there some merit to their argument, you may ask. What if the planet truly has a "fever" that portends worldwide destruction? Shouldn't we heed their warnings?

While it is beyond the scope of this book to debunk the scientific claims of global warmists, we'll take a brief moment here to note the fatal flaw of global warming alarmism: there is no scientific evidence indicating that carbon dioxide, much less manmade carbon dioxide emissions, control or even measurably impact global climate. This is true whether you look at data going back 650,000 years, data from the twentieth century, or even data from the past ten years.[2] Alarmist predictions of climatic doom are based exclusively on hypothetical mathematical models that have never been validated against the real world.[3] (For sources that disprove the many dubious claims of global warmists, refer to the *Suggested Reading and Viewing* section at the end of this book.)

So it's no wonder the greens resort to procedural hijinks like touting an imaginary United Nations consensus on global warming endorsed by 2,000 scientists, while ignoring a petition signed by more than 31,000 scientists rejecting global warming alarmism.[4] Then there's the infamous "hockey stick" graph, which UN and other alarmists often cited as the key evidence that global warming is occurring—until the graph was discredited by methodological flaws.[5] And let's not forget the British judge who barred teachers from showing Al Gore's global warming documentary *An Inconvenient Truth* without a disclaimer concerning all the film's errors, which amounted to nearly 100 percent of the film's scientific material.[6] With so little evidence on their side, it's unsurprising that global warmists are now reluctant even to discuss the science. "The debate is over," they insist.

How convenient.

The goal of the greens' global warming scare campaign is to create an overpowering sense of fear and urgency that we must act now *no matter what the cost*. Sparing no hyperbole or scare tactic along the way, the movement is now bigger and more influential than ever, easily co-opting politicians, CEOs, celebrities, and journalists. Just as the greens have increased their numbers in Congress and even captured the Oval Office, the current economic crisis has created an opportunity for them to use the hundreds of billions of dollars in government bailout funds as leverage to insist that recipient banks, auto makers, and other key industries adhere to green policies. The bailouts, along with President Obama's plans for a massive infrastructure investment program and a cap-and-trade carbon cutting regime, offer the greens a once-in-a-lifetime opportunity to advance their agenda dramatically.

Without a doubt, President Obama is a true believer in the green cause. Viewing our current living standards as excessive and immoral, he's determined to downsize our lifestyles—for the good of the planet. During his campaign, Obama warned that "we can't drive our SUVs and eat as much as we want and keep our homes on 72 degrees at all times . . . and then just expect that other countries are going to say OK. . . . That's not leadership. That's not going to happen."

So get ready—your choice of car, eating habits, and home energy usage are no longer your private business. Now it's the government's business.

If the greens succeed, we will see their vision for our future implemented with staggering speed. By the time you finish this book you may well be appalled by that vision, but you may also find yourself in awe of the sheer totality of the greens' agenda and their single-minded determination to achieve it. You might now associate the greens with their soft and fuzzy public image, but this will likely change as our new government adopts increasingly coercive policies to force the greens' idea of environmental virtue on you—whether you want it or not.

Don't say you weren't warned.

CHAPTER 1

THE RATIONING
RATIONALE

The greens have crafted an uplifting public perception of their goals. They offer nothing less than the sun, the wind, and the oceans—favorite subjects of the poets down through the ages—as our new sources of power. These sources are unlimited and come free to us all. Who wouldn't be seduced by the prospect that nature's clean and natural energy could lead us to a bright and prosperous tomorrow? And let's not forget, it's all "for the children."

They assure us that environmental protection need not constrain economic growth. Over the last few years, in fact, they have begun touting environmentalism as an economic godsend, promising the future creation of millions of "green-collar jobs." It all boils down to a choice of whether we want to live "sustainably" or "unsustainably," they say. That's hardly a tough call—who wouldn't choose to sustain a productive, clean, and prosperous society?

Well, let's let the greens answer that one in their own words. As you'll see, their happy rhetoric takes on a different tone when green academics, scientists, economists, activists, magazine editors, policy wonks, and social theorists talk amongst themselves.

Let's take a peek inside the October 2008 special issue of *New Scientist* magazine with its cut-to-the-chase special theme entitled, "The

Folly of Growth: How to stop the economy killing the planet." Arguing that economic growth has wreaked havoc on our planet and thus must be reduced, the issue's main editorial concluded, "The science tells us that if we are serious about saving the Earth, most of us need to accept the need for a more sustainable way to live."[1]

The issue's eight essays arrived at similar conclusions, providing a stark contrast to the smiley vision of our future that green activists present to the public. In the first essay, University of Surrey (UK) sustainable development professor Tim Jackson referenced a simplified version of a Stanford professor's formula for calculating the harm caused by human consumption: "people times wealth equals planetary disaster." Jackson made a crystal clear recommendation: "consuming less may be the single biggest thing you can do to reduce carbon emissions."[2]

The other essays echoed Jackson's prescription. Prominent Canadian green David Suzuki argued that we need to lower our standard of living because nothing is more important than the environment.[3] You need to judge your standard of living by "quality of life, your relationships with other people and your community," he said, not "illusions" like stores filled with food, lifespans, and wealth. University of Maryland ecological economist Herman Daly advocated cutting economic growth because we've allegedly passed the point where it provides benefits.[4] Yale University dean James Gustave Speth, co-founder of the Natural Resources Defense Council and former adviser to President Jimmy Carter, warned that economic growth "creates barriers to dealing with real problems," and he thus championed a "non-socialist alternative to today's capitalism."[5]

Promoting "redistribution" as a better way to fight poverty than global economic growth, Andrew Simms of London's New Economics Foundation promoted a "green new deal" that controls capital and raises taxes to create environmental jobs.[6] To improve the environment, Susan George of the Amsterdam-based Transnational Institute argued for cultivating a World War II-type mentality including rationing, victory gardens, and a government run by wealthy elites who are paid $1 per year.[7] London Metropolitan University "environmental philosopher" Kate Soper insisted on the need to "sacrifice some conveniences and pleasures: creature comforts such as regular steaks, hot tubs, luxury cosmetics and easy foreign travel."

This is an article of faith among greens—that saving the planet requires us to eviscerate our standard of living and societal freedoms. They deplore consumption of all kinds—and they'd like to see a lot less of it—never mind that our lives, our jobs, and our economic well-being depend on it.

And this belief is nothing new among greens. Since the 1968 publication of his gloom-and-doom manifesto, *The Population Bomb*, Stanford University population biologist Paul Ehrlich has railed against consumption virtually as a crime against humanity. Ehrlich is best known for his predictions of global famine back in 1968, predictions that proved so spectacularly wrong that one might have assumed he would have taken an early retirement—at least from making predictions. Not so. In his latest polemic, *Too Many People, Too Much Consumption*, Ehrlich recycles a 1970s-era mathematical equation (that he co-developed with President Obama's top science adviser, John P. Holdren) to predict, supposedly, the harm generated by human consumption: I = PAT

The "I" stands for our negative impact on the planet, "P" is the population size, "A" represents average affluence or consumption per individual, and "T" stands for technology that drives and services the consumption.[8] Since P, A, and T are multiplied together, more consumption means a greater negative impact on the planet. Ehrlich goes on to compare economic growth to a disease:

Perpetual growth is the creed of the cancer cell, but third-rate economists can't think of anything else. Some leading economists are starting to tackle the issue of overconsumption, but the problem and its cures are tough to analyze. Scientists have yet to develop consumption condoms or morning-after-shopping-spree pills.

To reduce consumption, Ehrlich suggests holding a UN forum in which people "decide whether they would like to see a maximum number of people living at a minimum standard of living, or perhaps a much lower population size that gives individuals a broad choice of lifestyles."[9]

So Ehrlich offers a stark choice for the future of humanity—either "a lot of us with a little" or "a few of us with a lot." We can either ration the goods or we can ration the people.

And Ehrlich's views are by no means extreme within the green movement. To the contrary, Ehrlich is a member of the prestigious National Academy of Sciences and has received awards from the Sierra Club, World Wildlife Fund International, the MacArthur Foundation, the United Nations, the Ecological Society of America, and the American Institute of Biological Sciences.[10]

We'll revisit Ehrlich later in this chapter, but for now he is—like the *New Scientist* crowd—useful in illustrating the rhetorical difference between green theorists and grassroots activists on the one hand, and those who act as the public voices of the green movement on the other. Image- and media-savvy greens want rationing as well, but unlike Ehrlich and company, they avoid the R-word in favor of euphemisms like "conservation," "smart growth," "carbon footprint," "sustainability," and "optimum population." Far be it from us to oppose anything "smart" or "optimum"—that is, until it becomes

clear that these terms all mean the same thing: *less* for us, and ideal-
ly, less *of* us.

Guess Where the Carbon Footprints Lead

The "carbon footprint" has been a clever gimmick for instilling green
guilt about the amount of energy that you use—that way you'll ration
yourself in the interim until the greens can set up a governmental
mechanism to compel it.

Here's how the Nature Conservancy positions "carbon footprint":

> Inevitably, in going about our daily lives—commuting, shelter-
> ing our families, eating—each of us contributes to the green-
> house gas emissions that are causing climate change. Yet, there
> are many things each of us, as individuals, can do to reduce our
> carbon emissions. The choices we make in our homes, our trav-
> el, the food we eat, and what we buy and throw away all influ-
> ence our carbon footprint and can help ensure a stable climate
> for future generations. [11]

The greens, you see, have personalized climate change. It's *your* fault.
It's *your* commute, *your* home, *your* purchases. Even *your* eating is a
problem. So you need to change *your* behavior. And the greens will
tell you how.

The first step is figuring out what your carbon footprint is, which
you can do by using online carbon footprint calculators. The calculators ask questions about your home energy usage, travelling habits,
whether you shop at second-hand stores, etc. Based on your responses,
the calculators estimate how many tons of carbon dioxide emissions
you are responsible for annually.

Think for a minute about how this works. Bigger carbon footprints are bad, and the footprints are largely based on how much energy you use. So in essence, these calculators serve as an anti-prosperity index: the more you travel, the bigger house you have, the more expensive shopping you do—in sum, the better you have it—the more immoral you are.

When I calculated my carbon footprint on CarbonFootprint.com, I was provided with a visual comparison showing my footprint to be about seven times bigger than the "world target." Apparently, the greens want me to reduce my personal energy use by around 87 percent. Based on my carbon footprint profile, to meet this goal I'd have to stop driving, flying, using electricity, and heating and cooling my home.

Or I could just buy "carbon offsets," which function as modern-day indulgences for green devotees. Let's say, for example, that you feel guilty about the twelve or so tons of carbon dioxide your SUV emits every year. To cleanse your conscience of your eco-sin, you can purchase CO_2 offsets from brokers who, in turn, take a commission and supposedly pay a third party to produce electricity with low or no CO_2 emissions or to plant trees that absorb CO_2 from the atmosphere.

The CO_2 offset marketplace is pretty shady. According to an August 2008 report by the General Accounting Office, carbon offsets have no uniform quality assurance mechanisms or standards of verification and monitoring.[12] "Participants in the offset market face challenges ensuring credibility of offsets," the GAO concluded.[13] In other words, buyers have little idea whether the offsets they buy actually reduce CO_2 emissions.

You need look no further than Al Gore's movie, *An Inconvenient Truth*, to get an idea of the flim-flammery behind carbon offsets. The movie's producers announced they purchased offsets from a broker called NativeEnergy to compensate for 100 percent of the CO_2 emissions involved in making the movie. Astoundingly, according to a

NativeEnergy website release—which has since been removed—it only cost forty tons of offsets (worth about $480) to make *An Inconvenient Truth* carbon neutral. It's an absurdly low figure given that producing a thirty-second television commercial commonly produces at least fifty tons of CO_2, and that making the movie *Syriana*—another NativeEnergy project—supposedly required 2,040 tons' worth of offsets. [14]

When I called NativeEnergy to inquire about the forty-ton figure, I was told that the company "does not share information about its clients without their consent." I found it strange that the producers of *An Inconvenient Truth* either withheld or revoked their consent, since so many of NativeEnergy's other clients predominately display their offset purchases on the company's website. NativeEnergy told me I would have to go through Paramount's legal department to obtain the necessary consent. Paramount never returned my calls—quite odd, given the movie's self-acclaim as the world's first carbon-neutral documentary. The NativeEnergy website still boasts about offsetting "100 percent of the carbon dioxide pollution" associated with *An Inconvenient Truth*—but it's unknown how many tons that "100 percent" actually represents.

What's more, it's unclear how much of NativeEnergy's income actually goes toward reducing CO_2 emissions and how much simply lines the company's pockets. This is a common problem among offset programs, as noted by the GAO. Former Clinton administration official Joseph Romm bluntly summed up the situation, writing that "the vast majority of offsets are, at some level, just rip-offsets." [15]

Rationing Energy

As dubious as they are, at least carbon offsets aren't mandatory—yet. Reducing your carbon footprint—read "energy use"—is still a voluntary exercise. But since not many are volunteering, the greens are trying to make it compulsory—starting in the United Kingdom, where the parliament's Environmental Audit Committee in May 2008 called for a "personal carbon trading" scheme.[16]

This would function similar to the kind of industrial carbon trading plans advocated by President Obama and other greens, but it would apply to *personal* energy usage. The government would place a cap on the amount of carbon-based energy—such as electricity from natural gas or coal, gasoline, and diesel fuels—and "travel services" available to the public. Individuals would be issued "carbon ration cards," enabling them to purchase a certain amount of energy or travel services. If you want or need more energy than your allowance, you have to buy carbon credits at the prevailing market price.[17]

Unsurprisingly, the greens are debate-shy in justifying their sweeping proposals. The committee wrote:

> What is needed is a shift in the debate away from ever-deeper and more detailed consideration of how personal carbon trading could operate towards the more decisive questions of how it could be made publicly and politically acceptable. It is these questions that will ultimately decide the viability of personal carbon trading.[18]

Translation: "By all means, steer the discussion away from how personal carbon rationing would actually affect the lives of individuals and their families, and instead focus on selling this to the public."

One type of organization acting to boost public acceptance of carbon rationing is CRAGs—Carbon Rationing Action Groups. CRAG members, mostly located in Britain, are the new carbon monks, voluntarily denying themselves the use of carbon-based energy while lobbying for wider systems of carbon rationing. There are also at least five U.S.-based CRAGs, in Maryland, Georgia, Oregon, Washington state, and the northern Kentucky/Cincinnati area. Interestingly, in America, where there is more public resistance to rationing, CRAGs tend to replace the term "carbon rationing" in their name with a softer sounding euphemism—"carbon reduction." Remember, the key is to sell this scheme to the public.

And in America, we've already witnessed attempts in Congress to reduce personal consumption for the sake of the environment. In August 2007, Michigan Democratic congressman John Dingell introduced a bill to increase gasoline taxes and also to remove the mortgage tax deduction for homes larger than 3,000 square feet.[19] "In order to address the issue of climate change, we must address the issue of consumption. We do that by making consumption more expensive," Dingell declared.[20]

Although Dingell's bill failed, in the near future having a small house or even a small apartment may not save you from the rationing police, who are aiming to enter your sanctum via your thermostat.

The first such proposal was made by the California Energy Commission in November 2007. It would have allowed California utility officials to require the installation in homes of so-called "programmable control thermostats" that would allow them to alter the thermostats remotely—as well as to control other electrical appliances such as your water heater, refrigerator, pool pump, lights, and the like—during an "emergency event" (a term that was left undefined).[21]

The purpose of the proposal, according to commission officials, was to allow utilities to reduce customers' electricity use during periods of peak demand for electricity, typically hot summer days when air conditioner usage places a heavy burden on the power grid. "If you can control rotating outages by letting everyone in the state share the pain, there's a lot less pain to go around," a commission member told the *New York Times.*[22] Perhaps, but the proposal sparked widespread criticism of the eerie "Big Brother" aspect of state regulators monitoring and controlling people's home energy use.[23]

The greens did their best to "sell" the proposal to the public. First, they adopted their usual smiley-face terminology, referring to the mechanisms that would allow state control of your home temperature as "smart thermostats." And second, they resorted to their typical scare tactics to justify their newest proposed intrusion. "Most people given a choice of two degrees of temperature setback and 14th century living would be happy to embrace this capacity," an "energy expert" with the Natural Resources Defense Council ominously told the *Times.*

In *Human Events,* columnist Walter Williams pointed out the slippery slope we create once we cede control of our thermostat to the state. What's next, Williams asked, will an energy czar turn our lights off at night? Will he switch off the TV at certain times to encourage kids to study more?[24]

Although the public outcry torpedoed the proposal, the energy rationers aren't giving up. While acknowledging broad public opposition to the scheme, California Energy Commission chairwoman Jackalyne Pfannenstiel continues to advocate "demand response"— another euphemism for rationing. She explained, "Demand response is ultimately about people's choices and decisions. In our society, it's not about government controlling the device in your house, it's about you choosing how you want to use your devices, including air conditioning."[25]

So allowing the government to cut your energy usage against your wishes is presented as a matter of *your* choice. Orwell would be proud.

What lessons did Pfannenstiel learn from this debacle? Unsurprisingly, it wasn't that government-controlled thermostats are an intolerable violation of personal freedom. Instead, she argued, next time the greens just need to do a better job selling the proposal to the public:

> The first lesson we learned was the need to get information out in advance, make sure people understand what [demand response] is and isn't, and why it makes sense .... Second I'd stress the economic benefits to customers, the potential savings that are available. Our society responds to prices but people don't know much about electricity prices. We need to compress the learning curve to have effective demand-response programs.[26]

You see, you just need to *learn* more about rationing to love it. You'd support it if only you *understood* your electric bill—as if having to pay it every month doesn't create familiarity.

And the greens aren't opposed to giving you a crash course in learning to love rationing, either. The British government is experimenting with so-called "smart metering," where a meter placed in your home not only displays how much electricity you are using, but has an alarm that goes off when your electricity use exceeds a preset limit. "I've become like one of Pavlov's dogs," one hapless victim of smart metering said. "Every time it bleeps I think I'm going to take one of those pans off the stove. I'd do anything to make it stop."[27]

A different form of energy rationing was recently adopted in Pennsylvania, where Governor Ed Rendell approved a law requiring utilities to cut their annual electricity use by at least one percent by May 31, 2011, or face fines of up to $20 million. As reported by the Associated Press, "Utilities will have to find ways to get people and businesses to use less electricity on the hottest summer days, when electricity is the most expensive. That could include enrolling the owners of homes and office buildings in a program to temporarily switch off hot water heaters or air conditioners."[28]

We are sure to see more of these schemes in the near future, carefully presented not to look like the energy rationing programs they really are. One can only wonder how much more energy we'd have if all the time and money sunk into the development of rationing plans were invested somewhere better—like removing the innumerable obstacles imposed by activist green groups that hinder the creation of new power plants.

Rationing Living Space

If you're old enough, you might remember that classic 1970s toy known as the Habitrail. It was a see-through hamster habitat that brought all your furry friend's living needs together into one compact living space. If you owned a hamster Habitrail, you no doubt enjoyed hours of wholesome fun observing everything that little guy was up to during his busy day.

Okay, while he's still fresh in your mind, imagine yourself trading places with him.

Welcome to "smart growth," the prevailing euphemism for "where the greens allow you to live." Smart growth is the ultimate in Soviet-style central planning. It aims to combat urban sprawl—in other words, to keep people from taking up "too much" space—by packing us into high-density urban areas and reducing our geographical mobility. By enacting local regulations, especially on housing and cars, smart growth planners seek to engineer confined urban living areas where houses give way to smaller, more "efficient" abodes like apartments and row houses. The main idea is to put you in a little geographical box—and keep you there.

Smart growth is the brainchild of 1970s-era social activists who, as Randal O'Toole of the libertarian Cato Institute puts it, "began to vilify low-density suburbs as 'sprawl.'"[29] The 1973 book *Compact City: A Plan for a Livable Urban Environment* "unleashed a large movement of planners and architects who endorsed government efforts to mandate high population densities, more multi-family dwellings, and severe limits on auto driving," according to O'Toole.[30]

Smart growth is packaged to sell. Marketing material positions smart growth as "a shot at the American dream of opportunity for all"; "safe convenient neighborhoods with homes that people can afford"; "development decisions that are fair to everyone"; and "investing tax-payer money wisely in our communities."[31] It may sound great, but beware. The smart growth crowd is pitching a combination of medievalism, misinformation, and doublespeak.

The Smart Growth Network (SGN), a coalition of environmental groups, local government groups, housing and transportation groups, and the Environmental Protection Agency, depicts so-called "live/work units" as the American dream. What's a live/work unit? It's a building where you can live *and* work—just like the village craftsmen in the days of yore. "Finding a good home in a safe neighborhood, convenient to jobs, good schools and other daily needs can be difficult," the SGN observes.[32] So its solution is for you simply to load up the family and move onto a postage stamp-sized lot or into the apartment above your workplace, behind the castle walls of high-density planned communities.

The SGN claims that smart growth, among its many virtues, saves tax-payer money. This has not been the result, however, in Portland, Oregon, a city with particularly aggressive smart growth policies that have actually driven up the cost of an acre of land available for housing from $20,000 in 1990 to $200,000 in 2001, reducing the number of households that can afford to buy a median-priced home by 50 percent.[33]

Much of the smart growth orthodoxy is rooted in the greens' disdain for the automobile. As Al Gore argued in his 1992 bestseller

Earth in the Balance, cars pose "a mortal threat to the security of every nation." As a result, he advocated a "global program" to eliminate completely the internal combustion engine within twenty-five years.[34]

The SGN takes a similarly dim view of car transport, lamenting that "in many places in this country, you must use a car, because other options are not safe, practical, or even possible."[35] It seeks to rectify this supposed problem by reducing driving in smart growth communities, but it wants to make the argument against cars with more subtlety than Gore does. So it refers to the curbing of driving as "the freedom to choose how we get around."[36] Yes, the smart growth folks want to liberate you from the chains of your car—and into mass transit.

Of course, smart growth advocates insist that you can still own a car in a living space-rationed community. But what's left unsaid is that owning a car in such a place will be completely impractical thanks to severe parking limitations placed at your home, workplace, and most other potential destinations. Car ownership is discouraged by making car usage as inconvenient as possible.[37]

Smart growth advocates also advertise their planned living arrangements as "healthy communities."[38] Without so many cars, you see, the streets are safer for pedestrians and bicyclists, while traffic and air pollution are reduced. "Children can get daily exercise by walking or biking to school," the SGN instructs.[39] That's true, but it brings up safety problems—school buses are safer for children than walking or biking. The SGN's "innovative" solution to this concern is the so-called "walking school bus," in which adult volunteers walk groups of children to school. Unsurprisingly, many parents have withheld their enthusiasm for the prospect of having volunteers, who are neither trained nor licensed to work with children, corralling kids along the roadside all the way to school—in rain or snow—as the kids drag their class projects and musical instruments behind them.

The SGN's health argument is also dubious. The basic idea is that eliminating cars improves health by reducing air pollution and forcing people to engage in physical exercise like walking and biking. It sounds quite plausible, but it's not. Of course, clean air and exercise are good for you, but there is simply no evidence that smart growth actually creates these benefits. In fact, Portland's "metropolitan planning organization"—the official name for smart growth bureaucracy—projects that under smart growth, congestion will actually grow worse in the city and smog will increase by 10 percent.[40] So much for cleaner air and better health from smart growth.

Smart growth revolves around the cult of planning, and not just for the short-term. It's about planning, as Buzz Lightyear might say, to infinity and beyond. "Planning for 50 or even 100 years into the future helps a community articulate the legacy it wants, set goals to achieve it, and create benchmarks it can use to check its progress and make necessary changes along the way," the SGN says.[41]

Now let me get this straight. Local bureaucrats will make plans for how we live that extend far beyond the lives of people yet to be born? Putting aside the arrogance of central planners depriving current and future citizens of the right to make their own decisions on where and how they want to live, let's ask some key questions the SGN doesn't like to consider: What if the central planners are wrong? What if their plans go awry? Remember, Portland's smart growth was supposed to lead to cleaner, not dirtier air.

"Smart growth," as it turns out, is looking like neither.

Rationing People

Let's compare how businesses view people versus how the greens do. To businesses, people are "human resources" (employees) and "markets" (customers). While a cynic may suggest that businesses only value people to the extent that they can be exploited as employees or customers, at least businesses generally recognize that resources such as larger employee pools and expanding markets are *good* things.

To the greens, in contrast, you are a "carbon footprint"—a burden on the planet that must be reduced or eliminated.

Modern worry-warting about overpopulation was brought into vogue by the English economist Thomas Malthus (1766–1834) in his treatise "An Essay on the Principle of Population." Simply put, Malthus hypothesized that population would grow geometrically while food production would only grow arithmetically, thereby leading to lots of people with little to eat—the so-called "Malthusian catastrophe" that, 200 years later, has still not occurred. But just because Malthusian thinking has discredited itself over time doesn't mean it's been entirely relegated to the dustbin of history—enter, once again, Stanford University's Paul Ehrlich.

"The battle to feed all of humanity is over"—that's how Ehrlich ominously began his 1968 book *The Population Bomb*, in which he predicted that hundreds of millions of people would die in mass famines in the 1970s and '80s. Along with increasing the food supply, Ehrlich argued, the only way to avoid these mass deaths was to reduce "the cancer of population growth" to zero or even negative growth. [42] How would Ehrlich and his life-rationing friends accomplish this?

Ehrlich dismissed the notion of adding chemicals to the water or to food that would temporarily sterilize people—not because he found the idea appalling, but because society lacked the technology to do the job properly. In fact, Ehrlich bemoaned this shortcoming as a "criminal inadequacy of biomedical research."[43] Ehrlich's plan B was to eliminate the tax deduction for children and to place "luxury taxes" on layettes, cribs, diapers, diaper services, and expensive toys.[44]

These measures and more would be established, coordinated, and enforced by a powerful new government agency called the "Department of Population and Environment"—we'll call it DOPE. As Ehrlich envisioned it, DOPE would aid Congress in developing population control legislation, including a federal sex education program beginning in elementary school and emphasizing "techniques of birth control."[45] While Ehrlich encouraged couples to limit themselves voluntarily to two children, the key for him was for the government to *mandate* population control. "We must change public opinion in this country, and through public opinion change the direction of our government," he argued.[46]

Ehrlich's goal when he wrote *The Population Bomb* was to maintain world population at "one or even two billion," which he suggested "could be sustained in reasonable comfort for 1,000 years if resources were husbanded carefully."[47] He acknowledged that we might "still have a chance" if the population stabilizes at four or five billion, but "of course, mankind's options will be fewer and people's lives almost certainly less pleasant than if the lower figure is attained."[48]

Well, it's been more than forty years since Ehrlich's tome was published. How have things turned out?

World population in 1968 was more than 3.5 billion—already way over Ehrlich's goal. Today, world population exceeds 6.6 billion—almost double what it was in 1968 and past the point of even having "a chance," according to Ehrlich. Did we run out of food or has the population become unsustainable? Hardly. According to UN statistics, the number of people in the developing world who were undernourished in 1968 was estimated to be more than 900 million.[49] That estimate is on track to be reduced by more than 50 percent by 2015.[50] So, while world population has just about doubled, global hunger is being cut in half.

Tremendous worldwide economic growth and technological advances—which Ehrlich failed to foresee—will have made this achievement possible. It looks like future editions of *The Population Bomb* ought to be re-titled as *The Prediction Bomb*.

So just imagine how different the present moment might be if we had listened to Ehrlich and thrown human procreation into reverse: right now Ehrlich would likely be hailed as mankind's savior for averting doom—an apocalypse we now know would *not have materialized anyway*.

Let's apply that same lesson to our current dilemma: what if we disassemble life as we know it in response to the greens' insistence, which echoes Ehrlich's insistence, that *"we must act now"* to save the planet? We could be signing up for an "all pain, no gain" reversal of human progress and freedom—and doing so on behalf of activists who aren't even willing to debate the scientific validity of their claims.

Now back to Ehrlich. Did the failure of his predictions chasten him and his adherents? Not at all—instead, the population control movement is growing even more influential. In fact, the premise of *The Population Bomb* was cited approvingly by John P. Holdren, President Obama's science adviser, in the published version of a major speech he gave in 2007 to the American Association for the Advancement of Science. In the text, Holdren perversely argued that "the elementary but discomfiting truth" of Ehrlich's insight "may account for the vast amount of ink, paper, and angry energy that has been expended trying in vain to refute it."[51]

While clinging to the "discomfiting truth" of their discredited predictions, population control advocates have revised their argument in one crucial way: they now cite global warming to justify population control.

The Britain-based Optimum Population Trust—a terrific euphemism for "stop breeding now"—laments that "in 2007, the world finally woke up to climate change. It has not, however, woken up to one of its fundamental causes—human population growth."[52] The trust says that "the most effective *personal* climate change strategy is limiting the number of children one has. The most effective national and global climate change strategy is limiting the size of population." After all, it observes, "a non-existent person has no environmental footprint."[53]

The author of that report, John Guillebaud, opined in the prestigious *British Medical Journal* that doctors need to get involved. Physicians should supply patients with information on population, the environment, and contraception—and set an example in their own personal lives—so as "to bring family size into the arena of environmental ethics, analogous to avoiding patio heaters and high carbon cars."[54]

America has its own advocates of people-rationing, which takes us back to Paul Ehrlich, who in 1968 co-founded a group called Zero Population Growth. While ZPG is still around, it is now known as the Population Connection—another terrific euphemism, since the last thing it wants people to do is *connect*. In the fortieth anniversary edition of its publication *The Reporter*, Paul Ehrlich was still at it—apparently he can never be wrong too often—writing that "ZPG's 1968 message that the population of the United States, as well as the global population, must stop growing is now more urgent than ever."[55]

Population Connection undertakes various activities in hopes of reducing the supposed disaster of too many people being born: It is working with Al Gore's Alliance for Climate Protection to promote global warming legislation that would ration energy use;[56] lobbying for the U.S. to fund international people rationing through the UN Population Fund;[57] and lobbying for taxpayer-funded family planning programs and against "abstinence-only" sex education programs in schools.[58]

A more radical course is proposed by the Voluntary Human Extinction Movement (VHEMT, pronounced "vehement"), whose manifesto states:

> As VHEMT Volunteers know, the hopeful alternative to the extinction of millions of species of plants and animals is the voluntary extinction of one species: Homo sapiens . . . us.
>
> Each time another one of us decides to not add another one of us to the burgeoning billions already squatting on this ravaged planet, another ray of hope shines through the gloom.
>
> When every human chooses to stop breeding, Earth's biosphere will be allowed to return to its former glory, and all remaining creatures will be free to live, die, evolve (if they believe in evolution), and will perhaps pass away, as so many of Nature's "experiments" have done throughout the eons. It's going to take all of us going.

Les Knight, founder of VHEMT, told the *Boise Weekly* that his convictions led him to get a vasectomy in the 1970s. "As long as there's one breeding couple, we're in danger of being right back here again," he declared. "Wherever humans live, not much else lives. It isn't that we're evil and want to kill everything—it's just how we live."[59]

Similar sentiments were voiced by James Lovelock, a founding father of the modern environmental movement and formulator of the Gaia Hypothesis. In a January 2009 interview, he predicted that global warming would "cull" the human population by 90 percent at the end of the twenty-first century. When the interviewer commented that this was a depressing outlook, Lovelock responded, "Not necessarily. I don't think 9 billion is better than 1 billion."[60]

For all its over-the-top extremism, at least VHEMT promotes a voluntary approach to population control. But others advocate more coercive policies.

The direct approach, of course, would be simply to revoke your right to have as many children as you want. That's crazy, you say? Well, it's not so crazy that the idea couldn't be floated in the *Yale Human Rights and Development Law Journal*. In an article entitled "Rethinking the Procreative Right," Carter J. Dillard claims that the U.S. constitution, international law sources, and even Lockean natural law do not provide people with the absolute and unfettered right to procreate as they wish. Rather, "these authorities merely provide for a right to continue the species, a right to perpetuate the race and have offspring, and the right to simply found a family, respectively."[61]

Once this right has been "fulfilled," it's over. What does "fulfilled" mean? According to Dillard, fulfillment could be either "a single act of procreation" or "procreation for optimized societal replacement." So your right to have children is limited to one child or perhaps more if it serves to "optimize society," whatever that means.[62] Dillard justifies this interpretation as necessary to protect people's "environmental rights," which are "potentially" infringed by the addition of each new human being.[63]

Fortunately, we don't have to speculate on how Mr. Dillard's one-child policy might work—China already provides an example.

Adopted in 1979, China's child rationing policy confines urban residents and government employees to one child with limited exceptions, while rural families, constituting 70 percent of the Chinese people, might be permitted to have a second child after five years if the first was a girl. A third child is permitted to some minorities in under-populated areas. The policy is enforced by rewards and penalties meted out at the discretion of local officials. Penalties could include fines, confiscation of personal property, and dismissal from employment.[64]

So how has this policy worked out after nearly thirty years? Chinese officials say the policy prevented 250 to 300 million births. This claim, however, cannot be verified because the Communist authorities are known to manipulate their statistics.[65] A more credible study in 2006 by a University of Geneva researcher estimated the number of births avoided at a much lower range of 50 to 60 million.[66]

An important side effect of the policy is that for every 1,000 live births, boys now outnumber girls by as much as 565 to 435. A study by the *New England Journal of Medicine* attributed the lack of girls largely to sex-selective abortion and non-registration of female births. Most disturbingly, the journal related, "Although infanticide of girls is probably very rare now, less aggressive treatment of sick female infants is known to occur."[67]

Reported consequences of the sex imbalance have included mental health problems and socially disruptive behavior among men unable to marry; increased kidnapping and trafficking of women for marriage; and increased rates of prostitution and the attendant sexually transmitted diseases. And the policy will probably have negative long-term economic effects, as the *NEJM* study observed that in the future "increasing numbers of couples will be solely responsible for the care of one child and four parents."[68]

You might think that China's depressing experience with people-rationing would dissuade people from advocating the same here in America. But you would be wrong. As Carter Dillard argues, "The issue of whether China's 'one child policy' as applied is justified or has been effective . . . differs from whether having any family-size limit violates its citizens' procreative rights. . . . Logically, one must first define the procreative right (a controversial enough undertaking) before determining how it is to be applied."[69]

But if you allow greens like Dillard to define what a "procreative right" is, you probably won't be keeping that right for long.

CHAPTER 2

POWER *IS* POWER

Historically, America has enjoyed access to cheap, abundant sources of energy. This has been vital in propelling our unprecedented technological progress, economic growth, and ever-rising standard of living. If our energy supply were threatened, then all our comforts and conveniences that stem from it—in other words, the American way of life—would be endangered as well. And today, our energy supply *is* becoming increasingly endangered as a deliberate result of the policies and actions of American greens.

The greens hurl their main arguments against fossil fuels—the oil, coal, and natural gas that comprise around three quarters of our energy supply. The use of these energy sources, the greens believe, irreparably "violates" the Earth. Furthermore, fossil fuels allegedly produce harmful emissions and waste products that kill and sicken people and harm the environment, as "proven" in green-touted scientific studies. As an alternative, greens have created the concept of "renewable" energy which, they say, simply harnesses natural forms of energy like sunlight, wind, tides, hydropower, and plant matter. This, they claim, is the key to solving our energy crisis.

But the green commitment to renewable energy is not what it seems. Even as the greens' media-friendly troops press for alternative energy, their activist allies undermine the cultivation of these very energy sources using their time-worn tactics of protest, litigation, and lobbying. That's right—the greens fight against the use of every type of energy, *including renewable energy*.

The War on Oil

While greens publicly claim to support the "sustainable use" of fossil fuels, in fact they're ideologically opposed to *any* use of fossil fuels. They engage in continuous campaigns to hinder any new development projects while doing everything possible to make these fuel sources—oil and coal, in particular—less available and more expensive. These actions have brought us to the verge of a true energy crisis and forced an ever-greater reliance on foreign oil to the detriment of our national security. Greens then point to this situation as evidence of the pressing need to find alternatives to fossil fuels.

Let's take a closer look at how this game is played.

The greens reflexively oppose any drilling for fossil fuels, working for decades to block oil drilling in the Arctic National Wildlife Refuge (ANWR). Until recently, they had similar success in preventing drilling for oil and gas offshore in the continental U.S. (thus leaving these resources to be tapped by our rivals like Cuba and China, which recently created a joint venture to drill just seventy miles off the Florida coast). In states like Florida and California, the greens are such a powerful political force that few politicians or even oil companies will risk angering them by pushing for offshore drilling.

The outlook for offshore drilling seemed to improve late in 2008 when public anger at spiraling gas prices forced Congress to allow the moratorium on offshore drilling to expire. This occurred a few months after President Bush had lifted the executive ban on offshore leasing. However, it's unlikely that significant offshore drilling will be allowed anytime soon due to lawsuits from green groups. In the *Wall Street Journal*, Arizona Republican congressman John Shadegg recounted some details of the greens' courtroom jihad against drilling:

> In February 2008, the administration issued 487 leases in Alaska's Chukchi Sea, which holds an estimated 15 billion barrels of oil and 76 trillion cubic feet of natural gas. The Sierra Club, the Center for Biological Diversity, and other groups used the National Environmental Policy Act and the Endangered Species Act to challenge and delay progress on all 487 leases. In a separate lawsuit, they challenged the entire national outer continental shelf (OCS) leasing program, seeking to block all future leases.
>
> Even if a lease makes it through these challenges, it isn't clear sailing. Right now, there are 748 leases in the Chukchi and Beaufort Seas. Exploration activities in every single one were challenged in May of this year by EarthJustice in conjunction with others.
>
> The Alaskan OCS contains 26 billion barrels of oil and 132 trillion cubic feet of natural gas. Not one offshore lease has escaped litigation.
>
> And it's not just Alaska. Wild Earth Guardians and others recently filed suit to block energy exploration on all leases in recent sales in Kansas, New Mexico, Oklahoma and Texas. Last year, almost 50% of gas leases in the Rocky Mountain states were protested in court.[1]

Sometimes even apparent breakthroughs in the drilling stalemate turn out to be nothing of the kind. For example, a July 2008 *Wall Street Journal* op-ed entitled "Environmentalists Say Yes to Offshore

Drilling" delightedly recounted how an oil exploration company reached an agreement with green activist groups to permit drilling off the coast of Santa Barbara, California—the first new wells since a January 1969 oil spill in that area.[2] "When an environmental group formed for the sole purpose of opposing offshore oil drilling warmly embraces a plan to drill off its own coast, you know something important has changed in our culture; Americans have recognized that offshore drilling is largely safe," the op-ed exclaimed.[3]

Perhaps Americans have recognized that, but the greens haven't. Less than a week later the greens wrote the newspaper to correct the record. "To be accurate, the [op-ed's] title should have read 'Environmentalists Secure End to Oil Development,'" wrote the greens' attorney who negotiated the deal. He revealed that the agreement would close "significant" existing oil production facilities in the next few years that otherwise would have operated indefinitely. He then frankly admitted that the green agenda was to eliminate *all* offshore oil development:

> We see this agreement as a direct complement to our support for the federal oil moratorium. Just as we need to say "no" to new oil development, we must put an end to existing development if we are to protect our coast from the risks of offshore oil and gas development, and protect society from climate change. . . . Environmentalists support actions that move away from, not toward, dependence on fossil fuels.[4]

So much for greens bearing gifts.

The greens' crusade against oil development has increased our dependence on the OPEC cartel and exacerbated the dramatic swings in oil prices we saw throughout 2008. One way to solve these problems would be to develop other forms of oil extraction. Since they're opposed to conventional oil development, one might think the greens would consider supporting other methods as an alternative.

For example, consider oil shale, which is a sedimentary rock that can be processed into a synthetic form of crude oil. More than 60 percent of the world's oil shale is found right here in the U.S., making us the Saudi Arabia of oil shale. In fact, our estimated shale reserves are seven times greater than the Saudis' proved reserves.[5] We have it—we just need to get at it.

But green groups oppose oil shale development, citing concerns about potential water and air pollution.[6] Influential greens such as Colorado senator Ken Salazar, whose home state holds huge deposits of oil shale, have fought tooth and nail against shale extraction.[7] Although in 2008 Congress allowed a long-standing ban on oil shale exploration in Western states to expire, green groups are already planning a campaign of lawsuits to halt any new shale development.[8]

Another immense oil resource is found in Canada, which holds as much oil in its tar sands—a mixture of sand and a thick petroleum— as is found in all the conventional oil reserves throughout the entire world. This concerns Americans, since every barrel of oil we buy from our friendly neighbor is a barrel we're not buying from OPEC's repressive sheiks and dictators. But Canadian greens are attacking tar sands projects and have already forced the Canadian government to divert $4 billion in revenues from them to fight greenhouse gas emissions.[9]

What's more, even if these projects were left alone to produce huge amounts of oil, U.S.-based greens are already working to put this supply off limits to Americans. A little-noticed provision of Congress's ironically-named "Energy Independence and Security Act of 2007" bars the federal government from buying fuels whose greenhouse gas emissions exceed those from fuels produced from conventional petroleum sources. This puts tar sands off-limits to the federal government. The greens' time-tested strategy in this situation is to lobby to extend the ban to contractors that do business with the federal government, to states and their contractors, and then, by default, to the nation as a whole.

While hindering the development of all forms of oil, the greens for decades have prevented the construction of new refineries that turn crude oil into gasoline. In fact, thanks to green obstructionism, we have not built a new refinery since 1976.[10] The severe danger of this policy became apparent in 2005 when the price of gas first spiked to over $3 a gallon after hurricanes Katrina and Rita damaged Gulf Coast refineries. Because U.S. refineries overall were already operating at or near capacity, the shutdown of Gulf Coast refineries forced us to import expensive gasoline refined abroad.

In addition to impeding the construction of new refineries, the greens have prevented the expansion of existing ones. The Sierra Club and the Natural Resources Defense Council (NRDC) in June 2008 blocked oil giant ConocoPhillips' expansion of its Roxana, Illinois, gasoline refinery. The project would have expanded the volume of crude processed from 60,000 barrels a day to more than 500,000 barrels a day by 2015. But after the state of Illinois approved the expansion, green groups successfully pressured the Environmental Protection Agency to stop it, alleging that ConocoPhillips' plan to reduce the refinery's sulfur dioxide emissions by 95 percent and nitrogen oxides by 25 percent was not green enough.[11]

This is happening throughout America. In California, green groups in June 2008 worked through the state attorney general's office to block an $800 million upgrade of a Chevron refinery in the city of Richmond.[12] Then in July, the NRDC sued the Indiana Department of Environmental Management to thwart BP from undertaking a $3.8

billion expansion and modernization of its refinery near Lake Michigan that would have boosted the refinery's annual production of gasoline, diesel, and jet fuel by 15 percent, making it the nation's top processor of heavy high-sulfur Canadian crude oil. [13]

But the greens don't even need direct activism to torpedo refinery construction. The myriad green laws that refineries must comply with are dauntingly expensive. As pointed out by the *Wall Street Journal*, refiners spent about $47 billion between 1993 to 2005 just to comply with the Clean Air Act, the Clean Water Act, the Toxic Substances Control Act, the Safe Drinking Water Act, the Oil Pollution Act, the Resource Conservation Recovery Act, and the Comprehensive Environmental Response, Compensation and Liability Act. And that's only the beginning, as a dozen more new major environmental programs are scheduled to come online by 2012.[14] All this regulation helped reduce investment returns in the refining industry to 5.5 percent between 1993 and 2002—less than half the return of the S&P industrials average. If investors can't earn a competitive return in the refinery business, they'll do something else with their money.

Despite their convoluted arguments for the "sustainable use" of oil, the greens' real attitude is actually pretty straightforward: "No oil. Period."

Lights Out: No to Electricity

Aside from curbing our use and development of oil, greens are diligently working to cut and control the electricity supply.

Just over half our electricity is produced by coal.[15] For decades the greens have tried in vain to reduce the use of coal, lobbying for regulations on how it is mined and the chemical compounds it emits when burned. But the global warming scare seems to have finally given them some traction. For the first time, applications to build new coal-fired power plants are being rejected based on their emissions of carbon dioxide (CO_2)—and not just a few plants. Of more than 150 coal plant proposals submitted to regulators for approval in recent years, by the end of 2007 just thirty-five had either been built or were under construction.[16] An astounding fifty-nine of the proposed plants were cancelled, abandoned, or put on hold because of concerns over CO_2 emissions. Many coal plants are falling victim to aggressive legal challenges by the Sierra Club, whose "Stopping the Coal Rush" website sports a database and map proudly showing the various plants being attacked by green groups.[17]

And lawsuits aren't the greens' only weapon in this campaign, as they now insert themselves directly into big business deals. Incredibly, greens played a key role in the $45 billion buyout of the electric utility TXU Corp by a group led by the private equity firm Kohlberg, Kravis, and Roberts in 2007. Prior to the buyout, TXU had angered greens by planning to build eleven new coal-fired power plants. So the KKR group reached out to the activists, who agreed to end their campaign against TXU and to support the buyout in exchange for KKR's capitulation to two green demands: not building eight of the eleven plants, and having TXU support federal carbon-reduction legislation.[18]

Burning natural gas, which accounts for 19 percent of our electricity, emits less carbon dioxide than burning coal, but that hasn't earned it much support from the greens. In February 2008 a Florida chapter of EarthFirst protested the construction of a natural gas-fired power plant. "I'm not willing to threaten the integrity of the Loxahatchee, one of the last large, intact pieces of the northern Everglades, so that people can fuel their greedy energy desires," declared one activist. Another green argued that "gas fired-power is not a clean or sustainable energy. It is a dirty and dwindling fossil fuel."[19]

An additional green strategy for attacking natural gas is to obstruct its supply, which is already limited due to green policies such as the recently expired ban on offshore drilling. A classic example was seen in Massachusetts, where Democratic congressman Barney Frank advocated dredging Fall River, a long-time industrial area, to preserve its viability as an industrial port. Six months later, however, a proposal emerged to build a terminal in Fall River for importing liquefied natural gas (LNG).[20] Once the LNG terminal was proposed, Frank suddenly reversed his position and introduced a bill to designate Fall River—the same area he had wanted dredged—a "wild and scenic river" protected by federal law. He also tried to block the LNG terminal by opposing the demolition of a decrepit—or would that be called "scenic"—bridge that would impede ship access to the area.[21]

If coal and natural gas are all off the table as electricity sources, surely the greens would support nuclear power, the one source of completely CO_2-free power generation not subject to resource depletion or dependence upon foreign suppliers? Wrong again. In fact, the greens have single-handedly made nuclear power so expensive and litigious that no new nuclear facility has been built in the U.S. in thirty years. Ignoring the extraordinary safety record of nuclear power throughout the world, greens have exploited decades-old accidents like the 1979 meltdown at Three Mile Island and the 1986 disaster at Chernobyl to scare the U.S. public away from nuclear power.

For example, a hoped-for addition of a third nuclear reactor at the Calvert Cliffs nuclear plant fifty miles southeast of Washington, D.C. evoked the typical green reaction. "Opponents hope to make the case in Maryland that despite safety innovations in the construction of nuclear reactors, a new plant would not be safe from a catastrophic accident or terrorist strike, would create evacuation problems and would add to the nuclear waste stored at Calvert Cliffs," reported the *Washington Post*.[22]

The Energy Policy Act of 2005 provided new incentives for expanding nuclear power, leading to some expectations of a nuclear

revival. As of the fall of 2008, twenty-one companies had applied to
the Nuclear Regulatory Commission to build thirty-four nuclear
power plants. However, the proposed plants still face innumerable
obstacles erected by the greens. "Many problems could derail the so-
called nuclear revival, and virtually no one believes all 34 proposed
plants will be built," the *New York Times* reported.[23]

But the real question is this: will *any* nuclear plants be built?

"Some people say they believe more political opposition will emerge
once some of the proposed plants move closer to construction," the
Times reported. A spokesman for the anti-nuclear power activist group
the Union of Concerned Scientists said that "it was too soon to say that
opposition was weaker now than during construction of the older
plants, when grandmothers tried to block bulldozers."[24] He continued,
"We've got the grandmothers; we just don't have the bulldozers.
There's not the Kodak moment that a lot of these protests need."

One of the most important aspects of the greens' anti-nuclear campaign is their obstruction of the building of a multi-billion dollar
nuclear waste facility slated for Nevada's Yucca Mountain. This site
would be crucial for collecting and securely storing spent nuclear rods
from U.S. power plants, which are now often stored separately at each
plant. But the Yucca site is being sabotaged by green advocates within the Environmental Protection Agency, which is responsible for setting the Yucca facility's construction standards. In August 2005, the
EPA proposed that public health should be protected from the
radioactive waste stored at Yucca for *one million years*—a period of
time more than 200 times the length of recorded human history. Since
it would be impossible for anyone to assure Yucca's safety for a million years, the site has been effectively annulled.

All the legal and regulatory obstacles have drastically driven up the
cost of building new nuclear power plants.[25] Perversely, greens argue

that the high cost of new nuclear power—which their own policies have brought about—should eliminate even the consideration of expanding nuclear power. Anti-nuclear researchers Amory Lovins and Imran Sheikh, for example, argue that nuclear power is "so hopelessly uneconomic that one needn't debate whether it's clean and safe." They go on to argue that nuclear power would worsen global warming.[26]

This is a tough argument to make since nuclear power puts out zero carbon emissions. But where there's a will, there's a way, and the greens are definitely not lacking in will.

Yes, Really: Greens Against Renewable Energy

So the greens oppose conventional oil, shale oil, tar sands, refineries, coal, natural gas, and nuclear power. As a substitute, greens say they support alternative energies like solar, wind, and biofuels. But do they *really*? One might ask outspoken global warming activist Robert F. Kennedy, Jr., who has vigorously campaigned against a proposed 130-turbine electricity-producing wind farm off Cape Cod because it would allegedly "impoverish the experience of millions of tourists and residents and fishing families who rely on the sound's unspoiled bounties."[27] Unmentioned in Kennedy's tirades, however, is that the windmill would obstruct the pristine view from his family's famed Hyannis Port compound nearby.

This may seem like a straightforward instance of individual hypocrisy, but it fits into a surprising pattern. Consider Maryland's green governor Martin O'Malley, who campaigned on promises to reduce emissions from coal-fired power plants and to secure the "right to breathe clean air."[28] But after winning election, in April 2008 he banned wind turbines from state-owned lands. In doing so, he sided with green activists who made arguments similar to those Kennedy made against the Cape Cod windmill: they claimed that windmills would reduce the land's recreational value, spoil the landscape, and lower property values.[29]

Other instances of green opposition to wind farms are strangely common. A proposed wind farm off the coast of Georgia was delayed when greens successfully lobbied to require a multi-year, multi-million dollar study of its potential impact on whale calving grounds and migratory birds. And Canada's *Globe and Mail* ran an article making a near-identical argument against a proposed wind farm off the coast of British Columbia that would supposedly threaten a flyway used by migrating birds.[30]

What about solar power? The greens say they are for it—so why did they resort to their usual obstructing tactics to delay a potentially huge expansion in solar power in the West? In May 2008, the Bureau of Land Management stopped accepting applications for solar energy projects' on public lands in six western states pending completion of a two-year, green-backed study on the projects' environmental impacts. Green activists had voiced concerns about the projects endangering local wildlife such as squirrels and tortoises.[31] "[The solar projects] cover [more than 500,000] acres potentially, and we need to determine what the environmental consequences are of that, and look at what it means when you spray the land with herbicides or remove vegetation," a BLM spokesman explained.[32]

The Bureau cancelled the moratorium on new applications after just five weeks due to pressure from the solar energy industry. But work will continue on the environmental study, whose sole purpose appears to be to provide a basis for denying permits for solar projects.

The Mojave Desert, with its sparse population and abundant sunlight, is a popular site for proposed solar energy projects, but greens have already laid the groundwork for protecting the desert against such encroachments with a 1998 study that estimated the Mojave

would need 1,000 years to recover from tank training exercises conducted there during World War II. "Deserts may be the best place for
tank exercises, but such use comes with a cost. If it hasn't recovered
in 200 years, maybe we're talking about a non-sustainable use," one
researcher told the media.[33]

If short-lived tank training has irreparably harmed the desert, what
would the installation and maintenance of thousands of square miles
of solar panels do?

The greens are also well-known backers of biofuels like ethanol,
which they tout as a clean replacement for gasoline that promotes
energy independence. But once again all is not as it appears, as the
greens insist that biofuels must be "done right," as the Natural
Resources Defense Council puts it.[34]

In practice, "done right" often means "not done at all." The activist
group Environmental Defense proclaimed in a 2007 report that
"renewable fuels produced with low greenhouse gas emissions are one
of our best opportunities to address global warming." However, the
report went on to warn of the dangers of using these very renewable
fuels, insisting that increases in ethanol production, for example, will
strain already stretched Midwest water supplies and involve the
apparently problematic conversion of grasslands into crop acreage.[35]

As ostensible supporters of biofuels, European greens had an unex-
pected reaction to the EU's decision in July 2008 to slow the expansion of biofuel use. Friends of the Earth Europe welcomed the move,
proclaiming, "This vote gives a clear political signal that an expansion
of biofuels is unacceptable. Politicians are waking up to the fact that
using crops to feed cars is a disaster in the making for both people and
nature."[36]

One of the key benefits of biofuels, according to greens, is their low
greenhouse gas emissions. Thus it was rather puzzling when the

director of the Sierra Club's Global Warming and Energy Program went on National Public Radio in February 2007 and bemoaned the fact that biofuels contribute to global warming because "the way we make ethanol now involves seven passes over the field with a diesel tractor, heating the corn to convert it into ethanol, and transporting the fuel in diesel-guzzling trucks."[37]

In the same vein, the *New York Times* reported in February 2008 that two studies—one of which was sponsored by the Nature Conservancy, a green activist group—had determined that "almost all biofuels used today cause more greenhouse gas emissions than conventional fuels if the full emissions costs of producing these 'green' fuels are taken into account." A Nature Conservancy scientist summed it up for the *Times*: "You're making climate change worse, just at the time when we need to be bringing down carbon emissions."[38]

The Hidden Agenda

All this brings up a burning question: why? Why would green activists lobby against wind farms, solar energy, and biofuels—the very alternative energies that their own movement claims to embrace?

Here's the answer: greens don't really want to increase our energy supply—whether with fossil fuels or renewable energy—because that would undermine virtually all of the greens' ultimate goals: zero population growth, limiting the development of physical infrastructure, impeding economic growth, and redistributing wealth. Solving our energy problems would mean making available vast supplies of cheap, reliable energy, and that would open the door to booming growth on every front—the absolute last thing the greens will tolerate. Their very use of the "energy crisis" as their rallying cry is replete with irony given that they have played a huge role in creating and perpetuating all our current energy-related problems.

Furthermore, by making energy scarce, the greens create larger avenues for expanding the government's power over the individual. It's extremely rare in history that a government responds to a crisis by lessening its own powers. Think about the Great Depression, which ushered in the massive government expansion known as the New Deal, or our major military conflicts—the Civil War, World War I, and World War II—which all ushered in the draft. An energy crisis would be very similar—it would create an opportunity, and even a public demand, for the government to do whatever it takes to solve the problem. When combined with the supposed crisis of global warming, energy shortages provide the greens with an urgent rationale for unprecedented government action.

Columnist George Will took note of this strategy, commenting that environmentalism is often a thinly-veiled form of collectivism:

> For some people, environmentalism is collectivism in drag. Such people use environmental causes and rhetoric not to change the political climate for the purpose of environmental improvement. Rather, for them, changing the society's politics is the end, and environmental policies are mere means to that end.
>
> ... One of the collectivists' tactics is to produce scarcities, particularly of what makes modern society modern—the energy requisite for social dynamism and individual autonomy. Hence collectivists use environmentalism to advance a collectivizing energy policy. Focusing on one energy source at a time, they stress the environmental hazards of finding, developing, transporting, manufacturing or using oil, natural gas, coal or nuclear power. [39]

The greens may be myopic, but they're not dumb. They realized long ago that power—the fuel and electricity that drive our economy—is power. When control over energy is disbursed among myriad competing private companies, there is a limited potential for abuse. But if the government were to use an energy crisis as a pretext to tighten its grip on the energy supply, it would vastly expand the state's ability to dictate the everyday parameters of how we live our lives.

Right now, individual Americans can choose what kind of fuel we use and how hot or cool we keep our homes. But government control of energy could quickly change that, ushering in "smart thermostats" and many other green-supported measures. Absent energy shortages, all this would be impossible to justify to the public.

So those of us who value individual autonomy and limited government should keep our eyes on the energy supply, remembering that energy—the very thing that has enabled the American way of life—can also be used to quash it.

CHAPTER 3

A MORE
PEDESTRIAN LIFE

It's no secret that we Americans cherish our cars. We see their mobility, functionality, and even their style as part of our national identity. And in the past few decades cars have become an increasingly important part of our daily routine; we now drive twice as much as we did in 1980 and four times as much as we did in 1957, when the interstate highway system was created.[1] In short, cars are a crucial element of the American way of life.

So it is unsurprising that the greens have put the automobile directly in their crosshairs. By making driving more expensive and more difficult, they seek to force us to drive less and drive smaller. For many greens, however, even that goal is too modest; they hope to get cars off the road altogether.

Paving the Way for a Car-Less world

America's love affair with the automobile is about a century old now, so it's going to take quite a lot to get us to abandon our wheels. Knowing this, the greens have constructed a global echo chamber reverberating with their "drive less" mantra. The National Resources Defense Council's "Drive Less and Drive Smarter" pitch to San Francisco Bay residents argues,

Like most of urban America, the Bay Area has a host of problems
that can be traced straight to one thing: too many automobiles.
Noise, congestion, sprawl, and other problems aside, cars create
enormous amounts of pollution, harm habitats and air and
water quality, and contribute to global warming. It's time to
rethink our relationship with the automobile.[2]

How should we "rethink our relationship" with cars? The NRDC
suggests that you use public transit, carpool, combine your trips (as
if you're not clever enough to do this without being told), join a car
co-op (where you can check out cars using a reservation system), and
"choose a compact neighborhood" where you don't need a car. The
commonality among all these recommendations is that they reduce
your independence and your freedom to do what you need to do
when you need to do it.

What's most astonishing about the "drive less" movement is how
widespread and active it is.

Dedicated to promoting "carfree" communities, the World Carfree
Network is an international coalition consisting of thirty-five European organizations, thirty-six groups in the Americas, and twelve
organizations across Africa.[3] The Network's screed against the automobile, as put forth in its "global charter," puts the NRDC's reproach
to shame. The car, according to the charter, "has led to the global
spread of an environmentally and socially destructive way of life";
kills people and animals in "truly catastrophic proportions"; "denies
free mobility to children, the elderly, the poor and the physically
handicapped"; harms "our physical and emotional health"; contributes to "a global obesity epidemic"; and transforms society into
"an urban wasteland" marked by "isolation and alienation."[4]

That's quite a jeremiad against a mode of transport that provides
nearly 200 million Americans with greater freedom to choose where

to live, work, and spend their leisure time. Neither the NRDC nor the World Carfree Network seem to notice that cars improve people's lives by making it much easier for them to get to work, take their kids to school, shop and run errands, act quickly in emergencies, and do countless other things.

Greens are free to eschew cars, of course, but they're bent on imposing their strange Luddite morality on the rest of us. To that end, the World Carfree Network is sponsoring a series of conferences around the world entitled "Towards Carfree Cities." The eighth such conference, held in Portland, Oregon in June 2008, featured a speech by a Sierra Club member who condemned road construction and advocated land use restrictions and a moratorium on new parking garages in downtown areas. Rather disturbingly, the speaker also serves on the citizens advisory committee of the Baltimore (Maryland) Regional Transportation Board.[5] Other participants proposed metered access to shared cars as an alternative to individual car ownership, and the increased use of speed bumps, traffic circles, and road closures to promote bicycle use. Freeway expansion, of course, was roundly condemned.[6]

There's more than talk behind carfree activism. In August 2008, the city of Seattle, Washington held the first of three planned car-free Sundays by blocking off five blocks of the city. Responding to complaints about the road closures, Seattle mayor Greg Nickels told residents to give their cars a vacation and "just chill."[7] The car-free Sundays cost the city a total of $45,000 for the permitting, barricades, and policing. "I think it's a total and complete waste of money," one resident who doesn't even own a car told the *Seattle Times*. Concerned that Seattle was turning into a "nanny city," she told the *Times*, "I don't like being told what to do."[8]

On the other coast, anti-car activists are lobbying New York City mayor Michael Bloomberg to close Brooklyn's Prospect Park to traffic even though it's a main thruway that eases congestion.[9] Meanwhile, Washington, D.C. is becoming "the most anti-car city in the country," a spokesman for the American Automobile Association told *The Washington Post* following the city's decision to close down a number of commuter routes there. D.C. officials lectured the *Post* that "there are plenty of ways for commuters to get into the city without bringing exhaust-spewing vehicles with them."[10]

Anti-car activism isn't just limited to the car. If the car-hating, anti-convenience crowd has its way, drive-thru businesses will go the way of the drive-in movie theater. "Given the concerns about all the carbon going into the atmosphere, I'm not sure we should be building more places for people to sit idling in their cars," said a spokesman for a citizen panel appointed by the mayor of Madison, Wisconsin.[11] The city is looking to follow in the footsteps of several Canadian cities and San Luis Obispo, California by banning drive-thru restaurants. Ask any mom with small kids strapped into their car seats whether she'd rather zip through the McDonald's drive-thru or corral her kids in and out of the restaurant. Is drive-thru banking the next convenience on the green hit list?

Some Americans even seek to impose their anti-car sentiments abroad. In November 2007, *New York Times* columnist Thomas Friedman cried out to India, "No, No, No, Don't Follow Us" in response to plans by India's Tata Motors to introduce the Nano, a car costing only $2,500. Though Friedman acknowledged that "we have no right to tell Indians what cars to make or drive," he went on to do just that, warning that "cheap conventional four-wheeled cars would encourage millions of Indians to give up their two-wheeled motor scooters and three-wheeled motorized rickshaws, could overwhelm India's already strained road system, increase its dependence on foreign oil and gridlock the country's megacities."[12]

So what does Friedman suggest? He wants India to "leapfrog us, not copy us"—like Indians allegedly did with their telephone system. According to Friedman's calculus, Indians went from no phones to 250 million cell phones because, apparently, they anticipated the advent of cellular technology and thus skipped landline telephones for over 100 years. Indians "should try the same with mass transit," Friedman admonishes. I suppose if the Indians were really clairvoyant, they could even skip mass transit and hold out for Star Trek-like transporter technology to become available—that way they could avoid mass transit's problems, too.

I thought of Friedman's piece when I saw a June 2008 *Washington Post* article about the rickshaw making a comeback in India because of high fuel prices and environmental activists. "'My rickshaw is my life. It's very cheap for my passengers,' said Saurabh Ganguly, a 27-year-old rickshaw cyclist whose shirt was sticky with dirt and grime," the *Post* reported.[13] While rickshaw transport may be this man's business, one can't help but wonder if he'd like the opportunity to escape the "dirt and grime" of being a human beast of burden and perhaps begin driving a Nano as a taxi?

But his chance of improving his lot in life is being sabotaged by greens who romanticize the rickshaw. "We must save the cycle rickshaw drivers," said a spokesman for the Institute for Transportation and Development Policy, a U.S.-based anti-car group. "Look at the soaring fuel price hikes. These bikes are wonderful alternatives. They provide an affordable, smog-free choice."[14] The Institute is most active in underdeveloped nations such as India, Senegal, and Ghana—doing its part to keep those countries from developing their way out of poverty.[15]

In a January 2008 piece, Bloomberg columnist Andy Mukherjee denounced Western criticism of the Nano. "This isn't a product for the West," he remarked. "It's aimed at a family of four that's current-ly forced to use a motorcycle or a scooter because it can't afford even the cheapest car on the roads and there's no reliable public transport where it lives."[16]

The greens shouldn't stand in that family's way—or yours.

Driving up the Cost of Driving

As previously discussed, green policies have deliberately driven up the cost of energy, resulting in the $4-per-gallon gasoline crisis of 2008. High fuel costs force people to drive less, and that causes numerous problems for many Americans: they have to limit their recreational activities and vacations; buy smaller, more dangerous cars; and cur-tail their business activities. But as we've seen, for many greens less driving—and preferably no driving—is an explicit goal, regardless of the consequences to you. And they're engaged in numerous cam-paigns to bring this about by increasing the cost of driving.

While you may think you can escape the next hike in gas prices by buying a more fuel efficient car, the greens are already working to thwart you. Fuel efficient cars may facilitate the green campaign against oil, but they don't further green efforts to reduce driving over-all. So some greens are working toward a more radical solution: ditch-ing the gas tax in favor of a per-mile driving fee. This is being tried in an Oregon pilot project, which the green-leaning *Washington Post* rec-ommended extending to the entire country:

> Roughly 300 Oregon motorists agreed to a per-mile fee that increased when they drove in congested areas or during rush hour. The result? Twenty-two percent of participants drove less during peak periods. Nine in 10 participants said that they preferred the mileage fee to the gas tax. The National Surface Transportation Pol-

icy and Revenue Study Commission recommended to Congress this year that the country transition to a mileage fee by 2025; the success of the Oregon program proves this is possible. [17]

The *Post* was apparently unconcerned by the gross invasion of privacy inherent in monitoring how much, when, and where every American drives his car. And although it's now being touted as a substitute for the gas tax, adopting a per-mile fee would more likely serve as an *addition* to taxes at the pump. In fact, the *Post* itself also advocates raising the gas tax. As gas prices tumbled in late 2008, the paper editorialized that "in a perfect world, we'd like to see a gas tax that was the equivalent of oil at $100 per barrel. This would send a loud-and-clear signal to drivers to continue eschewing gas guzzlers for fuel sippers and mass transit. . . . and it could all be returned to the American people in the form of tax rebates."[18]

In other words, punish drivers with high taxes and dole out that money as a virtuous reward for non-drivers and those with green-approved cars. We're all familiar with schemes to redistribute wealth from the rich to the poor, but now we're facing another concept: redistributing wealth from eco-sinners to the eco-saints.

Another program that would raise the cost of driving is road pricing. Now, some free marketers advocate road pricing as a market-based solution to congestion. These proposals usually take two forms: congestion pricing (charging motorists more to use a roadway, bridge, or tunnel during rush hour) and toll roads (charging for use of particular roads). These are the most limited of the road pricing systems, focusing on the modest goal of reducing traffic at the most congested times and on the most congested roads.

The greens support more radical road pricing schemes that serve a more ambitious goal: to get as many cars as possible off the road completely. The first of these, area pricing, seeks to reduce the number of cars in entire geographic areas by charging high fees for cars to enter those regions. The city of London adopted area pricing in 2003, charging five pounds (about $9) for entering drivers. Then in July 2005, the size of the restricted area was doubled and the charge was increased to eight pounds (about $14).

Although greens praise London's area pricing for successfully taking cars off the road,[19] others take a dimmer view. A report prepared for the advocacy group Keep NYC Congestion Tax Free concluded that the scheme hurt London businesses, was too expensive (costing $376 million to set up), was inefficient, and that congestion within London actually worsened even with reduced traffic volume.[20]

There have already been attempts to implement area pricing in major American cities. Mayor Michael Bloomberg proposed that New York City adopt a London-style scheme—$8 for cars and $21 for trucks to enter Manhattan—but his initiative failed due to protests about the economic consequences. A report from the Queens Chamber of Commerce noted the program's downside: less traffic would mean about 40,000 fewer people entering the city to do business, which would lead to an annual loss of $2.7 billion in economic output, 23,100 jobs, and $235 million in city and state tax revenues.[21] The report further noted that area pricing would particularly harm working- and middle-class New Yorkers who commute into the city, as well as small to mid-sized suburban companies whose business requires frequent trips into the city.[22]

And of course, once the program was in place, prices would inevitably rise. As Keep NYC Congestion Tax Free Coalition asserted, "Anyone who thinks it's going to be $8 is either delusional or they are deliberately trying to hoodwink the public."[23]

An even more sweeping program for getting cars off the road is universal tolling, which would charge drivers for using every road.

Though universal tolling is still, for the moment, a nascent concept, some greens have envisioned an electronic road-pricing system that uses GPS technology to charge drivers based on criteria such as their type of vehicle, driving location, and time of driving. The pricing scheme would incentivize everyone to drive, if at all, in small cars during off-peak hours in urban areas. The more you deviate from this set up, the more you pay. The Natural Resources Defense Council testified to Congress in June 2008 that universal tolling is one of several "established and growing means to address both congestion and financing in road transportation."[24]

In case expensive roads don't get you out of your car, the greens want to use car insurance for the same goal. Green activists in Environmental Defense, for example, promote so-called pay-as-you-drive insurance (PAYD), which would base your car insurance rate on the amount you drive—the farther you drive, the more you pay.[25] The group touts an estimate from the Brookings Institution, a left-leaning think tank, that a nationwide PAYD system would reduce overall driving by 8 percent.[26]

Some PAYD programs monitor not only your mileage, but *how* you drive. Auto insurer Progressive's PAYD program requires the installation of a monitoring device in your car that tells Progressive not only how far you drive, but when you drive, how fast you go, and how aggressively you drive—that is, how abruptly you brake and accelerate.[27]

If someone doesn't mind an insurer monitoring his driving this closely, then he's welcome to join a PAYD program (though one wonders about the effect on road safety when drivers try to minimize use of their brakes and gas pedals in hopes of saving money). But keep in mind that the program's benefits as trumpeted by greens, such as an 8 percent reduction in overall driving, won't be realized unless PAYD becomes America's *only* form of car insurance. And since tens of millions of Americans undoubtedly oppose this kind of intimate monitoring of their driving habits or simply don't want to be penalized for driving long distances, the only way greens can realize these benefits would be by making PAYD compulsory for everyone.

Hybrid Mania

Gas prices got you down? Then the greens have a solution for you. The Natural Resources Defense Council recommends buying a "smaller, more fuel efficient model or a hybrid" like the Toyota Camry hybrid, which the NRDC claims "boosts fuel economy by about a third compared to the conventional version. If you're paying $3.72 a gallon, that saves about $600 a year."[28]

Sounds great—until you do the math. As of this writing, the Manufacturers Suggested Retail Price (MSRP) for a 2009 Toyota Camry starts at $19,145, while the MSRP for that model's hybrid version costs $7,005 more.[29] Based on the $600 savings in gas estimated by NRDC, it would take more than *eleven years* of driving the hybrid to make up for its higher sticker price.

This is par for the hybrid course. According to a June 2005 analysis by Edmunds, the car buyers' information center, the price of gas would have to exceed $10 per gallon for a hybrid Toyota Prius to be as economical as a conventional Toyota Corolla, and a Prius would have to be driven at least 66,500 miles *per year* to match the savings achieved by buying a cheaper Corolla. Hybrids from companies like Honda and Ford offer a similar lousy pay off.[30]

Consider this: overnight delivery giant FedEx has the largest fleet of hybrid delivery trucks in North America. In logging more than 2 million miles of service, the trucks improved fuel economy by 42 percent. Sounds great, right? But when I asked FedEx CEO Fred Smith about the cost of the hybrid trucks at the 2006 FedEx shareholder meeting, he publicly admitted that they don't make economic sense.[31] His excuse for sticking with the hybrids was that the greens had forced his hand—he then muttered that environmentalism was a "cult."

Even though one of the world's most successful companies can't make hybrid trucks pay off, government agencies think they can do the trick.

Just look at California where, to comply with a state-mandated zero-emission demonstration program, the Santa Clara Valley Transportation Authority purchased three fuel cell buses in 2005. This has been a total economic failure: the fuel buses cost thirty-two times more per mile to operate than comparable diesel buses; they break down nearly six times more often and are way more expensive to fix ($34.40 per-mile parts costs versus 21 cents for diesel buses); and their hydrogen fuel costs about five times more than diesel fuel. Oh, and did I mention that the sale price of a fuel cell bus is almost ten times more than a standard diesel bus ($3 million versus $328,000)?[32]

In fact, the hybrid mania costs taxpayers in every state. Currently, Ford, General Motors, Honda, Nissan, and Toyota combined are eligible for nearly $1 billion in federal tax credits on hybrids.[33] The amount of this giveaway may rise further in the near future due to lobbying by carmakers. The Cato Institute's Jerry Taylor had an insightful response to a plea from Toyota for more aid for hybrids:

> By subsidizing people who buy Toyota products—products manufactured by one of the largest privately held corporations in the world—our taxpayers are supporting Toyota employees and stockholders at a time when GM and Ford are on economic life support.
>
> . . . Look, I have nothing against hybrid powered cars. There are even a number of Cato staffers who drive them. It's just that,

personally, I don't like being forced to pay for someone else's car. But that's just me.[34]

Perhaps you're thinking, "Okay, hybrids cost everyone more, but we'll be saving the planet, right?" Well, that's what the car companies claim. Toyota boasts, "We've sold over a million hybrids worldwide, more than any other car company—resulting in an estimated savings of millions of gallons of gasoline and billions of pounds of [carbon dioxide] being kept out of the atmosphere."[35]

Saving millions of gallons of gas sounds impressive—unless you know how irrelevant that is, since Americans use about 440 million gallons of gas *per day*.[36] Similarly, the atmosphere probably doesn't notice the "billions of pounds" of carbon dioxide not emitted over of a period of years given that natural decomposition from forests and grasslands alone emits about 440 *trillion* pounds of carbon dioxide each year.[37] Considering their huge cost and negligible environmental impacts, hybrids are a double rip off.

Drive Smaller, Drive Deadlier

When the greens aren't foisting hybrids on the public, they're trying to stuff you into smaller cars. Of course, there's nothing wrong with a small car if that's what you want. But larger cars, trucks, and SUVs are popular for numerous reasons: they're more comfortable, roomier, handle better in poor driving conditions, and are much safer.

All this leaves the greens unmoved. They've been trying to get big cars off the road for years by pressing the government to tighten fuel economy standards for new cars and light trucks. In 2007 Congress and President Bush obliged, raising the Corporate Average Fuel Economy (CAFE) standard from 27.5 miles per gallon for cars and 22.5 MPG for light trucks to thirty-five MPG for both categories by 2020.[38]

Greens claim the new CAFE standard will reduce U.S. oil consumption by about 5 percent by 2020.[39] And although carmakers are not sure they can meet such an ambitious goal, the greens are already advocating even higher standards—forty MPG by 2012, urges the NRDC.[40]

The government raised CAFE standards as if auto engineering wizards can easily invent some new technology to meet them. But in reality, the only practical way to meet higher CAFE standards is by the rather low-tech method of reducing car weight. And lighter cars are deadlier cars. A majority of participants on a National Academy of Sciences panel found in 2001 that the manufacture of smaller, lighter cars in the late 1970s and early '80s—partly due to CAFE standards— "probably resulted in an additional 1,300 to 2,600 traffic fatalities in 1993" and deprived drivers of desirable features like faster acceleration, greater carrying or towing capacity, and reliability.[41] In 2003 the National Highway Traffic Safety Administration similarly concluded that every 100-pound reduction in the weight of small cars increased annual traffic fatalities by as much as 715.[42]

The total cost to society of smaller cars is quite arresting. *USA Today* reported in 1999 that its analysis of previously unpublished government data showed that "46,000 people have died because of a 1970s-era push for greater fuel efficiency that has led to smaller cars."[43] Adding insult to injury (and death), the paper observed, is that small cars depreciate faster and are worth less at trade-in time, and insurers charge up to 45 percent more for collision and damage coverage.

According to the NRDC, the new CAFE standard will save us a million gallons of gas per day. That sounds like a great benefit, but how does it balance out against the 2,000 fatalities per year that the National Academy of Sciences attributes to the lighter cars resulting from that regulation? Let's charitably assume that the new CAFE standards reduce the price of gasoline by $1 a gallon. That would translate to daily savings of about $1 million. Is that worth the death of more than five people per day? The Environmental Protection Agency—for purposes of risk assessment—values a single human life at $6.9 million dollars. So it turns out that CAFE is likely to cost more than $35 million per day in human lives (not including non-fatal injuries) to save $1 million in gas.

What a bargain.

And if you survive CAFE, your job might not. A group of major automakers has warned the National Highway Traffic Safety Administration that new CAFE standards the agency imposed in 2008—4.5 percent annual increases in fuel efficiency between 2011 and 2015—would cost up to 82,000 jobs and reduce sales by 856,000 vehicles.[44]

But for greens, issues like job retention and even personal safety are of marginal importance. They're out to save the planet, you see, and if that costs a few jobs here or a few lives there, so be it.

Permanent Roadblocks

Although there are about 4 million miles of roads in the U.S., more roads are desperately needed.[45] According to the Federal Highway Administration,

> The Texas Transportation Institute estimates that, in 2003, the 85 largest metropolitan areas experienced 3.7 billion vehicle-hours of delay, resulting in 2.3 billion gallons in wasted fuel and a congestion cost of $63 billion. Traffic volumes are projected to continue growing. The volume of freight movement alone is forecast to nearly double by 2020. Congestion is largely thought of as a big city problem, but delays are becoming increasingly common in small cities and some rural areas as well.[46]

Adding new highways is a key strategy for alleviating these problems, since forty percent of the congestion problem is due to physical bottlenecks or highway capacity limitations.[47] However, a report prepared by transport engineers and planners for the Federal Highway Administration notes that "in some metropolitan areas...it is becoming increasingly difficult to undertake major highway expansions because of funding constraints, increased right-of-way and construction costs, and *opposition from local and national groups*" (emphasis added).[48]

Now, who might those "local and national groups" be?

Here's a hint: Deron Lovaas, the "Vehicles Campaign Director" and "Smart Growth and Transportation Program Deputy Director" of the Natural Resources Defense Council, laid out the greens' national highway strategy before the Senate Environment and Public Works Committee in June 2008. Needless to say, Lovaas did not enthusiastically endorse new highways. To the contrary, he called for a "minimization of the overall footprint of new and existing [roads]," and instead advocated the repair of existing infrastructure and providing "more travel choices," toll roads, and pay-as-you-drive insurance.[49]

In his testimony, Lovaas advocated a rail system as part of his suggestions for "more travel choices"—another euphemism for "no more roads."[50] But try to build a rail system and see what the greens have to say about it. In 2007, the Sierra Club successfully campaigned against a ballot measure in the state of Washington that would have created a $38 billion light rail system—ostensibly because the measure included funding for more roads.[51] Other environmentalists opposed the rail system with the bizarre argument that it would cause air pollution.[52] In another example, green groups are taking divergent positions on a proposed 800-mile rail system to connect California's Central Valley with the Bay Area. It's yet another green squeeze: some green groups champion the rail system as an alternative to roads, while others oppose it as likely to induce sprawl.[53]

As for Lovaas's recommendation of more toll roads, his own organization, the NRDC, shows a distinct lack of enthusiasm. For example, it opposed a proposal to build a toll road to relieve congestion in Orange County, California as a "threat" to a state park.[54] Not to be outdone, the Sierra Club and its allies filed a lawsuit that condemned the proposed road as "an ecological disaster."[55]

As it turns out, the greens only support converting existing roads into toll roads, which holds out the "benefit" of reducing driving overall by making it more expensive. In practice they oppose building new toll roads, because they see them as just another place for you to use your car. For the same reason, many greens now even oppose HOV lanes. "Widening the freeway, even with HOV lanes, allows more vehicles to get on the freeway, and we'll be back where we started—intolerable congestion requiring ever-greater expense to relieve it," argued a green activist in opposing a proposal to widen Highway 50 in Sacramento, California.[56]

As you may have noticed, California greens are particularly active in opposing highway construction—and the state has suffered the consequences. California State Senator Tom McClintock penned an essay in 1999 summing up the damage done by greens to the golden state's highway system. Noting that centerline mileage had increased by just sixty-four miles since 1974, McClintock wrote,

> California's transportation crisis is no mystery. It is the direct result of a critical shortage of highway lanes. California's highway system, once the finest in the world, has not merely been neglected. An ideological war has been waged against it for a quarter century. The refrain has been constant: "We just have to get people out of their cars."

... The practical effect of this ideological crusade against the car has been to bring new road construction in California to a virtual standstill.[57]

Of course, the greens' "ideological crusade" is not confined to California—it's just been particularly successful there. So look at the permanent gridlock that mars California's highways, despite the fact that Californians pay the third highest per-vehicle taxes in America.[58] There's a glimpse of the future the greens have in store for you.

CHAPTER 4

WATER, WATER... NOWHERE?

While the greens' campaign against cars, if successful, would encroach upon life as you know it, at least you might be able to scrounge up alternative solutions—who knows, perhaps you'll swap your car for a Schwinn three-speed and feel really good about it.

Yet there is no substitute for the single most essential substance for sustaining life—water. And it's an incredible testament to the greens' persuasive stagecraft that they have convinced many of us that water—by far the *most abundant substance on the planet*—will soon be in desperately short supply.

Conservation: A Fake Solution to a Fake Crisis

Much like the reporting on global warming, it's not unusual for stories alleging imminent water shortages to take on a quasi-apocalyptic tone, as in this Associated Press article from the fall of 2007:

> An epic drought in Georgia threatens the water supply for millions. Florida doesn't have nearly enough water for its expected population boom. The Great Lakes are shrinking. Upstate New

York's reservoirs have dropped to record lows. And in the West, the Sierra Nevada snowpack is melting faster each year.

Across America, the picture is critically clear—the nation's freshwater supplies can no longer quench its thirst.

The government projects that at least 36 states will face water shortages within five years because of a combination of rising temperatures, drought, population growth, urban sprawl, waste and excess.[1]

Such reports play into the greens' campaign against water usage. Much like the attacks on energy and carbon emissions, the anti-water offensive seeks to instill a sense of imminent crisis in order to force through dramatic, mandatory conservation laws.

In fighting the supposed villainy of casual water use, the greens make examples of high-profile people and companies who use large amounts of water, hoping that some public shaming will force them to repent for their eco-sins and will send the rest of us a strong message. Consider an article in an August 2008 issue of the *Austin-American Statesman* about cycling champion Lance Armstrong. The article begins,

Every minute, about five gallons of water passed through the sinks, sprinklers, fountain and pool at Lance Armstrong's house in June, making the retired professional cyclist Austin's biggest water-using individual that month.

A total of 222,900 gallons of water was used at Armstrong's home, according to the most recent city records available. That's about what 26 average Austin households use in a month. At a time when rainfall has been scarce and the city has imposed mandatory water restrictions, Armstrong is not the only Austinite using a lot of water.

... "I need to fix this.... I have no interest in being the top water user in Austin, Texas," the seven-time Tour de France winner told his local newspaper.[2]

Two months later, coffee purveyor Starbucks—which positions itself as an environmentally friendly and "socially responsible" company—got similarly hosed down for its water use. In an article titled "The Great Drain Robbery," a British newspaper blasted the company for "keeping a tap running non-stop at all its 10,000 outlets worldwide, wasting 23.4 million litres a day."[3] Starbucks maintains that the purpose of the policy is hygienic—to avoid the build-up of bacteria in the sink—but the article gave this consideration short-shrift. Instead, it heaped opprobrium on the firm's environmental evil-doing, barely stopping short of blaming the coffeemaker for the deaths of drought-stricken Africans. "A single Starbucks tap left running for just over three minutes wastes the amount of water one African needs to survive for a day in drought conditions," the article proclaimed, as if water would miraculously travel to needy Africans if only Starbucks would stop using it. Right on cue, the head of the UK environmental group Waste Watch denounced the company, admonishing that "leaving taps running all day is a shocking waste of precious water."

If we were really running low on "precious water," one would expect the greens to support an all-out effort to increase the water supply. But as you may have guessed, they have no interest in doing that. As they see it, more water would mean more economic development, more industry, and more people—all of which the greens oppose. So for the greens, "conservation"—in other words, limiting our usage—is the only acceptable solution. As a writer from Environmental Defense recently declared about a possible future drought in California, the answer is "what many environmentalists have been saying for decades. . . . water conservation, storm water capture, recycling and agricultural to urban transfers."[4]

In light of this emphasis on conservation, it was strange to see Environmental Defense condemn California governor Arnold Schwarzenegger's proposal to work toward reducing the state's per capita water use by 20 percent by 2020. According to the group, the proposal "would be neutralized about six years later, when population is supposed to increase by 25 percent above today's levels." It concluded, "Let's get serious about conservation goals."[5]

So in the end, even the greens don't *really* believe that water conservation is a long-term solution, since increases in population will eventually surpass conservation efforts. They advocate conservation programs until someone actually tries to implement them. Then, the programs suddenly become a ludicrous non-solution.

With the green campaign for water conservation, we see again that "conservation" is a convenient mask that hides a larger agenda—to limit our access to water. The Sierra Club has a laundry list of action items to achieve this, including: a nationwide moratorium on withdrawals from, and diversions of, rivers that could affect fish and wildlife or scenic values; groundwater use restrictions; a ban on transfers between watersheds; and redirecting federal efforts away from designing new water development projects and toward maintenance of existing projects.[6]

This campaign has had particular success in California, where in 2005 the NRDC and several other green groups sued the U.S. Department of Interior, the National Oceanic and Atmospheric Administration, and the National Marine Fisheries Service to force a cutback in the amount of water pumped from the Delta River. The greens' argument was that the pumping of the Delta for drinking water threatens the smelt—a three-inch fish—despite assurances from the U.S. Fish and Wildlife Service that smelt were adequately protected.[7]

A federal court in 2007 decided the case for the greens. The verdict has immense implications for California's water supply, seeing as 3 million San Francisco Bay Area residents rely on the Delta as their primary source of water, not to mention that water from the Delta constitutes about one-third of the water that northern California exports to southern California. Governor Schwarzenegger denounced the decision as "a devastating blow to our water system and state economy." As a result of the verdict, state water officials are predicting drastic declines of water exports to southern California, while some water districts are already discussing the prospect of mandatory water rationing.[8]

Another case occurred in Georgia, where a severe drought in 2008 provoked a local congressman to suggest that building dams along the Flint River might secure a better water supply. The mere mention of dams provoked outrage from the greens. Rebecca Wodder, head of American Rivers, asserted that the proposal was a "distraction that is diverting time from [real] solutions" like more efficient use of water, water reclamation and recycling, and—if Georgia really needs *more* water—capturing stormwater.[9]

It apparently didn't occur to Wodder that relying on stormwater probably isn't a productive strategy during a drought.

The Georgia greens even rolled out former president Jimmy Carter, who had helped kill a similar dam project in the 1970s when he served as the state's governor. Speaking in July 2008, Carter warned a crowd of local greens that it was up against a formidable foe—the promise to "let people sprinkle their lawns seven days a week."[10] He warned of other potential horrors as well: "We need to start arousing some opposition to let them know this is not a popular thing. You ought to prepare for a massive fight. Because you're up against the promise of employment and recreation and higher land prices—and more water for Atlanta."[11]

Indeed, what kind of social misfit would want to have a job, fun, wealth, and a green lawn?

Out with the Old Water, and Out with the New

The greens not only seek to limit the use of existing water supplies, but they also obstruct efforts to make new supplies available. For example, water officials in Las Vegas, Nevada hope that building a desalination plant will secure a reliable water supply for its booming desert economy, but they lament the obstacles erected by the greens. "If sited in California," Las Vegas' officials say, "a desalination facility large enough to provide a significant amount of water to Nevada would face significant environmental obstacles related to project footprint, power generation and brine disposal."[12]

Likewise, an August 2008 hearing of the California Coastal Commission discussed a private company's proposal to build the nation's largest desalination plant—one that could produce as much as 50 million gallons a day, or about 9 percent of local needs.[13] Environmentalists assailed the proposed plant, predicting it would increase energy use, kill sea life, encourage sprawl, privatize water, and waste money.[14] Fortunately for southern Californians—at least as far as this particular hearing went—the commission approved the plant. But this is probably not the last word on the subject. As a law professor noted, "Environmentalists opposed to the plant still have leverage through lawsuits, or merely threatening to file them as a bargaining tactic."[15]

Importing water is also a non-starter for environmentalists. Canada, for example, holds about 20 percent of the world's fresh water and could export huge quantities to the U.S.[16] But that's opposed by the Sierra Club, whose website states that "commercial bulk water export should not be allowed due to the serious ecological, trade and human rights ramifications."[17]

Simultaneously, the greens are working to close off the sale and pipelining of water within the U.S. With the approval of President George W. Bush and Congress, eight states—Illinois, Indiana, Michigan, Minnesota, New York, Ohio, Pennsylvania, and Wisconsin—are about to subject themselves to the Great Lakes Compact, which among other things would prohibit large-scale "diversions" of Great Lakes water by pipeline or ship. That's a lot of water to put off-limits to export; the Great Lakes, after all, is the largest fresh water system in the world, holding approximately 84 percent of North America's surface fresh water and about 21 percent of the world's supply.[18]

But even that agreement wasn't enough for some greens. "Loophole feared in Great Lakes accord," blared a headline in the *Buffalo News* in September 2008.[19] It seems that the compact allows water from the Great Lakes to be bottled and sold in containers no larger than 5.7 gallons—and this caused concern that bottled water from the Great Lakes would appear on store shelves. "Our bottom line is that water should not be a commodity," one green declared.[20]

As an alternative to increasing water supplies, greens claim to support water recycling (also called "indirect potable reuse" or "toilet-to-tap"). This entails used water, whether from your toilet, kitchen sink, or washing machine, traveling the sewer system to a sewage treatment plant that, in turn, superfilters the water. It's then pumped to a lake where it percolates into an aquifer that serves as a source of drinking water, and the cycle starts anew.[21]

Water recycling is problematic even aside from the "yuck" factor of drinking purified sewage—namely, it's very expensive. As the *San Diego Union-Tribune* remarked about a proposed water recycling plan in San Diego, at $238 million the plant would be a "costly boondoggle" that would require hiking water rates.[22] As an alternative, the paper suggested less costly methods of boosting the water supply, including bulk water imports and desalination.

Additionally, the greens' declared support for water recycling seems insincere at best. In the spring of 2008 when the mayor of Los Angeles proposed a water recycling plan, the *Los Angeles Times* reported that "some environmental groups have complained that the mayor's water plan—which includes crackdowns on wasters, incentives to replace water-guzzling washing machines and new storm-water-capturing reservoirs—does nothing to limit growth."[23] So we see that greens, while extolling water recycling in theory, oppose it in practice unless it's tied to an overall plan to limit water use.

Although it's indisputable that we need water from *somewhere*, the greens are agitating to ensure there is water *nowhere*. These efforts reflect the greens' negative view of humankind's very presence on Earth. Consider this: the Environmental Defense Fund concluded a 2008 report by stating, "For many years water users have maintained that water supply reliability is essential for the economic vitality of their industries and the State."[24]

"Water users?" Not "people?" Not to the greens. To them, you're just a "user"—a burden on the environment.

The Tap Water Scare

Alongside their efforts to reduce the water supply, greens have launched a shameful scare campaign about the safety of tap water.

One of the greatest overlooked achievements of civilization has been the establishment of a clean and safe drinking water supply. The crucial advance came in 1908, when Jersey City, New Jersey began disinfecting its drinking water with chlorine.[25] As the use of chlorine spread throughout America, cases of waterborne diseases such as typhoid fever declined from 43 incidents per 100,000 people in 1921 to less than 1 per 100,000 people by they mid-1950s.[26] It would be easy to say that the benefits of disinfecting drinking water with chlorine are indisputable.

But not to the greens.

The greens' war against chlorine extends back to Rachel Carson's 1962 book *Silent Spring*, in which she denounced chlorine-based pesticides like DDT as "elixirs of death" that allegedly cause cancer.[27] During the mid-1960s the Audubon Society and its spin-off group, the Environmental Defense Fund, began agitating to have DDT banned. After the Environmental Protection Agency prohibited the chemical in 1972, the relatively new agency, which was staffed with Rachel Carson acolytes, began investigating how other uses of chlorine might pose risks to health, including whether chlorinated drinking water causes cancer.

In November 1974, a day after the Environmental Defense Fund issued a report suggesting a link between chemical contamination in the Mississippi River and high cancer death rates in Louisiana, the EPA ordered a national study of chemicals in drinking water.[28] Thus began a smear campaign that continues to this day against one of the greatest achievements in public health. Despite a lack of scientific evidence that chlorinating drinking water causes cancer, the EPA now regulates chlorination as if it does. This scare has already had at least one tragic consequence—an early-1990s outbreak of cholera in Peru that was exacerbated by Peruvian officials who stopped disinfecting their drinking water with chlorine. An estimated 1 million people were sickened, and 10,000 died.[29]

The anti-chlorine campaign backfired again when the U.S. Army Corps of Engineers, which is responsible for much of the Washington, D.C. area's drinking water, switched its disinfecting agent from chlorine to chloramine—a combination of chlorine and ammonia. The ammonia, however, made the water more corrosive, which increased the level of lead leaching from the pipes into the water. The greens then stoked an entirely new panic about alleged lead poisoning of children. In January 2009, the *Washington Post* reported on a new study finding that "hundreds of young children in [Washington, D.C.] experienced potentially damaging amounts of lead in their blood." An outraged representative of the advocacy group D.C. Appleseed Center for Law and Justice declared, "We're talking about the health of little children. It's not like this is some insignificant issue."[30]

Predictably, the *Post* article vaguely attributed the heightened lead levels to the addition of "a new chemical" to the water supply—without mentioning that the move originated with the greens' campaign against chlorine.

The Environmental Defense Fund is not the only green group warning of the dangers of your tap water. In 2003, the NRDC issued a report claiming that "deteriorating water works, pollution and outdated treatment technology are combining to deliver water that might pose health risks to many residents in 19 of America's largest cities."[31] Despite all the NRDC's arm-waving about the grave danger presented by our drinking water, it cited no adverse health effects caused by the water systems it examined, reporting only a few technical violations of EPA regulations—standards that include a comfortable margin of error. No doubt, that's why the EPA states on its website that "the United States has one of the safest water supplies in the world."[32]

So what's behind the greens' drinking water scare? Could there be an ulterior motive? Interestingly, when the NRDC rated the nineteen cities on their water safety, only one city, Seattle, received a rating of "excellent" and just four were rated as "good." Looking into the criteria for the ratings, I found that in order to be rated "excellent" a municipality had to have "banned or all but banned" local development and have "no significant [water] pollution sources."[33] These criteria imply the need for a near-complete ban on agricultural and industrial operations in the cities. In essence, the NRDC punishes communities that allow development, farming, and manufacturing by raising doubts about the safety of their water supply.

As Goes Bottled Water, So Goes Everything Else

So if the greens don't want you to drink tap water, do they have an alternative? Are they for bottled water? Heavens, no! Bottled water contributes to global warming, they say—a ludicrous claim that's nevertheless caught some traction.

The greens have never liked bottled water—its availability weakens the impact of their scare campaign against tap water. The NRDC claimed in a 1993 report that tap water might be sickening as many as 900,000 and killing 900 Americans per year, but the group cautioned the public against switching to bottled water since it allegedly could be just as contaminated.[34] In a follow-up 1994 report, the NRDC claimed that more than 36 million Americans drank tap water that failed health standards, and 116 million drank water from systems that violated federal drinking water regulations. It then warned, "Bottled water is not regulated any more strictly than tap water. In fact, some bottled water manufacturers simply bottle tap water."[35]

Despite the NRDC's warnings, by 1999 bottled water had become a $4 billion-per-year business. Then the NRDC got serious, issuing a report on the bottled water "problem" that made the following claims:

- "bottled water should not be assumed to be purer or safer than most tap water"
- bottled water contamination with microbes may raise public health issues particularly for those who are immuno-compromised

• government bottled water regulation and programs have
  serious deficiencies
• voluntary industry standards are "an inadequate substitute for strong government rules and programs"
• bottled water marketing can be misleading
• the long-term solution to drinking water problems is to
  fix tap water—not switch to bottled water.[36]

But this effort didn't pay off either. By 2007, the U.S. bottled water industry had almost quadrupled in size to about $15 billion. That's when the greens unveiled their not-so-secret weapon—the global warming argument. And as hard as it is to believe, the greens are having some success making the ridiculous argument that bottled water is harmful because its production and transport both involve the emission of greenhouse gases.[37]

This campaign eventually began to impact public policy. In February 2007, the director of the San Francisco Department of the Environment and the general manager of the San Francisco Public Utilities Commission argued in an op-ed in the *San Francisco Chronicle* that "just supplying Americans with plastic water bottles for one year consumes more than 47 million gallons of oil, enough to take 100,000 cars off the road and 1 billion pounds of carbon dioxide out of the atmosphere . . . so it is clear that bottled water directly adds to environmental degradation, global warming and a large amount of unnecessary waste and litter."[38]

Two months later the city of Santa Barbara, California banned bottled water from city functions,[39] followed another two months later by a similar ban ordered by San Francisco mayor Gavin Newsome. "All this waste and pollution is generated by a product that by objective standards is often inferior to the quality of San Francisco's pristine tap water," Newsome declared.[40]

It's amusing to note that while Newsome regurgitated the NRDC's claims about the dangers of bottled water, he ignored the group's derogatory comments about the quality of his own city's tap water. In a June 2003 report, the NRDC rated the quality of the city's tap water as "poor" due to its allegedly dangerous levels of cancer-causing contaminants and lead.[41]

Undaunted, Mayor Newsome took his anti-bottled water crusade to the 2008 annual meeting of the U.S. Conference of Mayors where he introduced, and the conference approved, a resolution calling for the phase-out of bottled water purchases by municipalities.[42] According to the conference's media release, the resolution "will send the strong message that opting for tap over bottled water is what's best for our environment, our pocketbooks and our long-term, equitable access to our most essential resource."[43]

The American Beverage Association—a trade group representing the soft drink and bottled water industry—chided the conference's resolution as "sound-bite environmentalism" done "in their zeal to appease liberal activist groups that are pedaling misinformation about bottled water."[44]

So the greens are finally making progress in their war against bottled water. By September 2008, St. Louis and Seattle had passed their own bans on city purchases of bottled water, while Chicago now taxes the product.[45] The Canadian city of London, Ontario ordered a ban on bottled water sales at municipal facilities and the installation of new water fountains at its properties and mobile tankers to distribute water at its parks.[46]

So what are the implications for you of the war against bottled water?

For the most part, bottled water offers convenience and reliability. More important, it can help travelers avoid serious sicknesses. As pointed out by the travel advisory service IndependentTraveler.com,

Contaminated drinking water is one of the leading sources of health problems for travelers, and can cause anything from mild gastrointestinal distress to serious bacterial diseases.

The most common cause of water-borne illness is bacteria, such as E. coli, cholera and salmonella, but illness can also be caused by protozoa (including giardia and cryptosporidium), viruses (like hepatitis A, polio and rotavirus) and chemical pollutants.

The best way to protect yourself is to avoid local tap water and instead seek out bottled water.[47]

The availability of bottled water is crucial during outbreaks of water-borne disease and natural disasters. For emergency preparedness, the Centers for Disease Control and Prevention recommends keeping a supply of water that is "preferably in store-bought, factory-sealed water containers."[48] That sounds a lot like bottled water, which will become awfully hard to find if we continue down the current road of restricting its availability in order to fight the chimera of global warming.

Perhaps you don't drink bottled water so you couldn't care less if it's banned. But the implications of the greens' war against bottled water are larger than you may think.

Bottled water only constitutes 14 percent of the market for fountain and packaged beverages, which typically come in aluminum, plastic, and glass containers.[49] While consumers see a big difference between bottled water, soft drinks, and beer, wine, and liquor, greens only perceive that all these beverages are produced, packaged, and transported in the same environmentally destructive, global-warming-causing way.

The Sierra Club warns that it takes 17 million barrels of oil and 2.5 million tons of greenhouse gas emissions to make one year's worth of plastic water bottles.[50] Just imagine how much oil and emissions are involved in producing the other *86 percent* of the market. Once drinking bottled water is established as an eco-sin, there's no logical justification for allowing the consumption of coke, beer, or any other bottled or canned beverage. It's pretty easy to foresee that if bottled water goes down to the greens, other beverages won't be far behind.

CHAPTER 5

DIETING FOR THE PLANET

If you think your diet is nobody's business but your own, then you're in for a surprise. According to the greens, the food you choose to eat has dramatic ramifications for the environment—and therefore your diet is the rightful focus of public policy. The animals that provide your meat, the way your food is transported to the supermarket, how your food is grown and harvested—all these issues are of intimate concern to those seeking to mitigate the ravages of human existence on Earth.

And if the end result of green food policy is more expensive food, less culinary variety, and less food overall, well hey, a little forced dieting is a small price to pay for saving the planet, now isn't it?

Vegetarianism for Me—And for Thee

In a famous 1984 Wendy's TV commercial, an old lady insistently asked, "Where's the beef?" It was funny then, but don't laugh now. You may be asking that question one day, courtesy of the global warming scare.

The greens claim that, after energy, meat production is the next largest source of greenhouse gas emissions, responsible for about 20 percent of the total. Although data from the Environmental Protection Agency indicates this figure may be exaggerated by almost ten-fold,[1] the greens have decided on the superiority of a meat-free diet—for them and for you.

An anti-meat manifesto was succinctly laid out in a January 2008 column by *New York Times* food columnist Mark Bittman, who lamented that Americans eat about twice as much meat as the global average, consuming about 15 percent of the world's beef though we're just 5 percent of the world's population. Bittman went on to allege many wrongs done to the planet and its people by our voracious appetite for beef, including global warming, global hunger, water quality problems, and an assortment of health problems such as heart disease, cancer, and diabetes.[2]

Claiming we could get by on almost a quarter of our present meat intake, the author asked, "What can be done?" An economist told Bittman we should try to reduce the demand for meat (or in his strange wording, to ensure "the burden is put on eaters"). And Mark Rosegrant of the International Food Policy Research Institute suggested a plan to accomplish that: "a stronger public relations campaign in the reduction of meat consumption—one like that around cigarettes—emphasizing personal health, compassion for animals and doing good for the poor and the planet."[3]

I guess Rosegrant is hoping to see Big Macs and Whoppers carry a warning from the Planetary Surgeon General, Al Gore:

WARNING: EATING THIS BURGER INCREASES
THE THREAT OF PLANETARY DESTRUCTION

With the global warming scare, vegetarian activists have found a great pretext to force their eating habits on the rest of us. Natural Resources

Defense Council advisor Sheryl Eisenberg outlined this strategy in a blog post in November 2007:

> The one thing that critics on both sides seemed to agree on was that the problems associated with livestock farming—air and water pollution, deforestation and groundwater depletion—were not serious enough to warrant compromise on what, for them, were more important goals.
>
> My question is: what if we added global warming to the mix? Could everyone get behind the idea of changing our diets—not completely, but just a little—if it would help with the biggest, scariest environmental problem of all? Because it could.[4]

In making the dubious connection between meat and global warming, greens decry emissions of methane gas from livestock. Cow burps and farts may seem like an unlikely threat to our existence on Earth, but scientists are actually working on "solving" the "problem." Australian scientists reported in May 2008 that they are developing a grass that will reduce the amount of methane that cows belch.[5] Another researcher reported in a scientific journal in July 2008 that a certain dietary supplement could increase cows' milk production by about 7 percent and reduce greenhouse gas emissions by a similar amount.[6] Like meat, however, milk has also fallen out of favor with the greens; the British government is gearing up for action against the insidious drink after issuing a report in July 2008 concluding that the price of milk, meat, and other farm products should increase to reflect the *environmental* cost of producing them.[7]

Then there's the ex-wife of former Beatle Paul McCartney, Heather Mills, a vegan activist who, in November 2007, spoke in London's Hyde Park to launch a campaign against livestock. Wearing a T-shirt reading, "VEGAN, YOU CAN'T GET GREENER," Mills declared that, because livestock emit more greenhouse gasses than cars, we should all go vegan or at least give up cows' milk. "There are many other kinds of milk available," she proclaimed. "Why don't we try drinking rats' milk and dogs' milk?"[8]

You first, lady.

Eating Close to Home

Do you enjoy Chilean grapes, Australian oranges, or French wine? Well you shouldn't, according to the NRDC, because all these imports cause global warming. In a November 2007 report, the NRDC asserted that these products, as well as Chinese garlic, Mexican and Dutch tomatoes, and Thai rice, travel long distances by planes, trains, trucks, and ships, all of which "consume energy and spew pollution that contributes to global warming."[9] And in case you're not panicked by global warming, the NRDC also argues that the importation of fruits, vegetables, cereals, nuts, and wine causes air pollution that leads to asthma and other respiratory disease, and ultimately to school absences.[10]

So what can you do to save the planet from the scourge of imported fruit? Why, shop locally, of course. You should "look on the labels to see how far your food traveled and ask your favorite grocery stores, restaurants—even the cafeteria in your office—to carry more local foods." Whatever you do, "avoid buying produce that has been flown in from abroad."[11]

This all might be mildly amusing if greens followed such advice as a matter of personal choice. But that's hardly ever the case, and the campaign against imported food is no exception. The NRDC advises you to "encourage businesses and *government bodies* to adopt procurement policies favoring locally grown, organic, and sustainably harvested foods that are minimally processed"[12] (emphasis added).

The shop-local or "locavore" campaign dramatically constricts a consumer's food choices. Since many fruits and other foods cannot grow in the U.S. during certain seasons, shopping local for out-of-season fruit really translates into doing without that fruit. It also means that foods not produced in the U.S. at all—including many kinds of cheeses, olives, coffee, spices, chocolates, and fruits—are totally off-limits. And wine is also taboo unless you live near a vine-yard.

Additionally, shop-local implies not buying in-season produce that is not locally produced. So they may have nice summertime oranges in many parts of the U.S., but if you live in New York City then you'll have to do without them—and without many other fresh fruits. There is, after all, no emission-free magic carpet to transport citrus from Florida, Texas, and California to the northeast. We need greenhouse gas emitting trains and trucks to do that.

Notice that the rationale for eschewing imported food—that it causes greenhouse gas emissions during transport—also applies to every other imported product. Why would buying a New Zealand kiwi be any worse than buying a New Zealand-made sweater or piece of furniture that was imported by the same pollution-causing ship or plane? It's not. The shop-local campaign in fact, really reflects a wider agenda against *all* foreign trade, and even against long-distance domestic trade. The NRDC food report makes this point in a paren-thetical remark: "As foreign trade increases dramatically (and the global warming pollution and harmful health effects that go along with it do as well), you can make a real difference by taking simple steps in how you shop for your food."

So if you enjoy good French wine, reliable Japanese cars, or even cheap clothes made in China, know that your favorite commodities are squarely in the green crosshairs.

Farming As a Societal Ill

Oftentimes even locally-grown food is not green enough for the greens. In its food report, the NRDC produces some statistics showing how growing various foods and wine in California is better for the environment than importing them into the state. The NRDC, then, clearly promotes local agriculture in California, right? Wrong. In attacking the alfalfa crops used to feed dairy livestock, the NRDC condemns the use of water by California farmers:

> California's rivers and wetlands, and the critical San Francisco Bay-Delta ecosystem, have suffered serious degradation as a result of excessive water diversions. Much of the water taken out of the ecosystem goes to support California's industrial agriculture. Agriculture now uses approximately 80 percent of California's developed water supply, but produces less than 2.5 percent of California's income.[13]

Rather than alfalfa farms, the NRDC recommends establishing semiconductor plants that would supposedly generate more revenue while using less water. It makes you wonder if the NRDC realizes that, despite its name, you can't eat a microchip.

In another report fretting about the energy used to produce California's water supply, the NRDC not only advocates the permanent retirement of swathes of California farmland, but notes that this step would be ineffective unless water is permanently diverted from that farmland to ensure it won't be used for any agricultural purpose:

> Retiring land and allowing water to remain in the district for agricultural use would likely result in an increase in permanent

crops, such as orchards, which under plausible assumptions would increase electricity use by 48 percent and total energy use by 16 percent. [14]

California food crops targeted for extinction by the NRDC land retirement proposal include rice, corn, grapes, fruits, tomatoes, and a multitude of row crops.[15] Note that this proposal would make these foods totally unavailable to California's shop-local adherents.

This is yet another classic green squeeze. What exactly are Californians—or for that matter the rest of us—supposed to eat? The greens say you must eat locally—but wait!—farming, local or not, is bad because it uses water, electricity, and other energy. So does that mean they want you to grow your own food? Oh, but you would need a front or back yard for that, and the greens say that yards are a waste of land better used for high-density housing.

What will satisfy their endless nay-saying? Must we all stoop over urban, communal garden plots, tending to the few vegetables that can be grown organically under such conditions?

It seems so.

"Slow Food" Means "No Food"

To convince you to deprive yourself of meat and imported food and drink, the greens employ a variety of tactics ranging from scares to seductions.

Some of these attempts are comically crude. In a December 2007 presentation at the annual Technology, Entertainment, Design (TED) conference in Los Angeles, Mark Bittman—the *New York Times*' anti-meat crusader—began a slideshow with an image of a cow that he said was "this year's version of this," whereupon he showed a slide of a fiery atomic bomb blast.[16] Over the top, you say? Bittman said the comparison "was only a little hyperbolic," calling the eating of meat "a holocaust of a different kind."[17]

On the more sophisticated end of the scale is the so-called "slow food" movement. Slow Food USA, the nation's premier slow food group, is consistently vague about its agenda. It advocates "clean" food, defined as "nutritious food that is as good for the planet as it is for our bodies. It is grown and harvested with methods that have a positive impact on our local ecosystems and promotes biodiversity."[18]

Let's decipher these euphemisms one at a time. The group explained what it believes is "good for the planet" in its blog posting for Earth Day 2008:

> Did you know that our current food system is the single largest contributor to greenhouse gases? Protecting our planet requires action by everyone, and supporting local food systems and sustainable food production will help value and protect the land that feeds us all.[19]

So "good for the planet" means engaging in global warming alarmism as a means to provoke action "by everyone." That includes *you.*

How about "positive impact on the ecosystem"? For Slow Food USA, this primarily means a ban on biotech food, which slow food activists consider abhorrent. For example, when the New Mexico state legislature passed a bill to provide $250,000 for the genetic engineering of chile peppers, members of a New Mexico chapter of Slow Food USA threatened a boycott of New Mexican chile products unless Governor Bill Richardson vetoed the bill.[20] Slow Food members, who advocate "locally derived" food, apparently didn't appreciate the irony that the bill's rejection would keep the state dependent on chilies imported from Peru.

The final explicitly-stated Slow Food USA goal is promoting "biodiversity." That's admirable, if it means reasonably balancing the wants and needs of society with a biologically diverse environment. But if "biodiversity" means being told what you can eat as part of a naïve effort to return the planet to a utopian, Eden-like state that never really existed, that's something entirely different. So what's Slow Food USA's vision?

Well, it's a little odd.

The group has a program called Renewing America's Food Tradition (RAFT) to help "preserve America's endangered foods."[21] You're probably wondering what an "endangered food" is. According to RAFT, America has more than 1,000 unique seeds, breeds, fruits, nuts, fish, and game that are "threatened or endangered," such as the Stayman apple, Makah Ozette potato, and Navajo-Churro sheep.[22] And just like endangered wild animals, "endangered foods" require radical protective actions. RAFT declares, "While all species and varieties on the list should be recovered and their habitats restored, not all should be eaten in the immediate future, if ever within our lifetimes."[23]

Thus, for slow food adherents biodiversity means, at least in part, putting some foods off-limits to humans. You can save them, but you can't savor them. You're just supposed to feel good knowing that the flavor exists somewhere on the planet.

At its core, the slow food movement is political, designed to introduce a new kind of "food activism," as one writer put it.[24] Eco-activist Vandana Shiva told the *Wall Street Journal* of her concern that if the slow food movement focused on "the pleasure derived from good tastes," it would not reach its potential—which she sees as advocacy on issues such as "migrant Mexican workers in Florida and Washington [who] are being exploited by multi-national corporations."[25]

Slow Food Nation executive director Anya Fernald told the *Journal*, "This is not just about wine and cheese. It's about the world's agricultural system and how it's breaking down."[26]

Did she mean "how the world's agricultural system is breaking down" or "how the greens are planning to break it down"? It seems that the world's agricultural system is doing just fine, judging from the Chilean grapes, Australian oranges, and other imported foods available in our supermarkets in wintertime. A broken agricultural system would be one in which there is no long-distance or foreign trade, and therefore there is no food available other than what's grown locally—the precise vision the greens are struggling to realize.

Poisoning the truth

Though global warming alarmism is a major new tactic in the green war against our food supply, they haven't given up on their traditional attacks on the use of pesticides. My first personal experience with this campaign came in the early 1990s when I was doing consulting work on an insecticide called Aldicarb. Crops that were legally treated with Aldicarb had never been linked to any adverse effects in humans, but a group of greens in the Environmental Protection Agency was inexplicably bent on banning the chemical anyway. So the agency rejected the results of tests that Aldicarb's manufacturer had performed on human volunteers, requiring instead that the pesticide be tested on dogs. The key test was whether a given dose caused diarrhea, leading to some comical disputes between the EPA and the company about how soft is too soft when it comes to dog poop. In the end, both sides compromised so that Aldicarb use was restricted but still allowed.

Today the European Union is at the forefront of the war against pesticides, especially with the imminent decision in Brussels to apply

the "precautionary principle" to pesticide testing.[27] This will funda-
mentally change the way pesticides are approved. Instead of evaluating health or environmental risks based on the real-world use of a
pesticide, the precautionary principle will require that a pesticide be
proven to cause no harm whatsoever under virtually any circum-
stances. This is a "negative proof"—a logical fallacy considered an
impossible and invalid standard. European greens support the precautionary principle because it replaces science, risk assessment, and
reality with the arbitrary and unchallengeable power of regulators to
deny any or all pesticide use.

European farmers rightfully protest that adopting the precautionary principle will ban the use of most pesticides and decimate crop
yields.[28] A report by a farmers' association estimates that the principle
will reduce production of wheat, potatoes, and green vegetables such
as cabbage and broccoli by 25 to 50 percent.[29] The UK pesticide regulatory authority predicts "major impacts on crop yield and food quality."[30] The Scottish Consumer Council is warning of the effect on
Scottish families, especially poor ones, of the rise in food prices—as
much as 50 percent for staples such as cereals, potatoes, and fruits—
likely to accompany the adoption of the precautionary principle.[31]
And Scotland's representatives to the European Parliament point out
that the banning of fungicides will increase the presence in food of
toxic mycotoxins, which are linked to liver damage and cancer.[32]

This should worry Americans because EU regulations habitually
find their way to the U.S. For example, in June 2008 the EU began
implementing the precautionary principle on industrial chemicals,
which meant U.S. companies that do business in the EU had to comply. "The European Union's tough stance on chemical regulation is the
latest area in which the Europeans are reshaping business practices
with demands that American companies either comply or lose access

to a market of 27 countries and nearly 500 million people," reported the *Washington Post* in June 2008.[33] So these U.S. companies adopt EU standards and then, by marketing their product back in the U.S. as "extra safe," force their U.S. competitors to adopt the same standard. And voilà—a de facto regulatory change has occurred despite its total circumvention of the normal U.S. regulatory and political process.

But even without official or unofficial importation of EU regulations, we've already begun slouching our way toward banning pesticides in the U.S. for no good reason. In 1993, a panel of the National Research Council, the for-hire arm of the National Academy of Sciences, produced a report on the effect of pesticides on children. The report strongly insinuated all kinds of dangers, even though it failed to produce one iota of evidence that any child, or anyone else for that matter, has ever been harmed by the legal use of a pesticide—a fact reluctantly admitted by pesticide alarmist Phillip Landrigan, the chairman of the committee that produced the report.[34]

The report sparked a public panic about pesticides that culminated in the enactment of a new federal law, the "Food Quality Protection Act of 1996," which empowered the EPA to *assume* that children are far more sensitive to pesticides than adults. This assumption enables the EPA to reduce the permissible levels of pesticide residues in food, also called "tolerances," by a factor of ten—which can easily result in pesticides being removed from the market with no real scientific basis. In fact, in a report on the tenth anniversary of the Food Quality Protection Act, the EPA cited as an "accomplishment" its cancellation of about 4,400 pesticide registrations, comprising about a quarter of the registrations then in existence.[35]

The U.S. government inadvertently boosted the campaign against pesticides in January 2001 when the Department of Agriculture allowed the "USDA organic" label to be applied to foods produced without the use of pesticides or other politically incorrect technologies such as irradiation, genetic engineering, and growth hormones. Admitting that the label is little more than a marketing gimmick, then-Secretary of Agriculture Dan Glickman asserted, "The organic label is a marketing tool. It is something that I think consumers want. It is not a statement by the government about food safety; nor is organic a value judgment by the government about nutrition or quality."[36]

But the organic foods industry pitches its product as being safer than conventional food specifically because of the absence of pesticides. The website of organic food giant Whole Foods claims that organic farmers "strive to . . . eliminate the use of toxic and persistent chemical pesticides and fertilizers."[37] Horizon Organic Dairy brags that its farmers don't use "dangerous pesticides."[38] In recommending that consumers look for the "USDA Organic" label, the NRDC resorts to this panic-inducing exclamation:

> Heavy reliance on pesticides by conventional farmers is suspected of leading to increased rates of cancer and reproductive problems in humans. More than 80% of the most commonly-used pesticides today have been classified by National Academy of Sciences researchers as potentially carcinogenic—and are routinely found in mothers' milk.[39]

These claims are part and parcel of the greens' fear-mongering tactics. They deliberately choose their words to instill fear, knowing that few people other than scientists understand that saying a pesticide is "potentially carcinogenic" does not mean that it is harmful or even potentially harmful. The same goes for finding traces of pesticides in mother's milk—this is a function of the amazing technology that allows us to detect in humans some particle in such an infinitesimal amount that it's scientifically impossible for it to cause any harm.

But all this fear-mongering has paid off handsomely. The organic foods industry was a $7.4 billion business in 2001, when the USDA introduced the label, but had grown into an estimated $25 billion business by 2008.[40] What a difference a label makes.

So organic food has been great for its purveyors, but has it been great for you?

If you've ever been in Whole Foods, then you know that organic food is more expensive. Maybe you're willing to pay more for food that's grown without pesticides, but what's the real benefit? The food isn't safer. There is no difference in taste from trace levels of pesticide residues. And there's no nutritional difference between organic and conventional crops. The only difference is the "USDA Organic" label and the accompanying higher price.

And get this: organic crops can actually be worse for the environment than conventional crops.

Pesticides and fertilizer facilitate more intensive farming—that is, more crops on less land with greater yields. As the *Economist* notes,

Following the "green revolution" of the 1960s greater use of chemical fertilizer has tripled grain yields with very little increase in the area of land under cultivation. Organic methods, which rely on crop rotation, manure and compost in place of fertilizer, are far less intensive. So producing the world's current agricultural output organically would require several times as much land as is currently cultivated. There wouldn't be much room left for the rainforest.[41]

Britain's Department of Environment, Food and Rural Affairs recently reported that a liter of organic milk takes twice as much land to produce than conventional milk while releasing 20 percent more greenhouse gases and 60 percent more runoff to rivers and surface waters. It also found that raising free-range chickens uses 20 percent and 15 percent more energy to produce meat and eggs, respectively.[42]

In other words, organic food violates the greens' own tenets of conservation. Organic consumers are paying more for food of equal quality that is produced less efficiently, on more land, using more water, with lower crop yields. Organic food, in short, is a rip-off—for you *and* the environment.

Franken-Foods or Franken-Greens?

Agricultural biotechnology is another target of a green campaign that could make food more scarce and more expensive. Biotechnology has been a tremendous boon to food production, allowing scientists to develop crops that are resistant to both pests and pesticides. Biotechnology, like pesticides, allows farmers to produce more crops on less land with less environmental impact. The technology is so successful that in the U.S. 80 percent of the corn crop, 86 percent of the cotton crop, and 92 percent of the soybean crop is biotech.[43]

Naturally, the greens oppose biotechnology. It's simply too productive and far too efficient for meeting the world's food demands. Although they lost most of the early battles over biotech crops at the end of the 1990s, they've recently had some success. Monsanto Corporation withdrew biotech wheat in 2004, for example, citing declining demand.[44] Greenpeace, however, attributed the move to a green pressure campaign, calling Monsanto's decision "a hard-won victory for every environmental group, every consumer, every cyberactivist who has said 'no' to genetically engineered foods."[45]

Deprived of any evidence that biotechnology is unsafe, greens have taken to demonizing biotech companies. Britain's Prince Charles, perhaps the most prominent anti-biotech activist, has led the way. In

August 2008 he accused biotech companies of conducting a "gigantic experiment . . . with nature and the whole of humanity which has gone seriously wrong." Apparently seeking to outdo Al Gore in a doom-mongering contest, the prince declared that relying on "gigantic corporations" for food would result in "absolute disaster," and that we will "end up with millions of small farmers all over the world being driven off their land into unsustainable, unmanageable, degraded and dysfunctional conurbations of unmentionable awfulness."[46]

These apocalyptic lamentations provoked some dissent. A columnist for *The Guardian* noted the ahistorical nature of Charles's conception of small farming. "The classic way of ensuring there is no food in the future," she wrote, "is to grow it all by hand on small inefficient farms . . . leaving matters entirely at the mercy of a bad harvest."[47] The science correspondent for *The Times* noted frankly that the prince "belies a lack of understanding of the scientists whose work he is seeking to criticize."[48]

The greens, however, rushed to Charles' defense.[49] Their frenzied opposition to biotechnology seems inexplicable, since biotech reduces our "farmprint" by allowing much more efficient food production on smaller plots of land. But this is precisely what the greens oppose: rising food production could sustain more people and more economic growth. That makes biotechnology a non-starter in their book.

Burning Food for Fuel

A final threat to our food supply comes from the greens' campaign to use corn-based ethanol as a "renewable fuel." Congress first mandated the use of ethanol in the energy bill of 2005, then increased the requirement in 2007 so that 36 billion gallons of ethanol must be blended into U.S. gasoline by 2022.[50] Positioned as a green means to energy independence, ethanol enjoys generous government subsidies (equivalent to 51 cents per gallon) and therefore is heavily supported by business interests and farmers—despite the fact that its use is driving up the cost of food.

Because of the ethanol mandate, corn production was diverted from food to congressionally mandated fuel production; the portion of corn production dedicated to ethanol rose from 20 percent in 2006 to an estimated 33 percent for 2008.[51] This dramatically increased corn prices, from about $2 per bushel in 2005, when the energy bill was passed, to over $5 per bushel in early 2008.[52] As a result, food riots broke out in various parts of the world, even leading to the toppling of the Haitian government.[53]

The effect of rising ethanol use on food prices hardly came as a surprise, even to the greens. Long-time green and Worldwatch Institute founder Lester Brown wrote an article whose title said it all: "Why Ethanol Production Will Drive World Food Prices Even Higher in 2008."[54] Even the ethanol industry couldn't deny that ethanol caused higher food prices, so it simply tried to divert attention to other issues. "Though much attention has been focused on the rising price of food, the increase in gas prices is by far a heavier burden for Americans," the American Coalition for Ethanol lamely argued.[55]

Looking closer, we find that greens display their typical schizophrenic attitude toward ethanol. Even while touting its supposed superiority to gasoline, greens denounce ethanol for the environmental damage it causes. The Environmental Defense Fund complains that growing corn for ethanol requires that more land be farmed. "When food-producing land is diverted for energy production, the food that would have been grown on that land must be grown elsewhere," bemoans the co-director of the group's Land, Water & Wildlife Program. "This prompts farmers to convert land not currently in production into cropland. When grassland or forestland is cleared to grow crops, the carbon sequestered in the soil and trees is released into the atmosphere."[56]

Then there's all the water required by ethanol-destined corn crops—that's bad too, according to the greens. Environmental Defense Fund fellow Martha Roberts complains, "Nine new ethanol plants are already planned for some of the most water-depleted areas of the Ogallala Aquifer, even though those areas are vulnerable to erosion and the entire region's water resources are stretched thin."[57]

And Christopher Cook, author of a book with the charming title *Diet for a Dead Planet*, bewails the overall use of energy in ethanol production:

> Ethanol processing plants gobble up vast quantities of water, electric power, and, at some facilities, coal. All told, there is considerable debate among researchers about whether ethanol uses up as much or more energy than it saves: Estimates vary widely, from a 29 percent net energy loss to a 67 percent gain.[58]

So although greens sweat the impact of corn ethanol on the planet, they seem to care little about its impact on the price and availability of food—except to the extent, perhaps, that corn ethanol can reduce food consumption. In a March 2007 posting, TreeHugger.com blogger John Laumer noted that demand for biofuel feedstock has driven down corn and wheat supplies and pushed up their prices. The rise in corn-sweetener prices, Laumer argued, will raise the price of snack foods, resulting in healthier eating. He concluded with a reference to Gaia, a Greek goddess now claimed as a symbol of environmentalism: "Stop complaining about the net energy transfer rate of ethanol. Gaia rules."[59]

Indeed. And if she does, we're all going to be mighty hungry one day.

CHAPTER 6

KISS YOUR HEALTH AND SAFETY GOODBYE

Judging by the dismal outcome of many green attempts at over-hauling your lifestyle, the greens are remarkably negligent toward your health and safety. Nothing personal, mind you—it's all just collateral damage on the way to the great Green Transformation.

We've already mentioned the appalling result of green campaigns such as the attack on chlorine, which exacerbated the 1991 Latin American cholera epidemic. But let's take a quick look at a few more highlights of past product "improvements" brought to us by the greens.

Consider the 1986 explosion of the space shuttle Challenger, which was ultimately blamed on faulty O-ring seals meant to contain hot gasses. What happened? NASA decided to stop using tried-and-true, asbestos-containing putty for sealing joints, opting instead for a "green" alternative material.[1] The disastrous result failed to dissuade NASA from a similar attempt to go green by substituting politically-correct chlorofluorcarbon-free foam in space shuttles' heat-absorbing tiles. This may have caused the tiles' mysterious disintegration and the resulting explosion of the Columbia space shuttle seven years later.[2]

The anti-asbestos campaign may also have played a tragic role on September 11, 2001, when the eco-friendly, asbestos-free fireproofing of the World Trade Center towers succumbed before the buildings could be fully evacuated. Simulations conducted after the attack by the National Institute of Standards and Technology revealed that the "green" fireproofing was inferior to that of asbestos, which was used only on one-third of the floors in the first tower and was totally absent from the second due to environmental concerns.[3]

And let's not forget the worst green tragedy of them all—the joint crusade by the Audubon Society and the Environmental Defense Fund that led to the ban of the insecticide DDT in 1972, which eventually caused tens of millions of deaths in Africa due to the proliferation of malaria-carrying mosquitoes.[4] Tragically the death toll continues to mount—a million children under five every year—even though the World Health Organization recently lifted the DDT ban. This is a testament to the effectiveness of green demonization campaigns—when something gets demonized, it stays demonized. As a result, to this day international charities and multinational companies continue to eschew DDT, focusing their aid efforts instead on providing ineffective bed nets that are more useful in helping the greens save face than in protecting people from malaria-carrying mosquitoes.

With this record, you might guess that the greens would show some humility when recommending further safety innovations. Guess again.

Road Safety? That's Out the Window

Let's begin with bicycling, which the greens incessantly tout as an eco-friendly alternative to driving. What they don't like to talk about, however, is the attendant safety risks. On May 17, 2008, the *Providence*

Journal-Bulletin reported that the mayor and other state officials led a pack of about fifty cyclists through downtown Providence as part of the city's annual Bike to Work Day. The mayor endorsed biking to work as a simple way to decrease congestion and to improve air quality. A rider who belonged to the Sierra Club noted that Rhode Island's transportation sector is the largest emitter of "global warming pollution" in the state.

At the very end of the article was an interesting note: "Wednesday, Rhode Island will hold a local observance of the worldwide event, Ride of Silence, to remember cyclists killed in auto accidents."[5]

One person who will have to be commemorated at the next Ride of Silence will be Miles Coburn. Cleveland's *Plain Dealer* reported in August 2008 that "a popular John Carroll University biology professor with a passion for the environment [and who taught about global warming "before it became a trendy topic"] died Saturday while riding his bicycle." Despite wearing a helmet, the 58-year-old Coburn was struck and killed by a car.[6]

Indeed, biking on roadways—where most people would have to travel in order to bike to work, as the greens exhort—is much more dangerous than driving. The *San Francisco Chronicle* reported that there have been more than 2,000 deadly and near-deadly roadway accidents involving bicycles since 1998 on roads just in the Bay Area.[7]

The point of this is not to scare you away from bicycling on roads if that's what you want to do. But there's a certain hypocrisy evident here. Greens play up the most minute health risks—and sometimes, as you will see below, simply make them up—in order to get products banned that they claim harm the environment. But in encouraging people to trade in their relatively safe cars, and especially their even safer SUVs, for the dubious protection of a bicycle helmet, greens willfully ignore the obvious safety risks of the actions they're promoting.

And of course, the risk of injury is even higher if parents are towing their children on bikes behind them.

And for you recalcitrants who insist on driving, the greens have some safety "innovations" in store for you, too. Aside from trying to herd you into small, less-safe eco-box cars, there are initiatives like the one recently undertaken by the city of Seattle. While most local governments use salt to help keep icy and snowy roads drivable, Seattle has abandoned salt, claiming it's bad for the environment.[8] So a "plowed" street in Seattle now means a hard, snow-packed street with perhaps a sprinkling of sand.[9] What does this policy mean for the city's drivers? Consider this CNN report about a December 2008 snowstorm: "In Seattle about 75 bus passengers had to be scared out of their wits when [their] bus was dangling over a freeway. . . . It's not clear if the weather was to blame or something else. But the roads were icy at the time."[10]

As the seventy-five passengers sat suspended over a precipice, I wonder if they were feeling good about Seattle's new contribution to a healthier environment.

Take Your Pick: Pesticides or Pests?

Although we once believed the use of DDT would eliminate bedbugs for good, the annoying critters have recently begun hitchhiking their way back across Europe and beyond thanks to the pesticide-free mantra of the greens. The British newspaper *The Guardian* reported in September 2008 that pesticide bans, increased foreign travel, and a lack of awareness are contributing to an increase in bedbug infestations on European planes, trains, and buses.[11] In 2005 Italian rail officials even had to pull 508 cars out of circulation due to protests from angry riders bitten by bedbugs.[12] While bedbug infestations are up 40 percent across Western European trains, buses, and planes,[13] closer to home there has been a resurgence in the pests in New York and else-where over the past few years.[14]

While at least bedbugs are not deadly, the same can't be said for the West Nile virus—a mosquito-transmitted disease that first appeared in the United States around a decade ago. The Centers for Disease Control and Prevention reported 1,370 cases of West Nile in the Unit-ed States in 2008, including thirty-seven deaths.[15]

The CDC says the best way to avoid the virus is to prevent mos-quito bites. Of course, rather than trying to outrun mosquitoes, the far easier way would be to use pesticides with proven effectiveness and good safety records. But the greens want that option off the table entirely. Spraying insecticides is now politically incorrect—and in some cases, illegal—so the CDC offers this advice for avoiding bites by West Nile virus-carrying mosquitoes:

- stay inside during dusk and dawn when mosquitoes are most active
- wear long pants and shirt sleeves
- eliminate mosquito breeding sites by emptying standing water from flower pots, buckets, and barrels
- change the water in pet dishes and replace the water in bird baths weekly
- drill holes in tire swings so water drains out
- keep children's wading pools empty and on their sides when they aren't being used[16]

This is primitive advice, identical to the strategy systematically used over 100 years ago to reduce the incidence of yellow fever during con-struction of the Panama Canal. It's hard to believe that a century later this is the best we can do to fight disease-carrying mosquitoes—but it's the only course of action acceptable to greens like the Pesticide Action Network.[17] All these methods are not only inconvenient but also largely ineffective—some mosquito species feed at times other than dusk; long pants and sleeves don't protect your face, neck, and hands from mosquitoes; and eliminating standing water is only useful until the next rainfall.

The proven, effective way to protect you and your family is simply to use pesticides. With the West Nile virus, using pesticides can literally be a life-or-death decision. No one has ever been killed or even sickened from the proper application of a pesticide, but the West Nile virus kills on average more than three Americans a day.

West Nile virus is not the only threat the greens are willing to countenance for the sake of the environment. Consider the activist group the National Coalition Against the Misuse of Pesticides, also known as Beyond Pesticides, which considers *any* use of a pesticide as misuse. Armed with that viewpoint, the group is effectively trying to make schools safer for wasps and cockroaches, yet much more dangerous for children.

On its website, Beyond Pesticides urges parents to send postcards asking school officials to "please ensure that my child is not exposed to toxic pesticides." The group then touts a study published in the *Journal of the American Medical Association* (*JAMA*) that found that "children and school staff nationwide are being poisoned by pesticide use at schools."[18]

The *JAMA* study, published in 2005, identified 1,972 cases of school children allegedly sickened by pesticides during the period 1998 to 2002. There is much less to this result than meets the eye— the figure is largely unsubstantiated, since 87 percent of the cases are self-reported by the patients or their relatives without verification by a doctor or other expert that a pesticide caused the illness. What's more, the researchers themselves acknowledged that their methodology may have counted some false positives—illnesses that were caused by something other than pesticides. Nevertheless, the study's publication was seized on by green groups that deliberately stoked a public panic over pesticides in schools.

Eliminating the false positives and incorrectly self-diagnosed cases would leave some small number of school children who were sickened, probably by the misapplication of pesticides. What the researchers failed to consider, however, is how many illnesses would be caused if pesticides were actually eliminated from schools. Schools and other institutions use disinfectants, insecticides, rodenticides, fungicides, repellants, and fumigants to combat dangerous and unsanitary pests such as cockroaches, fire ants, bees, wasps, mosquitoes, poison oak and ivy, rats, mice, and bacteria. In reality, pesticides provide significant health and safety benefits to school children with minimal risk. Beyond Pesticides would apparently send your kid to school armed with a flyswatter and a prayer.

An official for Anne Arundel County, Maryland, public schools spoke about the precision of the extermination process: "We take a hypodermic needle with a gel bait and inject it right into the cracks and crevices when a roach problem exists." Before the Maryland legislature passed the School Pesticide Notification Act in 1998, that would have been a fifteen-minute job. Thanks to the green law, though, it now takes about a week and mounds of paperwork. Meanwhile, notifying parents costs schools tens of thousands of dollars per year.[19] The piling on of all these hassles and expenses is a deliberate attempt to force schools simply to abandon pesticides altogether.

The anti-pesticide campaign reached Congress years ago. From 1999 to 2003, Democratic senators repeatedly tried to pass a bill to restrict severely pesticide use in schools.[20] One such proposal made it

out of the Senate as part of the No Child Left Behind legislation only
to be omitted in the final bill.[21]

The kinds of anti-scientific scare tactics that underlie the green
campaign against pesticides are encapsulated in a single image—a
photo of an asthma inhaler featured on the postcard that Beyond Pesticides recommends you send to schools. The photo, meant to imply
that pesticides are causing asthma in school kids, is problematic for
multiple reasons. First, asthma is not known to be caused by expo-
sures to chemicals at all; it's a physical response to exposure to an
allergen. There are, in fact, no scientific studies credibly linking pesticides with childhood asthma.[22] Second, the allergens that do cause
asthma are often carried by mice, roaches, and other pests that will
only multiply in schools if pesticides are banned.[23]

And finally, if anything is threatening asthmatics right now, it's the
greens themselves. On January 1, 2009, the standard propellant that
pushes the asthma medication, albuterol, out of inhalers was banned
because it was made with chlorofluorocarbons (CFCs), which the
greens claim causes ozone depletion. "Inhalers are going green," is
how the media welcomed the switchover.[24]

As dubious as that claim is, what's clear is that the new propellant
is an inferior product. Asthmatics must be trained to use the new
inhalers. With the CFC propellant, one could just stick the inhaler in
the mouth, squeeze it, and a rush of cool relief was on the way. With
the new inhalers, the medication comes out slower and is harder for
the user to detect because it lacks the rush of coldness. The new
inhalers also clog easily and must be cleaned frequently. Asthmatics
need to pump them four times before use—which may not be very
convenient when the user is gasping for air and perhaps not familiar
with the way the new inhaler works.[25] Oh, and for the privilege of
using the inferior, green inhaler, asthmatics pay $45 or more, com-
pared to just $12 for the old version.

Chicago's local ABC affiliate reported that "chronic obstructive pulmonary disease patient Alice Burgess is furious" about the new inhalers, declaring, "I don't know how I'm going to handle it but you know you have to breathe."

The ABC reporter didn't ask Ms. Burgess whether the fact that her new inhaler was "green" made her feel any better. It's hard to imagine that a more awkward and cumbersome inhaler will make too many children or their parents happy either.

Light Bulbs from Hell

It used to be that when you broke a light bulb, your only worry was cutting yourself on a piece of glass. You could just sweep up or vacuum the shards and the clean-up was done. But Congress has decided to phase those days out in the name of fighting global warming. As part of the Energy Independence and Security Act of 2007, standard incandescent light bulbs are being eliminated in favor of more energy efficient bulbs. Under the law, light bulbs will need to be 25 percent more efficient starting in 2012. Most incandescent bulbs can't meet this standard and will most likely be replaced by compact fluorescent bulbs (CFLs).

CFLs are a poor substitute for incandescent bulbs: they cost a lot more, give off lower-quality light, trigger migraines, can't be connected to dimmers, and don't turn on right away when you flip the light switch. But a bigger problem is that, like all fluorescent light bulbs, they contain mercury—the same mercury that the greens have been warning us against using for several decades. We've been told to worry about mercury emissions from power plants and mercury contamination in fish. There have been campaigns to get people to stop using mercury thermometers. Now the greens have successfully gotten a law passed mandating that a mercury-containing product be used throughout your home.

If you break a mercury bulb, you could be in for quite a hassle. Consider the case of Brandy Bridges of Ellsworth, Maine, who had the misfortune of dropping a CFL that shattered on the carpet in her daughter's bedroom. Aware that CFLs contain potentially hazardous substances, Bridges called her local Home Depot for advice. The store told her that the CFL contained mercury and that she should call the poison control hotline, which in turn directed her to the Maine Department of Environmental Protection. The DEP sent a specialist to Bridges' house to test for mercury contamination. The specialist found mercury levels in the bedroom in excess of six times the state's "safe" level for mercury contamination. The specialist recommended that Bridges call an environmental cleanup firm, which gave her a "low-ball" estimate of $2,000 to clean up the room. The room then was sealed off with plastic and Bridges began "gathering finances" to pay for the costly cleaning.

Given that greens claim the replacement of incandescent bulbs with CFLs will save the average U.S. household up to $180 annually in energy costs—and assuming that Bridges doesn't break any more CFLs—it will take her more than eleven years to recoup the cleanup costs of breaking a single bulb.[26]

Even without a deluxe $2,000 cleanup, the do-it-yourself approach is still somewhat intense, if not downright alarming. Consider the fourteen-step procedure listed on the website of the Maine DEP for cleaning up a broken bulb containing "a small amount of mercury":

- Do not use a vacuum cleaner to clean up the breakage. This will spread the mercury vapor and dust throughout the area and could potentially contaminate the vacuum.
- Keep people and pets away from the breakage area until the cleanup is complete.

- Ventilate the area by opening windows, and leave the area for 15 minutes before returning to begin the cleanup. Mercury vapor levels will be lower by then.
- For maximum protection and if you have them, wear rubber gloves to protect your hands from the sharp glass.
- Carefully remove the larger pieces and place them in a secure closed container, preferably a glass container with a metal screw top lid and seal like a canning jar. A glass jar with a good seal works best to contain any mercury vapors inside.
- Next, begin collecting the smaller pieces and dust. You can use two stiff pieces of paper such as index cards or playing cards to scoop up pieces.
- Pat the area with the sticky side of duct tape, packing tape or masking tape to pick up fine particles. Wipe the area with a wet wipe or damp paper towel to pick up even finer particles.
- Put all waste and materials into the glass container, including all material used in the cleanup that may have been contaminated with mercury. Label the container as "Universal Waste—broken lamp."
- Remove the container with the breakage and cleanup materials from your home. This is particularly important if you do not have a glass container.
- Continue ventilating the room for several hours.
- Wash your hands and face.
- Take the glass container with the waste material to a facility that accepts "universal waste" for recycling. To determine where your municipality has made

arrangements for recycling of this type of waste, call your municipal office or find your town in this list municipal collection sites.

- When a break happens on carpeting, homeowners may consider removing throw rugs or the area of carpet where the breakage occurred as a precaution, particularly if the rug is in an area frequented by infants, small children or pregnant women.
- Finally, if the carpet is not removed, open the window to the room during the next several times you vacuum the carpet to provide good ventilation.

The DEP continues with these recommendations:

The next time you replace a lamp, consider putting a drop cloth on the floor so that any accidental breakage can be easily cleaned up. If consumers remain concerned regarding safety, they may consider not utilizing fluorescent lamps in situations where they could easily be broken. Consumers may also consider avoiding CFL usage in bedrooms or carpeted areas frequented by infants, small children, or pregnant women. Finally, consider not storing too many used/spent lamps before recycling as that may increase your chances of breakage. Don't forget to properly recycle your used fluorescent bulbs so they don't break and put mercury into our environment.[27]

The only step the DEP omitted was the final one: keep your fingers crossed that you did a good enough cleanup job so that you, your family, and your pets aren't poisoned by any mercury you missed.

Keep the Home Fires Burning

Should your house catch fire the greens may have helped it to burn faster thanks to their campaign against flame retardants. At a November 2007 meeting at the Consumer Product Safety Commission, Dr. Arlene Blum of the University of California at Berkeley marked thirty years of research-activism against flame retardants by asking the CPSC to require that all flame retardant chemicals be proven safe to human health and the environment before they are used; that more money be devoted to research and development of "green" flame retardants; and that a moratorium be imposed on new flammability regulations until "green" flame retardants are developed or existing ones are shown to be safe.

This is essentially a request to ban flame retardants for the sake of the environment. Does this sound like a good idea? Is there a reasonable basis for it? As for the value of flame retardants, EPA officials state that

Every year, fires kill more than 3,000 people, injure more than 20,000, and result in property damages exceeding an estimated $11 billion in the United States alone. Fire incidence has dropped over the past 25 years, which is partly because of the fire prevention policies requiring the presence of flame retardant chemicals in many industrial products.... Thus, not only do flame retardants save lives and prevent harm, but they also reduce the economic cost of fires.[28]

In 2003, then-California governor Gray Davis signed a bill to phase out two so-called "brominated flame retardants," which are widely used in furniture and electronic equipment. While bromine is not the only type of flame retardant, the chemical has saved thousands of lives since the 1960s and is the most effective flame retardant. So why do the greens oppose it? Has it harmed anybody? No. Not a single study has ever linked the use of brominated flame retardants with adverse health or environmental effects.[29] So why do the greens attack a chemical that is both beneficial and safe?

"Californians have highest U.S. levels of toxic flame retardants, study claims," blared a headline in the October 2, 2008, issue of San Jose, California's *Mercury News*. According to the article, the study reported that household dust in two California towns contained four to ten times more brominated flame retardants than other American homes, and that Californians had twice as much of the chemical in their bloodstream.

This may be perfectly true, but once again, a key bit of information gets lost in the panicked headlines: namely, that there is no evidence at all that this level of bromine causes any negative health effects. Greens are simply trying to scare people with the notion that their bodies are teeming with manmade chemicals, which *must* be harmful because, well, they're manmade.

This is an anti-scientific line of argument, since a fundamental principle of toxicology is that mere exposure to any particular substance does not mean that exposure is harmful. In fact, substances like water, salt, and sugar can all be "poisonous" if you consume enough of them. The concept that "the dose makes the poison" has been fundamental to science since at least the sixteenth century, when the Swiss physician who called himself Paracelsus wrote that "all things are poison and nothing is without poison, only the dose permits something not to be poisonous."

And if chemical flame retardants are politically incorrect, what could a "green" alternative possibly be? With the exception of water and stone, every other "natural" substance burns—and water and stone are hardly suitable for flame retardants.

Burning to Be Green

Those who live near forests now face an increased risk of their home burning down, thanks once again to misguided green policy. In recent decades, overgrowth of federal forests and the presence of dead trees, fallen branches, and other debris have fuelled devastating wildfires, including a 1994 outbreak that burned 3 million western acres and killed fourteen firefighters. Over 700,000 acres burned that year in California alone, causing the loss of twenty lives and more than 2,600 homes. In 2003, wildfires burned nearly 7 million acres, killed twenty-three firefighters, destroyed more than 800 homes, and cost taxpayers more than $1.5 billion.

Some politicians have advocated the common-sense solution of thinning forests and clearing the debris as a means to prevent wild-fires. In August 1994 California congressman Wally Herger declared, "Our forests are detonating like napalm bombs. We need to remove dead and dying bug-killed timber."[30] But such efforts are resisted by the greens; a spokesman for the Natural Resources Defense Council condemned Herger's demand as "a pretext for accelerated logging in the Sierra Nevada"—as if it's better to let forests burn and risk the lives of firefighters rather than prevent these fires by turning wood into a useful product. That's green logic for you.

"Politicians who call for firing a magic bullet, such as thinning the forests, are simply grandstanding," a Sierra Club representative told the media, adding that California is "a fire-adapted ecosystem that's always going to burn."[31] Aside from the lives, money, and useful natural resources that go up in smoke every year, you'd think the greens would be less blasé about forest fires—that is, if they're truly worried about global warming. A study published in November 2007 by researchers at the National Center for Atmospheric Research and the University of Colorado at Boulder reported that U.S. forest fires release about 290 million metric tons of carbon dioxide into the atmosphere annually—equivalent to about 5 percent of the nation's carbon dioxide emissions from fossil fuel burning.[32]

Being green is so hard—there are just so many contradictions to balance.

First, Do No Harm

Your health and safety could also be compromised by green mucking in the fields of medicine and public health. Notwithstanding the aforementioned effort to force CFLs into your house, the greens have a decades-old campaign to rid the world of the element of mercury.

The campaign has resorted to the basest kind of fear-mongering, even perpetuating the groundless scare that thimerosal, a mercury-containing vaccine preservative, causes autism. The NRDC website states,

> Medical scientists do not know what causes autism. Some people have speculated that vaccines containing thimerosal may be linked to this disease. Although a few studies have suggested such a link, the best studies so far have not found one. The Institute of Medicine of the National Academies of Science has reviewed the scientific evidence on this topic and concluded that probably no link exists between vaccines and autism.[33]

After relating that no scientific link exists between mercury-containing vaccines and autism, the NRDC then warns that mercury causes all kinds of *symptoms* of autism:

While the causes of autism remain unknown, there is no question that mercury is a neurotoxin which can cause serious harm to the developing nervous system. Children exposed to mercury early in life can develop neurological delays that may appear as subtle learning disabilities. Children's exposure to toxins such as mercury should be limited in every way possible, and the removal of mercury from childhood vaccines was an essential advance.

NRDC attorney Robert F. Kennedy, Jr. has tried to exploit the alleged link between thimerosol and autism. In a 2005 *Rolling Stone* article he wrote,

> It was only after reading the [testimony of an epidemiologist from the Centers for Disease Control] studying the leading scientific research and talking with many of the nation's pre-eminent authorities on mercury that I became convinced that the link between Thimerosal and the epidemic of childhood neurological disorders is real.[34]

Kennedy's article had so many inaccuracies that *Rolling Stone* was forced to append to it *five paragraphs* of corrections. Undeterred, in 2007 Kennedy wrote an article on the Huffington Post blog that recounted the onset of autism in a 2-year old:

> After hearing that story a couple dozen times, a rational person might do some more investigation. That's when one encounters the overwhelming science—hundreds of research studies from dozens of countries showing the undeniable connection between mercury and Thimerosal and a wide range of neurological illnesses.[35]

Kennedy went on to allege that the Centers for Disease Control and Prevention and the pharmaceutical industry had "ginned up" studies "designed to disguise the link between autism and Thimerosal."[36]

As it turns out, the alleged link between thimerosol and autism was debunked in early 2008 by a study conducted by the California Department of Health.[37] In a classic use of epidemiology, the researchers showed that even as thimerosol disappeared from vaccines, the prevalence of autism did not decline. But for the NRDC and Kennedy, the thimerosol-autism scare was a useful controversy to exploit in their ongoing campaign against coal-fired electricity plants, which emit small amounts of mercury.

In case you're confused, let's review: the greens' anathema on mercury applies as long as that mercury comes from potentially life-saving vaccines or energy-providing coal—but not if it comes from light bulbs.

The main problem is this: when the greens are wrong about science, they tend to be wrong in a spectacular way that causes real harm. In August 2008, the Centers for Disease Control and Prevention reported that the national measles rate had surged from an average of sixty-three cases annually between 2000 and 2007, to 131 cases reported for just the first six months of 2008.[38] The CDC attributed the increase to parents choosing not to have their children vaccinated.[39] The report declined to speculate as to *why* fewer parents are vaccinating their children, but an October headline in a Florida newspaper offers a pretty good hint: "Florida parents weigh vaccinations against perceived autism risk."[40]

Thus, the fear remained even after the thimerosol-autism link was debunked, and many parents are now refusing *all* vaccines for their children, even though thimerosol has long since been eliminated from the few vaccines that contained it.

Good Day, Sunshine

Undeterred by their uncanny knack for getting it wrong, some greens now advocate subjecting our entire planet to their experiments. Ever heard of geo-engineering? Well, maybe you'll get some idea of its pretensions from the headline of a September 2008 op-ed in the *New York Times* by a pair of Canadian academics: "Blocking the Sky to Save the Earth."[41]

Still don't get it? To fight global warming, the authors suggest loading the atmosphere with dust particles that would shade the Earth from sunlight. "Of course, flooding the atmosphere with manmade particles poses real risks," they magnanimously concede, but "the reduction in climate risk from even a small scale sun-shading scheme could easily be larger than the increase in risk from the scheme's possible side effects."

One thing the authors don't discuss is what to do if their "scheme" goes awry. We would need an awful large vacuum cleaner to clean up the mess. When the Tambora volcano erupted in 1815 putting sunlight-reflecting sulphate particles into the atmosphere, the next year became known as the "year without a summer."[42]

Another colossally ambitious green scheme to fight global warming is "fertilizing" the oceans with iron to encourage the growth of planktonic algae to remove carbon dioxide from the atmosphere.[43] Although preliminary experiments have shown that iron will make plankton grow, no one knows what would happen to the carbon when the plankton die. Researchers hope that it sinks to the ocean floor and stays there—but what if it doesn't? Would it acidify the ocean? Then there's the problem of shallow-water algal blooms swamping local environments.

Luckily, it appears unlikely that geo-engineering will be used anytime soon. As the *Economist* put it, "The other fear is of moral hazard—the possibility that people would see the promise of geo-engineering their way out of trouble, despite the risks and uncertainties, as an excuse to continue to pollute the atmosphere as usual."

Translation: geo-engineering doesn't solve what the greens believe to be the crux of the global warming problem: their lack of control over the way we live.

CHAPTER 7

SAY HELLO TO BIG GREEN BROTHER

We've already discussed green attempts to introduce various types of technological surveillance into our lives. The unpopularity of green-touted devices like "smart thermostats" and GPS systems monitored by car insurers show that most Americans regard such initiatives as unacceptable intrusions on their privacy.

And this Orwellian greening of society doesn't stop with gadgets. Hardcore greens also have intolerant and even authoritarian conceptions of things like free speech, childhood education, and even personal relationships. For the greens, personal freedom is all well and good. But when it obstructs their mission of "saving the Earth," then like everything else, freedom has to go.

Silencing the Heretics

The greens reserve a special kind of vituperation for global warming skeptics.

They demonize those who question global warming alarmism as corrupt lackeys who spread lies at the behest of big business. For example, the Union of Concerned Scientists (UCS) issued a report complaining that "ExxonMobil had funneled nearly $16 million between 1998 and 2005 to a network of 43 advocacy organizations that sought to confuse the public about global warming science."[1]

It's interesting to note that these free-market, libertarian, and conservative organizations, some of which I have been affiliated with, received what averages out to $46,500 per group per year, an amount that pales in comparison to the income of the top ten green groups—roughly $1.36 billion in 2007, an average of about $136 million each.[2] Ironically, much of the greens' largess comes from businesses with enormous financial interests in pushing green images and technologies. S.C. Johnson & Sons, for example, gave $100,000 to the Nature Conservancy and was permitted to use the group's logo in ads for toilet cleaner and other products.[3] Between 1994 and 2003, General Motors gave the Nature Conservancy more than $19 million.[4]

So, in the greens' view, businesses can try to make a buck by funding the greens, but they're insidiously confusing the public if they fund the other side.

For extremist greens, doubting global warming is worse than a heresy—it's a *crime*. Take, for example, this exclamation about the "denial industry" by David Roberts, a writer for *Grist Magazine*: "When we've finally gotten serious about global warming, when the impacts are really hitting us and we're in a full worldwide scramble to minimize the damage, we should have war crimes trials for these bastards—some sort of climate Nuremberg."[5]

Roberts eventually retracted his demand, but still insisted that people who question global warming alarmism "deserve to be held publicly accountable."[6]

NASA scientist James Hansen issued a similar call in his June 2008 presentation at the National Press Club. Speaking of coal and oil company executives who "spread doubt about global warming," Hansen declared, "These CEOs should be tried for high crimes against humanity and nature."[7]

In a naked effort to silence dissent, greens frequently label skeptics, including scientists, as "deniers"—an attempt morally to equate the questioning of global warming alarmism with Holocaust denial. Doubting predictions of a global warming catastrophe, of course, is perfectly consistent with scientific methodology, but green extremists are now trying to outlaw such expressions. Perhaps before long we'll see demands that such dissent be categorized as a "hate crime" against the planet.

Having condemned global warming skeptics as criminals, it's only logical that some greens insist that skeptics be censored. It is surprising, however, that such demands are even voiced within the field of journalism—a profession that's usually at the forefront of free speech advocacy.

Consider Cristine Russell, president of the Council for the Advancement of Science Writing, a group that describes itself as being "committed to improving the quality of science news reaching the public." In the *Columbia Journalism Review*, Russell pleaded for the media to stop reporting on the arguments of skeptics, arguing that "the era of 'equal time' for skeptics who argue that global warming is just a result of natural variation and not human intervention seems to be largely over. . . . The he-said, she-said reporting just won't do. The public needs a guide to the policy, not just the politics."[8]

Yes, that's right, Cristine. A public that hears *both* sides of the argument might run the terrible risk of deciding for itself. Therefore, we must slash and burn the creed of journalistic objectivity in order to "guide" the public toward the correct thinking on global warming.

On the other side of the pond, British journalism professor Alex Lockwood also recently suggested that global warming skeptics be silenced, possibly by limiting their right to post their opinions on the Internet. Now that the United Nations has declared that the debate over global warming science is over, Lockwood observes, "Do we really have time for ill-formed skepticism and disinformation?"[9] In addressing this supposed problem, Lockwood floats two ideas without overtly endorsing them: nationalizing the Internet as a public utility, and requiring blog publications to register with an Internet watchdog.

Free speech? Who needs it when the future of the Earth is at stake?

Staying on Message

The greens emphasize the need to "stay on message." This sometimes means keeping the facts from falling into the wrong hands—as in, the *general public's* hands—even when those facts emerge as a result of taxpayer funded research. Such was the case when a British government report found that the "carbon footprint" of reusable cloth diapers is 75 percent bigger than the footprint of disposable diapers. *The Sunday Times* reported that the government, which had promoted the supposed green benefits of reusable diapers, reacted by suppressing the embarrassing report and ending any further environmental research on diapers.[10]

The greens' creepy fixation on message management comes through in a report by a British think tank, the Institute for Public Policy Research, on how to induce "mass behaviour change" to combat global warming:

> The task of climate change agencies is not to persuade by rational argument but in effect to develop and nurture a new "common sense".... [We] need to work in a more shrewd and contemporary way, using subtle techniques of engagement.... The "facts" need to be treated as being so taken-for-granted that they need not be spoken.... It amounts to treating climate-friendly activity as a brand that can be sold. This is, we believe, the route to mass behaviour changes.[11]

As *Spiked Online* editor Brendan O'Neill noted, "The IPPR proposes treating us not as free-thinking citizens who should be engaged, but as consumers who should be sold these 'unspoken facts.'"[12]

Of course, the greens have to determine *which* message is most likely to induce compliance. And here the greens have received assistance from a surprising—and disturbing—source: the American Psychological Association. As *USA Today* reported in August 2008, the APA is "stepping up efforts to foster a broader sense of eco-sensitivity that the group believes will translate into more public action to protect the planet."[13]

The APA's website discusses one such project, in which psychology researchers worked with a hotel to determine what message would be most effective in goading guests into reusing their towels. The researchers ultimately recommended encouraging social conformity with messages such as "Everybody's doing it!"[14]

In a similar vein, the APA proudly reports that a researcher "has developed a handbook to help environmental managers in local government, national parks and the like to develop scientifically sound pro-environment interventions. The handbook encourages resource managers and community leaders to apply social-science findings to remove barriers to pro-environmental behavior and to develop interventions that promote those behaviors, including carefully designed persuasive messages."[15]

When did coaxing "green" behavior become a legitimate goal of psychologists?

Compliance Starts Young

We've seen in earlier chapters that greens have a decidedly unsentimental take on children, whom they view as little planetary burdens in training. Yet once these pint-sized resource-siphons reach a certain age, the greens are not above using them strategically as cute, cuddly messengers of planetary doom.

A prime example is the Rainforest Action Network (RAN), which has insinuated itself in schools across the country. Through its "Rainforests in the Classroom" program, RAN claims to have a network of more than 5,000 teachers propagating its views. One of RAN's common activities is sponsoring letter-writing, poster drawing, and other campaigns "designed to encourage decision-makers to think about how their actions will affect future generations." Through one such program, the "Kids Action Team," school children sent over 10,000 letters and posters to "decision makers" and raised $250,000 for RAN. RAN also encourages kids to raise funds for the group by sponsoring "Rainforest Read-A-Thons" and selling rainforest magnets and wristbands.[16]

And then there are RAN's "direct action" campaigns. Working with a sympathetic public school teacher, RAN diverted a field trip of Fairfield, Connecticut second graders in December 2004 so that the kids could protest the international lending policies of JPMorgan Chase at the bank's Manhattan headquarters.[17] Writing at the time, Canadian business columnist Terence Corcoran called RAN's actions "ideological child abuse."[18]

RAN preaches a message of green extremism to your children. According to RAN, greedy oil companies destroy millions of acres of rainforests so they can "get oil . . . [and] sell it to make a lot of money." This is foolish, argues RAN, since "oil is not necessary. . . to drive our cars, fly our planes, operate our factories and warm our homes. . . . We can use different things—or alternative resources—like the sun and the wind to make energy."[19] And of course, no green appeal is complete without a swipe at meat-eaters. While "many of us love to eat hamburgers, hot dogs, bologna and other items made from beef or red meat," RAN instructs, "fifty-five square feet of rainforest is destroyed for every quarter pound hamburger that comes from a cleared rainforest."[20]

RAN further admonishes kids to shun private cars and glass bottles. Paper is also to be avoided—unless you're participating in a RAN poster contest or willing to donate $25 or more to RAN, in which case you'll receive a paper certificate of thanks for helping to protect rainforests.

Many other green groups strive to indoctrinate children into going green. The Natural Resources Defense Council, Defenders of Wildlife, National Wildlife Federation, World Wildlife Fund, Environmental Defense Fund, and Greenpeace all have programs aimed at kids. The Children's Environmental Literacy Foundation, according to the *New York Times*, has "trained hundreds of teachers from Massachusetts to New Jersey in issues of sustainability and environmental science. More than 1,500 students attended the group's annual expo, Students for a Sustainable Future, at Pace University this spring."[21] In none of these programs are children provided balanced views of environmental issues. Instead, they are bombarded with the simple message that nearly any productive economic activity degrades Mother Nature.

Encouraged to think they know and care more about environmental issues than parents, corporate CEOs, and other presumed authority figures do, kids are urged in these programs to spread their "awareness" through letter-writing campaigns, fund raising for green groups, and other kinds of activism. It's like turning children into mini-lobbyists. And there are indications that this indoctrination is causing real psychological harm to kids.

In April 2007, the *Washington Post* began an article entitled "Climate Change scenarios Scare and Motivate Kids" as follows:

The boy has drawn, in his third-grade class, a global warming timeline that is his equivalent of the mushroom cloud.

"That's the Earth now," the 9-year-old says, pointing to a dark shape at the bottom. "And then," he says, tracing the progressively lighter stripes across the page, "it's just starting to fade away."

Alex Hendel of Arlington County is talking about the end of life on our beleaguered planet. Looking up to make sure his mother is following along, he taps the final stripe, which is so sparsely dotted it is almost invisible. "In 20 years," he pronounces, "there's no oxygen." Then, to dramatize the point, he collapses, "dead," to the floor. [22]

And that child seems composed compared to another one spotlighted in the article. A 9-year-old "cried very hard" when her mother brought home a T-shirt of a colorful frog and the words 'Extinction is forever." "I don't like global warming," the little girl said, "because it kills animals, and I like animals." She declared that she "dreams of solar powered cars," has made recycling baskets, persuaded her mother to start composting, and spends her recess time picking up playground trash. "I worry about it because I don't want to die," she said.[23]

As the *Post* reported, "For many children and young adults, global warming is the atomic bomb of today. Fears of an environmental crisis are defining their generation in ways that the Depression, World War II, Vietnam and the Cold War's lingering 'War Games' etched souls in the 20th century." This anxiety is not confined to youngsters in America: a survey of 1,150 7- to-11-years olds in the UK reported that 50 percent feel anxious about global warming, and many lose sleep worrying about it.[24]

In children, green activists in Hollywood have discovered a captive audience for scary doomsday messages. The Paramount Classics 2007 live-animal action drama *Arctic Tale*—co-written by one of Al

Gore's daughters—follows a walrus and polar bear from birth to maturity as the Arctic ice melts beneath them. The movie's cinematographer told the movie trade press, "As we started to craft *Arctic Tale*, we really thought we had a responsibility to deal with the issue of climate change. We didn't want to tell a story about the Arctic and say to everybody, 'Everything's okay, look how beautiful this place is.' No, we wanted to show what's happening in real time."[25]

The film's director specified that the movie aims to promote green activism among children: "We're using the animals as a metaphor, really, for human beings, especially young people, to be inspired by the animals and see they can take initiative and they can take the bold steps that are going to be necessary for us to change the way we live; in response to climate change."

During the credits, the moviemakers used children to "describe ways the audience can help stop global warming, by turning off the lights, using less water, and making their parents buy hybrid cars," according to the *Los Angeles Times*.[26] Or, as the *New York Post* described it, "At the end, a parade of multiracial cherubs marches in to try to turn your kids into roboscolds who will accuse you of killing polar bears if you buy frozen food, use bright light bulbs, stay in the shower too long or fail to buy a Prius."[27]

"Roboscolds" turns out to be a pretty accurate description. The *New York Times* reported in October 2008 on the "growing army of 'eco-kids'—steeped in environmentalism in school, houses of worship, scouting activities, and via popular culture." One parent described how her "environmentally-conscious children," 10- and 7-year-old girls, scorned the car she drives, the relaxing bath she takes at night, and her forgetfulness in using reusable shopping bags. "They're on my case about getting a hybrid car. They want me to replace all the light bulbs in the house with energy-saving bulbs," she remarked ruefully.[28]

The *Times* offered further examples: a father whose 15-year-old son "yells at him for leaving the car idling for a few seconds in the driveway," and a mother whose 10-year-old son chastised a neighbor for watering his lawn after it rained. "I just sat there and cringed," the mother said.[29]

The greens are proud of their success in indoctrinating kids, viewing these efforts as a perfectly legitimate way to get their message to parents. A spokesman for the Natural Resources Defense Council told the *Times*,

> Kids have really turned into the little conscience sitting in the back seat.... One of the fascinating things about children is that they don't separate what you are doing from what you should be doing.... Here's this information about how we can help the environment, and the kids are not able to rationalize it away the way that adults do.[30]

The British energy company npower has become particularly enamored by the idea of turning kids into little green shock troops in the home. Launched in July 2008 with full-page ads in British newspapers, npower's "Climate Cops" campaign makes a game of turning kids into energy police in order to "cut down on the climate crimes that are taking place in your home." What's a "climate crime"? According to npower, the following qualify: leaving the TV on standby; using your clothes dryer on a sunny day; not using compact fluorescent light bulbs; leaving a cell phone charger plugged in; leaving the lights on; letting the water run while brushing your teeth; taking a bath; putting hot food in the refrigerator; not cleaning your windows; boiling a kettle of water for just one cup of tea; and leaving room doors open.[31]

These are all infractions for which your child should write you a citation, forms for which are available online. Children are supposed to download the so-called "Climate Crime" cards and use them to search your home to make sure that none are happening under your own roof.

> Then build your 'Climate Crime Case File' and report back to your family to make sure they don't commit those crimes again (or else!). You may need to keep a watchful eye over them by revisiting the case every week or two to make sure they don't slip back into any of their old habits.
>
> You can spread your search even wider by adding even more "Case Files" to your notes. What about the homes of your uncles, aunts or friends from school?[32]

What? No search warrant? No Miranda warning?

Let's hope all these kiddie stakeouts and sting operations under the family roof won't be too stressful on mom and dad's marriage. Why? Because the greens want you and your spouse to stay together no matter what. This is not for the sake of your personal happiness or the welfare of your children, mind you, but because divorce is a "resource-inefficient lifestyle" that splits one household into two, thus doubling a family's carbon footprint. This was the ludicrous finding of a 2007 study conducted by two Michigan State University researchers and edited by the usual suspect, Paul "Population Bomb" Ehrlich.[33]

There Goes the Neighborhood

Some green policies are placing new kinds of stresses on social interactions beyond the family sphere—those between neighbors, throughout neighborhoods, and between citizens and their local officials.

Having decided that private people's garbage is now a public issue, British greens are sending out "garbage police" to enforce intrusive new trash collection regimes. As the *New York Times* relates, "Many [local governments] now collect trash every other week, instead of every week. They restrict households to a limited amount of garbage, and refuse to pick up more. They require that garbage be put out only at strict times, reject whole boxes of recyclables that contain the odd nonrecyclable item and employ enforcement officers who issue warnings and impose fines for failure to comply." The *Times* reports on one resident who was fined the equivalent of $215 for the high crime of leaving his trash container lid open three inches—and then fined an additional $225 and given a criminal record for failing to pay.[34]

The *Times* notes, however, that the greens' intrusive zeal has provoked resistance from irritated citizens:

> Britons do not like being told what to do. Encouraged by anti-government newspapers, they particularly resent government meddling, as they see it, in such intimate matters as the contents of their garbage cans. As regulations get more stringent and enforcement more robust, there have been reports across the country of incensed residents shouting and throwing trash at garbage collectors, illegally dumping and burning excess garbage, and even surreptitiously tossing trash in—or stealing—their neighbors' garbage cans.
>
> "It's like something out of 'Mad Max'" Paul Nicholls, a resident of Cannock, near Birmingham, told the newspaper *The Guardian* recently, describing the free-for-all in his town at garbage-collection time. "Every man for himself, scavenging for an extra bin."[35]

The garbage police have already come to America. But instead of relying on British-style fines and citations, in Seattle, Washington they resort to another method to enforce compliance: public humiliation. In that city, if you mix your trash with recycling the garbage men tag your bin. "When you're the one guy on the block with the little tag on your garbage can, everyone knows you screwed up," a Seattle official said. "There's a little bit of shame, a 'Scarlet Letter' effect, to this program that seems to work with people."[36]

San Francisco mayor Gavin Newsom, however, aims for more robust enforcement. In July 2008 he proposed to have garbage collectors inspect trash and recycling bins to ensure trash isn't mixed up with recyclables. Repeat offenders would be fined up to $1,000 and risk having their trash pick-up halted. Newsom claimed that fines would only be levied in egregious circumstances, but some residents oppose the invasive nature of the entire effort. "I will stop recycling if this law goes into effect just to become an eventual test case," vowed one uppity San Franciscan. "Dictators are anathema, no matter which side of the political spectrum they come from."[37]

In a typical example of voluntary participation giving way to compulsory green living, the town council of Marburg, Germany in June 2008 moved from mere encouragement of solar panels on homes to a first-of-its-kind mandate.[38] New homes and those with renovated roofs or heating systems must install solar panels or face a $1,500 fine. Although the mandate had one local politician accusing the town council of operating as a "green dictatorship," the local greens are unfazed. "What they are doing in Marburg is good and progressive, and we, and other cities, need to move forward with similar initiatives as well," a Green Party member declared.

I suppose the greens really are "progressive," in that we're steadily "progressing" toward a dystopia of green government micro-regulating your life.

Full Court Press

As we anticipate ever-increasing green regulations and eventually some form of sweeping global warming legislation, it's important to note that environmental laws enjoy a special enforcement mechanism: so-called "citizen lawsuits."

Virtually every environmental law—including laws covering air quality, toxic waste sites, pesticides, drinking water, and chemicals— provides "any person" with the right to sue to ensure its enforcement. Greens make prolific use of such citizen lawsuits to force the Environmental Protection Agency to take action against alleged polluters.

As described in the Environmental Law Institute's "A Citizen's Guide to Using Federal Environmental Laws to Secure Environmental Justice," there are two basic types of citizen lawsuits. "Any person" can either sue to force the EPA to carry out a duty lawfully required of it, or "any person" can sue other "persons"—typically businesses and government agencies—for a variety of environmental infractions.[39]

While there's nothing theoretically wrong with such provisions, as Florida State University professor Bruce Benson explains, in practice they allow greens to engage in "environmental bounty-hunting"— extorting money out of private companies. Citing the research of James May in the *Widener Law Review*, Benson notes that between 1993 and 2002, 75 percent of all environmental federal court decisions started out as citizen suits, mostly brought by green groups, not private citizens. He finds that 4,438 notices of intent to sue were filed for four environmental statutes, but only about 670 resulted in federal court decisions. Benson safely presumes that most of the others resulted in cash settlements to the green plaintiffs.[40]

These suits are really just overkill, since the government is an overzealous enforcer of environmental laws. This was made shockingly clear in the case of Gaston Roberge, who was charged with having an illegally filled wetland—a 2.8 acre commercial lot that he allowed his town in Maine to use as a dump. As R. J. Smith reported in 2006 in *Human Events*, an internal government memo was subsequently obtained through legal discovery that read, "Roberge would be a good one to squash and set an example [for other landowners and developers]."[41]

And the EPA is quite good at setting examples. Consider the case of John Pozsgai, who operated a small truck repair business in Pennsylvania.[42] Between July 1987 and September 1988, Pozsgai removed more than 5,000 old tires, rusted auto parts, and debris that had piled up on his property, spreading dirt where the junk had been. For these actions, Pozsgai was indicted on September 29, 1988, for criminal violations of the Clean Water Act. Although Pozsgai's land was bordered by two major highways, a tire dealership, and an automobile salvage yard, the EPA considered his land a "wetland" because of a drainage ditch running along the edge of his property that flooded when it rained. Though the ditch was mostly bone-dry, the EPA classified it as a stream.

When Pozsgai began filling the ditch without a permit, EPA undercover agents secretly filmed the dump trucks that delivered the topsoil. Even though Pozsgai's land was not listed on the Department of Interior's Wetland Inventory Map, and his actions didn't create any pollution or endanger any species or water quality, Pozsgai was sentenced to three years in prison and fined more than $200,000. He eventually served eighteen months in jail, another year in a half-way house, and then five years of probation—and was forced into bank-ruptcy.[43]

Pozsgai's prosecution is unexceptional for the EPA. Bill Ellen, a Maryland conservationist who ran a nonprofit wildlife rescue mission, was sentenced to six months in jail for trying to construct a 103-acre wildlife refuge including ten duck ponds on Maryland's Eastern Shore. Ellen had held long discussions with various federal agencies about the convoluted legal definition of a wetland. After receiving a cease-and-desist order for alleged wetlands violations, Ellen allowed two loads of dirt to be dumped on an area that had been designated as uplands.[44] That's when he was arrested. Another Maryland developer who created some wildlife ponds on his land, and apparently contra-vened the Clean Water Act, was sentenced to twenty-one months in federal prison and fined $4 million.[45]

The EPA's zeal got the better of it in 1997, when nearly two dozen federal agents armed with semiautomatic pistols raided James Knott's wire-mesh manufacturing plant in Riverdale Mills, Massachusetts. Knott was indicted about a year later on two counts of violating the Clean Water Act for allegedly pumping highly acidic water into the town sewer system.[46] The EPA issued media releases condemning Knott and warning that a conviction could result in up to six years in prison and a $1.5 million fine. The case, however, was dropped when it was discovered that the EPA's search warrant had omitted informa-tion indicating that Knott, in fact, was *not* in violation of the Clean Water Act.[47]

Green government may be Earth-friendly, but it's armed and dan-gerous where humans are concerned. As columnist Joseph Farah com-mented,

I suspect that most Americans would be shocked to learn that agents of the EPA, the U.S. Fish and Wildlife Service and the

Army Corps of Engineers are packing heat. Has the protection of spotted owls and kangaroo rats become a matter of life and death? Why do EPA agents need to be armed? Well, if you were in the business of seizing people's personal property in the name of saving endangered species, you might want to be armed, too.[48]

Green law is a one-way street. The EPA can come after you, and green groups can sue the EPA to compel the agency to come after you. But can you go after the EPA? Not really. There is no environmental law that permits parties aggrieved by overzealous EPA action a meaningful opportunity for timely redress. It is well-understood among the regulated community that only the very brave or the very foolhardy challenge the EPA in court. The EPA is a $7 billion dollar government agency with its own lawyers who are backed up by those of its law firm—the U.S. Department of Justice. So the agency can afford to out-wait and outspend virtually anyone who attempts legal action against it.

Greenlighting Green Vigilantism

So what happens to companies that stand up to the greens? Doesn't the law protect them? In Britain, the answer is apparently no. In October 2007, twenty-six Greenpeace activists broke into the Kingsnorth coal-fired power plant in southeastern England to protest the plant's proposed expansion. The protesters, who caused about $60,000 worth of damage to the plant, were arrested the next day for criminal trespass.[49]

At their September 2008 trial, the activists offered the laughable argument that their actions were legal because they aimed to prevent environmental damage throughout the world.[50] British multimillion-aire environmentalist Zac Goldsmith, who was not involved with the protest, testified to the jury, "Legalities aside, which I don't know, I suppose if a crime is intended to prevent much larger crimes, I think then a lot of people would consider that as justified and a good thing."[51] NASA scientist James Hansen, fresh from his public call for prosecuting CEOs who doubt global warming, made the outrageous claim at the trial that the Kingsnorth plant would, by itself, be responsible for the extinction of 400 species.[52]

Shockingly, the jury acquitted the activists, citing a 1971 British law allowing someone to damage property if it's done to prevent even greater damage. The law was meant to eliminate liability for actions such as breaking down the door of a burning house in order to fight the fire.[53] This was a completely new interpretation of it—one might call it "green justice."

The verdict sparked calls for similar acts of green vigilantism in this country. Two weeks after the greens were acquitted, Al Gore sparked loud applause at the annual meeting of the Clinton Global Initiative when he declared, "If you're a young person looking at the future of this planet and looking at what is being done right now, and not done, I believe we have reached the stage where it is time for civil disobedience to prevent the construction of new coal plants that do not have carbon capture and sequestration."[54]

Thus spoke our esteemed winner of the Nobel Peace Prize.

While it may be discouraging to think of our rights and legal traditions being eroded by the greens, let's close this chapter on a happy note. Even though human rights may be on the wane, some other species with which we share the planet are actually enjoying the dawn of their own civil rights movement—at least in Switzerland. As the *Wall Street Journal* reported in October 2008,

> For years, Swiss scientists have blithely created genetically modified rice, corn and apples. But did they ever stop to consider just how humiliating such experiments may be to plants?

That's a question they must now ask. Last spring, this small Alpine nation began mandating that geneticists conduct their research without trampling on a plant's dignity.[55]

And the Swiss are energetically enforcing their plants' new rights. When a group of scientists wanted to conduct a field trial of wheat that was genetically modified to resist a fungus, they first had to explain to the government why the trial wouldn't "disturb the vital functions or lifestyle" of the wheat. When the scientists applied for permission for a larger trial, the issue of plant dignity came up again, and they had to argue that they were actually furthering the wheat's dignity by making it fungus resistant. None of this mattered in the end, as a group of anti-biotech activists invaded the test field and trampled the plants.

"They just cut them," a scientist told the *Journal*. "Where's the dignity in that?"[56]

CHAPTER 8

WELCOME TO THE NEW SOCIAL ORDER

An entertaining diversion can be found in reading media accounts of individual eco-philes in their backward-thinking quest for an ever-smaller carbon footprint. You simply can't make this stuff up.

In October 2008 the *New York Times* profiled numerous such activists. We met Sharon Astyk, whose farmhouse relies on a home-made composting toilet and is heated by a wood stove. She has unplugged the family refrigerator, using it instead as an old-fashioned icebox, and relies on frozen water jugs as the home's coolant. Her family grows its own produce and spends only $1,000 a year on consumer goods—mostly used. They air dry their clothes, and Astyk's four sons sleep huddled together to pool body heat. Simon, her six-year-old son, wants to play in a baseball league, but is prohibited because doing so would require a long drive. "I say that it isn't good for the planet," says Astyk, "so we play catch in the yard." Despite these measures, Astyk admits she is not "pure" since she sometimes shops at Amazon.com.[1]

Another eco-monk, Jay Matsueda, eschews heat and air condition-ing in his home. He runs his Mercedes on waste oil obtained from a restaurant and favors reusable bamboo cutlery. To save water on toi-let flushes, he says he occasionally relieves himself on his front lawn—which, since he lives in a condo, apparently means the condo association's front yard.

Other amusing characters include David Chameides, who collects in his basement all the waste he generates in a year, and Colin Beavan, whose family is trying to live for a year with no trash, elevators, subways, packaged products, plastics, air conditioning, TV, or toilets.[2]

Other media outlets describe the travails of Steve Bernheim in relying on an electric car that gets just twenty-five miles per charge (which takes eight to twelve hours); the joy of John-Paul Flintoff after receiving a "Wrapsack"—a fabric cover for gifts that can replace wasteful wrapping paper; and the challenges of Jay Schaefer, who lives in a self-built eighty-nine square-foot house—"smaller than some people's closets," he proudly notes. Deciding that he could make do with even less, Schaefer later downsized to a seventy square-foot home on wheels.[3]

The humble commode—and the minutiae of how you use it—seems to be a primary focus of the new green asceticism. There's World Toilet Organization founder Jack Sims, who pronounced the flushing toilet to be "unsustainable" at the 2008 World Toilet Summit. Conference attendees called for various solutions such as the use of a "dry" toilet that separates the two kinds of human waste, or a "toilet tax" to discourage flushing.[4]

And finally, pop singer Sheryl Crow's admonition that we should use only "one square of toilet paper" was only to be outdone by the anti-toiletry of actress Drew Barrymore, who bragged that she once "took a poo in the woods hunched over like an animal"—and it was "awesome."[5]

Meet the Green Elite

What's missing from these reports on eco-phile role models is any indication that certain high-flying, well-connected greens among us—

make that *above* us—are set to live even more luxurious lives in a future green America. As they preach to us the virtues of a smaller, humbler, sweatier existence—and work to usher it in—the green elite are carefully building in loopholes, dispensations, and licenses to transgress their own orthodoxy. The key to securing these exemptions is money—lots of it—but this presents little obstacle, since these elites stand to grow even richer from the new regime.

Just consider how a personal carbon trading scheme would work, as discussed in chapter one. A rich man can "emit" all he wants simply by purchasing CO_2 emission rights from the poor. Likewise, if public utilities ration energy to consumers, that same rich man can just install whatever obscenely expensive renewable energy device is needed to keep his personal estate buzzing with power—and to hell with the mandatory conservation rituals forced onto others. In this plutocratic game of eco-Monopoly, cash will be the magic get-out-of-green-hell-free card.

In fact, it already is.

Consider the World Wildlife Fund (WWF), one of the most well-known environmental charities. Its website asserts that "it clearly is time for all Americans to roll up their sleeves, to take steps to reduce emissions, to prepare for climate change, and to encourage others to do the same." Lamenting that the average American produces 19.6 tons of CO_2 annually, WWF advises you to use less heat and air conditioning, install low-flow shower heads and faucets, and commute by car pool or mass transit, among other acts of self-denial. The website provides a handy carbon offset calculator so you can crack down hard on yourself.[6]

And yet, what a strikingly different message WWF promotes to its donors. Driving your own car may be an eco-sin for the average slob, but WWF donors are encouraged to travel in style. "Join us on a remarkable 25-day journey by luxury private jet," begins WWF's glossy travel brochure hawking a 'round-the-world trip in April 2009 to visit "some of the most astonishing places on the planet to see top wildlife, including gorillas, orangutans, rhinos, lemurs and toucans."[7] For a price tag starting at $64,950 per person, travelers will meet at the Ritz-Carlton in Orlando, Florida, then fly to "remote corners" of the world on a "specially outfitted jet that carries just 88 passengers in business-class comfort." During the jaunt, "a professional staff will be devoted to making your global adventure seamless and memorable."[8]

Using WWF's own carbon footprint calculator, the 36,800-mile trip in a Boeing 757 jet will burn about 100,000 gallons of jet fuel, producing 1,231 tons of CO_2 in just over three weeks. That's the equivalent of putting about 1,560 SUVs on the road during that time, and is nearly sixty-three times the amount of CO_2 that WWF's website berates *you* for using over the course of an entire year!

The trip's carbon emissions average out to fourteen tons of CO_2 per person. That's three-and-a-half times the *annual* footprint of the average Earth-dweller. But who's counting—especially when you're kicking back in "19 rows of spacious leather seats with full ergonomic support" enjoying "gourmet meals, chilled champagne [and] your own chef."[9] Maybe they plan to use carbon sequestration to capture all the champagne bubbles.

Neither the brochure nor the WWF website indicate that the group will even go through the charade of buying carbon offsets to make up for the trip—and there may be a good reason for that. According to WWF's calculator, it would cost in excess of $44,000 to offset the air travel.

Perhaps the greens' pleas that we all refrain from air travel are not meant to "save the planet," but to "save the donors"—from suffering overcrowding while they revel in exotic animal life in the "remote corners" of the world.

One Pristine Tract Coming Right Up

And if you think that the WWF caters to the wealthy, get a load of the Nature Conservancy (NC), the world's richest green group. While the greens are trying to corral you into vertical living in planned communities, NC hotshots are treating themselves to scenic lots through backroom deals at cut-rate prices—as reported by *The Washington Post* in a stunning series of articles in May 2003.

NC's stated mission is to buy land and preserve it in perpetuity—not to operate as a real estate brokerage for green elites. But some of this land can be awfully nice—the kind that's perfect for a vacation home for the über-wealthy and well-connected. In 2000, NC bought ten undeveloped acres on New York's Shelter Island near the exclusive Hamptons. Less than two months later it sold the land to the former chairman of an NC regional chapter for $500,000—$1.6 million *less* than what NC had paid. To make up the loss, the buyer donated about $1.6 million to the group—allowing him to take a tax deduction on the donation probably worth about $500,000. So in the end, the former NC official bought a $2.1 million parcel of land for about $1.6 million.[10]

And for what green cause was the land to be used? The deed specifically authorized construction of a single-family house of unrestricted size, a swimming pool, a tennis court, a guest cottage and a writer's cabin, the cutting of firewood for personal use, tree cutting, hillside terracing, gardening, lawn planting, and virtually everything else people can do to their own property. So what's the preservation aspect of this deal? It's this: the deed also prevents public access. In the end, taxpayers subsidized the NC bigwig's right to exclude them from the "preserved" land.[11]

Then in 2001, NC bought 215 acres of rare open sand plain for $64 million. At the time NC characterized the purchase as "an important victory for conservation on Martha's Vineyard," which was part of its campaign to save the Earth's "Last Great Places." NC immediately resold half the land to others, "paving the way for Gatsbyesque vacation houses on pristine beach and grasslands," according to the *Post*. Who were the buyers? They were "a pair of Oracle software tycoons, a retired Goldman Sachs executive and comedian David Letterman."[12]

The *Post* also reported that, under the guise of land preservation, NC has logged forests and drilled for natural gas under the last breeding ground of an endangered bird species.[13] It seems that the only thing being preserved in all this is NC's wealth—to the tune of $3 billion as of 2003.

Nobel or Nobility?

The hypocrisy of green organizations is matched—and often exceeded—by that of the movement's individual leaders. Let's begin with the man who has emerged as the most famous spokesman of the global green movement.

It seems that the more Al Gore scares us, the richer he gets. Gore's estimated net worth has ballooned from $1–2 million in 2000 to more than $100 million by December 2007.[14] He made $30 million as an adviser to Google, another $6 million as a board member of Apple Computer, co-founded a $1 billion investment firm called Generation Investment Management, launched a cable TV channel, co-produced an Academy Award winning documentary, and authored a bestselling book, to name a few of his accomplishments. Ordinarily, I would applaud his success—except that it is largely built on his advocacy of reduced living standards for the rest of us.

Gore has traversed the world preaching the need for major lifestyle changes in order to forestall a global warming catastrophe. Just before the credits roll at the end of his dubious global warming documentary, *An Inconvenient Truth*, viewers are asked starkly, "Are you ready to change the way you live?" On the movie's website, Gore specifies what he has in mind: using less heating and air conditioning, buying fluorescent light bulbs, using less hot water, using a clothesline rather than a dryer, carpooling, flying less, buying cost-inefficient hybrid cars—in other words, downsizing your lifestyle.

In light of these entreaties, one might naturally assume that Gore had changed the way *he* lives. And one would be wrong. A month after his movie won the Academy Award for best documentary, the Tennessee Center for Policy Research reported that Gore's mansion in Nashville, Tennessee consumed more than twenty times the national average of electricity. In August 2006 the Gore mansion burned more than twice the electricity in a single month as the average American family uses in an entire year. Gore's heated pool house alone used more than $500 in electricity every month.[15]

Though Gore's spokesman protested that Gore made up for his profligacy by buying carbon offsets, this wasn't quite true. His offsets were actually bought by Gore's London-based investment firm, Generation Investment Management, which bought offsets to cover the personal energy use of all twenty-three of its employees. These offsets, then, were provided to Gore as a kind of employee benefit, thus requiring very little sacrifice on his or his family's part.[16]

Two weeks later, while testifying on Capitol Hill about global warming, Gore was asked about his eco-hypocrisy point blank by Republican senator James Inhofe. This time, Gore argued that his mansion ran on so-called "green energy"—electricity produced by wind turbines, solar panels, or methane gas. This was true, although Gore failed to mention that he'd just started buying green energy a few months before. What's more, Gore's own utility admitted that Gore's "green energy" supply still used some coal.[17]

And Gore stands to reap even greater rewards from global warming alarmism. In November 2007, he became a partner in the well-heeled venture capital firm of Kleiner Perkins. As of October 2008, the company had raised over $1 billion in financing for forty so-called "green-tech" companies. One of the firm's managing partners told *New York Times Magazine* that Kleiner Perkins expected the world's multi-trillion dollar energy market would "undergo a wholesale eco-transformation" and that Gore "would help address some of the most vexing problems of the modern era—namely climate change, fuel costs and energy independence."[18]

Gore, of course, will be addressing these topics by pressing the federal government for new laws that will make Kleiner-Perkins' investments extremely profitable. Without such legislation, you see, the products funded by Kleiner Perkins would not have much of a future.

One such product is the Think, a Norwegian-made compact electric car made out of plastic and other recyclable materials. Before taking a Think for a test drive, a *New York Times Magazine* reporter said he had "the sense that we were about to drive a milk carton rather than a car."[19] It may very well take a federal law to get people to drive an electric milk carton, since the last time U.S. manufacturers offered electric cars—thanks to a mandate from the state of California—they sold poorly, were withdrawn from the market, and even destroyed by their manufacturers.

Another Kleiner Perkins investment is in a solar power company called Ausra. As the *Times Magazine* reporter noted, investments like Ausra are unlikely to be profitable now, but "there would be virtually no limit to the demand for Ausra power" if the government were to begin taxing carbon emissions—a policy that Al Gore just happens to advocate.[20]

And that's how higher electricity bills for you could turn Al Gore into a billionaire.

Do as I Say, Not as I Do

Another member of green royalty is Robert F. Kennedy, Jr., who serves as chairman of the activist group Waterkeeper Alliance, is an attorney with the Natural Resources Defense Council, and was named by *Time* magazine as one of its "Heroes for the Planet." Kennedy rails against the use of coal as a "criminal enterprise,"[21] though we've already seen his resistance when an alternative—a wind farm—was proposed for Cape Cod that risked blocking the view from his own family's compound.

But that doesn't mean Kennedy is against windmills blocking *other people's* views. In fact, he touts the American Midwest as "the Saudi Arabia of wind," insisting that "North Dakota, Kansas, and Texas alone produce enough harnessable wind to meet all of the nation's electricity demand."[22] In advocating the Midwest as a suitable location for erecting gigantic wind farms to power the whole nation, he also proposes reconfiguring the national power grid to accommodate them—an action that would likely impose hundreds of billions of dollars in costs on the rest of us.[23]

This kind of green hypocrisy now reaches all the way to the presidency. As previously noted, on the campaign trail then-senator Obama proclaimed, "We can't drive our SUVs and eat as much as we want and keep our homes on 72 degrees at all times . . . and then just expect that other countries are going to say 'OK.'. . . That's not leadership. That's not going to happen."

Once elected, however, Obama found the oval office to be a wee bit chilly for his tastes. So he ratcheted up the heat to the point that he broke protocol and removed his suit jacket. "He likes it warm," remarked his advisor David Axelrod. "You could grow orchids in there."[24]

You got that? Orchid-growing heat for Obama, less than 72 degrees for the rest of us.

Then there's billionaire chairman of the Virgin Group Richard Branson, a self-styled eco-activist who once declared that "global warming could snuff out humankind."[25]

In March 2008, Branson held a luxury confab to discuss green strategies at Necker Island, one of his two private isles in the British Virgin Islands. Numerous green plutocrats put aside their jeremiads against carbon emissions and hopped on carbon-spewing planes to attend the gathering, including Google co-founder Larry Page, former UK Prime Minister Tony Blair, and Paypal co-founder Elon Musk. Although Microsoft co-founder Paul Allen moored his gas-guzzling 198-foot yacht off Necker Island, he apparently never made it onshore.[26]

The eco-hypocrisy of the entire scene was captured in a single moment: according to the *New York Times*, Branson asked his fellow magnates, "So, do we really think the world is on fire?"—as "a manservant scurried off to fetch him another glass of pinot grigio."[27]

Branson claims that he bought his second island, Moskito Island, because "I didn't want it to fall into the wrong hands and get ruined. . . . It has the only pristine rainforest in the Caribbean."[28] So naturally, Branson plans on building there permanent family houses, wind turbines, salt water swimming pools, and a wastewater treatment plant.[29] The island won't be so "pristine" after that, but at least it'll be "the right hands" that ruined it.

Branson is building luxurious resorts on both his islands, but these are not just meant to indulge wealthy celebrities. You see, they're a model of green activism: they'll be powered by wind turbines and solar panels, serve organic food, and have cars that run on biofuels.[30] The resorts are an example of a growing phenomenon among the super-wealthy—"luxury eco-tourism."

This line of business offers some great benefits to Branson. Not only will he make a pretty penny from his fabulously wealthy clients, but the operation exempts Branson from green protests and pressure campaigns that target other corporate magnates, especially those who, like Branson, commit the cardinal eco-sin of running an airline. As *Luxury Travel* reported, "Thanks to the efforts of its talismanic founder, Virgin seems to enter the public consciousness separate from being a marauding corporate monster."[31]

Luxury eco-tourism is not Branson's only green money-making scheme. In September 2006 he pledged $3 billion over ten years to combat global warming.[32] However, as Steven Price noted in 2008 in the *Sunday Business Post*, "the money would go to a new division of the Virgin conglomerate, called Virgin Fuel. Branson was simply gearing himself up to make more money."[33]

Branson responded with a strange letter. While ostensibly disproving Price's claims, he simply confirmed that the money would be funneled to Virgin Fuels and to another Virgin endeavor, the Virgin Green Fund, which both stand to profit from their investments.[34] So two years and almost $250 million later, Branson has only invested in himself.

Then there's Branson's fledgling space business, for which he hopes to launch tourists into space for two hours at a hefty price of $200,000 per person. As Price observed, "Spraying huge amounts of jet fuel into the atmosphere, purely to allow rich people to look down on an overheating planet, is about as stupid and hypocritical as it gets."[35]

Sky Pigs

Google brags about its dedication to fighting global warming, announcing in 2007 a commitment to investing in "clean energy and green technology." Its eco-sensitivity has earned the company praise from the heads of the World Wildlife Fund and the Climate Group.[36]

This is a bit hard to square with the 2005 purchase by Google moguls of a gargantuan airplane known as the "Google party jet." As reported by the *Wall Street Journal*, Google co-founders Larry Page and Sergey Brin bought a decidedly un-green Boeing 767 wide-body air-liner that is seventy percent longer and three times heavier than a more conventional Gulfstream jet. The plane, used for the co-founders' personal travel, consumes more than 1,500 gallons of fuel per hour, whether carrying Google partiers to Greenland for some kite-boarding and Sergey Brin's bachelor party, or former president Bill Clinton and his entourage on a July 2008 media tour of Africa.[37] A blogger at Tree-Hugger.com observed, "In general, it's difficult to determine the company's motivation for its sustainability initiatives, but this certainly suggests that Google may be more interested in public relations than becoming a true model of sustainability."[38]

You think?

But at least Page and Brin don't fly their plane to work every day like California governor Arnold Schwarzenegger does. Tired of living alone in a hotel penthouse across from Sacramento's Capitol building, Schwarzenegger decided to live in his Los Angeles mansion and spend three hours a day commuting in his private Gulfstream jet. The *Los Angeles Times* noted that the plane "does nearly as much damage to the environment in one hour as a small car in a year." Although he ostensibly buys carbon offsets to make up for his unusual commute, even the greens aren't buying it, telling the *Times* that the governor "is essentially attempting to buy a clean conscience with carbon offsets, which cost about $43 an hour."[39]

This is the same Governor Schwarzenegger who on June 2, 2005, announced at the United Nations, "Today, California will be a leader in the fight against global warming. I say the debate is over. We know the science, we see the threat and we know the time for action is now."[40] And Schwarzenegger meant it. Unwilling to wait for congressional action, the governor has signed legislation that effectively increases the price of electricity on Californians and limits their options on where to live—in order to fight global warming.[41]

This sort of green hypocrisy is not just anecdotal. A study of more than 200 people by researchers from the UK's University of Exeter Business School concluded that "even the most 'eco-conscious'" are unwilling to give up flying, even though they're "deeply skeptical" that carbon offsets or higher taxes can mitigate the environmental impact of air transport.[42]

Wind for Profit

Most green elites are liberals, but some rich folk on the right are also getting into the green game—at your expense. The most prominent example is billionaire oilman T. Boone Pickens, who in 2008 began a $58 million ad campaign to promote his "Pickens Plan" to get America off foreign oil. His plan is to substitute wind power for the natural gas used to produce about 22 percent of our electricity, then to substitute natural gas for the conventional gasoline used to power vehicles. And what's more, says Pickens, this will cost you nothing: "It will be accomplished solely through private investment with no new consumer or corporate taxes or government regulation."[43] What's not to like?

Well let's see, wind power is expensive and unreliable, and it would cost billions to restructure the national energy grid to accommodate it. And natural gas cars are also expensive. All these costs would trickle down to you—the taxpayer and consumer—while billions of dollars in taxpayer subsidized profits trickle up to Pickens. Not only does Pickens aim to build the largest wind farm in the world on 200,000 acres covering four Texas counties, but he also hopes to earn $1 billion by selling the groundwater underneath that land.

Additionally, in order to build the necessary pipelines, Pickens would almost certainly have to rely on the government to invoke eminent domain to confiscate lands from their current owners. Pickens already has some experience with this, having lobbied the Texas legislature to change state law to allow the *two* residents of an eight-acre parcel of land in Roberts county, Texas to vote to create a municipal water district—a government agency with eminent domain powers.

Who were the two resident-voters? They were Pickens' wife and the manager of his nearby ranch. And who was appointed to sit on the board of directors of this new water district? They were the parcel's three other non-resident landowners, all Pickens' employees. So by essentially turning himself into a water district, Pickens obtained the power to condemn land anywhere in Texas in order to build pipelines for his water.[44]

But that still left the wind power transmission problem. Pickens then lobbied the Texas legislature to change the law so that rights-of-way for renewable energy projects—like his wind farm—could piggy-back on a water district's eminent domain rights. So Pickens can now use his water district's authority also to condemn land for his future wind farm's transmission lines.[45]

Adding taxpayer injury to the insult of Pickens' ability to turn himself into a for-profit government, the Texas legislature gave his water district the authority to sell tax-free, taxpayer-guaranteed municipal bonds to finance the $2.2 billion cost of the water pipeline, and it voted to spend $4.93 billion of public money for wind farm transmission lines.[46] Although the latter sum was not specifically earmarked for Pickens, he plans to build the world's largest wind farm, so he can expect to get his fair share of it.

Because Pickens is championing wind power, he's picked up some otherwise unlikely support—green groups like the Sierra Club. Although Pickens hopes to sell as much as $165 million worth of water annually to Dallas alone, as of October 2008 no Texas community had yet signed on, partly because they don't currently need the water and partly due to resentment against water profiteering by the Sierra Club, which has long opposed further exploitation of the very groundwater Pickens wants to use—the Ogallala Aquifer.[47] The Sierra Club once slammed Pickens as a "junk bond dealer" who wanted to make "Blue Gold" from the Ogallala.[48] But oh, how things can change when agendas intersect. Since Pickens' pushing for wind power helps the green global warming agenda, which in turn helps Pickens' push to become a wind power baron, Sierra Club president Carl Pope and Pickens became fast friends. Pope has flown in Pickens' private jet and publicly lauded him.

What can come from this merger of Big Green with Big Bucks? Higher electricity prices for you, another billion or two for Pickens, and politically empowered greens.

The Price of Green

The greening of America will shift our socio-economic boundaries. Green mandates that apply to everyone but the green elite will look and feel a lot like downward mobility to most Americans. Prominent greens may get propelled to stratospheric heights of wealth and power, but there will be a pronounced "flattening" effect for the rest of us.

Overall, the greens show little concern for your financial well-being which, in their view, is just another realm that will require some sacrifices from you in order to save the planet.

So what might that look and feel like?

One of the strategies the greens use to change behavior is to try to price consumers out of an "undesirable" behavior—thus their tendency, and their intention, is to promote inflationary policies across the board. Although greens haven't yet gained the power to implement rationing on food, water, energy, and land, they have succeeded in doing the next best thing—creating the perception of scarcity (and in the case of oil, natural gas, and nuclear power, some actual scarcity)—and that can only translate to higher prices for the basics in life. The greens don't particularly mind if such policies reduce your disposable income, since you'd only spend it committing some kind of carbon sin anyway.

So you can expect to pay a lot more in a future green America. Green policies will dramatically increase the price of electricity through laws penalizing carbon emissions, whether through high taxes or a cap-and-trade scheme, and through mandates for using renewable energy. They intend to abolish coal-fired electricity, which currently costs only one-fifth of natural gas power. And the removal of coal, which accounts for half our electricity supply, would dramatically increase the demand for, and thus the price of, other fuel sources. Furthermore, rising demand for electricity will push prices even higher as greens make progress in replacing gas-powered cars with electric and other kinds of vehicles.

It doesn't end there. The much-touted "renewable" energy sources of our future are heavily dependent on taxpayer subsidies. A megawatt hour of wind power is now subsidized at $23.37 while solar power earns $24.34, compared to just 44 cents and 25 cents for coal and natural gas, respectively.[49] So the increasing reliance on expensive renewable energy will require Uncle Sam either to divert money from other government programs or raise your taxes—most likely the latter.

The rising cost of fuel will ripple throughout the economy, raising the cost of almost any product that requires energy in its production or transport to market—in other words, *virtually everything*.

Tough going isn't it? Feeling like you're going to need a vacation? Maybe you should make that a stay-cation. In addition to more expensive fuel, global warming regulations will likely require airlines to buy greenhouse gas emissions permits as in the European Union. In October 2008, the EU approved airline emissions limits that are estimated to cost the industry $4.4 billion per year. "The system will raise costs for passengers if airlines, as expected, pass on the costs by raising ticket prices," reported the *New York Times*.[50] This may take a bite out of your wallet, but it's unlikely to do much harm to millionaires like Al Gore, Larry Page, Sergey Brin, and Arnold Schwarzenegger, as they board their jets to their next speech on the need for you to "change the way you live."

So with everything around you costing more, how will you cope with less? You could always downsize dramatically like the eco-philes mentioned earlier. Sure it might involve growing your own food or rethinking your relationship with your toilet, but that's not too much to ask for the planet, is it? Or perhaps you could join the grassroots Freecycle movement, whose members use the Internet to scrounge up free, surplus used items like mattresses, clothes, and furniture. Freecycle, however, is likely to be an ironic casualty of our green future— scarcity, rationing, and inflation will all cut into the amount of "surplus" goods any of us will have to go around.

CHAPTER 9

TURNING BUSINESS UPSIDE DOWN

Business has emerged as a primary target of the greens. They are coaxing, cajoling, and coercing CEOs into putting green interests ahead of shareholder interests. They're turning business upside down and whether you're an investor, an employee, an employer, or a consumer, you're going to feel the effects.

Scattered green protests against the business sector coalesced during the 1990s into the movement for so-called "corporate social responsibility" (CSR), which adherents euphemistically define as "aligning a company's activities with the social, economic and environmental expectations of its 'stakeholders.'"[1] In reality, this means intimidating companies into capitulating to green demands on environmental, labor, and human rights issues.

· The CSR movement today is active among corporations, mutual funds, state pension funds, and investment advisories that manage portfolios with assets in the trillions of dollars. In other words, CSR is an enormous industry that touches the lives of tens of millions of Americans who have investments, retirement savings, or pension plans but may not even be aware that their nest eggs are entrusted to activists pursing a political agenda.

For example, public pension funds worth about $1.2 trillion in assets under management—representing about 45 percent of the total assets managed by state and local governments as of 2006—are lobbying *for* global warming regulation. They do this through Ceres, a coalition that addresses global warming by lobbying and pressuring corporations and governments, holding investor "summits," and directing a coalition of institutional investors focused on climate change.

Rather than agitating for global warming regulation, these fund administrators might want to focus more on managing their portfolios, many of which are in financial trouble, such as the plans in Connecticut, Illinois, Kentucky, Massachusetts, New Jersey, New York City, Rhode Island, and Washington State. Perhaps they should start by no longer lobbying against their own investments. ExxonMobil Corporation, for example, is the single largest equity position in most, if not all, of the portfolios of public pension fund systems.[2] Given that the stock price of ExxonMobil is likely to be harmed by global warming regulations, does it really make sense for pension funds to be lobbying against the company and its entire industry?

The corporate social responsibility movement influences business institutions far beyond pension funds, forcing CEOs to adopt policies that forgo huge revenues and damage their own stock prices. As businesses sabotage their own bottom lines to curry favor with the greens, one might wonder what exactly is "responsible" about their actions.

Enter the Stakeholders

Businesses, of course, exist to make money. They act responsibly when they strive to earn profits and maximize shareholder value within the confines of the law. Following this model makes businesses the cornerstone of our economy—they create wealth, supply needed goods and services, spur technological innovation, create jobs, pay salaries, and fund government services by paying taxes. In doing so, American business is the epitome of social responsibility.

But the CSR movement has no use for such trivialities. Either a company toes the green line—acting at various times as a charity, government, and community activist group—or it is, by definition, irresponsible. The CSR modus operandi begins with the partial shifting of a business's focus from its shareholders to its "stakeholders." What's a stakeholder? As it turns out, virtually any pressure group that wants to be one. In the case of General Electric, its 2006 stakeholders included global warming pressure groups Ceres and the World Resources Institute; human rights advocates Amnesty International; and People for the Ethical Treatment of Animals (PETA).[3] So a "stakeholder" is essentially anyone who claims some sort of interest in a business's activities.

Many corporations now humor their CSR "stakeholders" by issuing annual reports under headings such as "corporate citizenship" or "social responsibility" in which they tout their achievements in the realms of the environment, human rights, and so on. A recent survey shows that 70 percent of the 100 largest companies in the Fortune 500 engage in this sort of reporting.[4] Although these reports are usually vapid public relations exercises, they sometimes reveal some interesting aspects of a company's management. In its 2006 "Citizenship Report" GE, for example, elevated "stakeholder impact" to a level of equal importance with "strong economic performance," indicating that the company views satisfying the greens as an equally important task as making money for its shareholders.[5]

There is little empirical evidence proving that CSR adds to a company's bottom line, as its advocates claim. In 2005, a study by renowned economist Arthur Laffer found no evidence that CSR initiatives enhance business profitability. To the contrary, Laffer noted that CSR imposes significant costs on business, including the direct costs of the programs, administrative costs, and most important, the very real cost of distracting management's attention from its core businesses.[6]

One cost overlooked by Laffer is that of foregoing profit-generating business in the name of corporate social responsibility. Take the case of banking giant Citigroup. In 2003, Citigroup adopted the green-backed Equator Principles as a means of evaluating the environmental and social impacts of its lending for energy, infrastructure, telecom, and mining projects in the developing world. Under Equator, Citigroup takes candidate projects that are deemed financially viable and then reviews them for their potential environmental and social impacts. Projects that are deemed to have adverse impacts are flagged as high risk and are unlikely to get funded. It all sounds eminently reasonable—that is, until you look at the results the Equator Principles produce, conveniently reported in Citigroup's "Citizenship Reports."

Citigroup disclosed that in 2005, seventy-four projects were subject to review under Equator, of which fifty-four, or 73 percent, were rejected—representing about $73 billion of potentially income-generating loans that were not made. Of eighty-six projects reviewed the following year, sixty-six were refused, worth perhaps more than $100 billion. In 2007 just nine of sixty-four applications survived the review, thus foregoing perhaps another $100 billion.[7]

The amount of potential lost revenue is so staggering that I decided to look into it. I did this through the auspices of the first pro-free market activist mutual fund, the Free Enterprise Action Fund. I co-founded the fund with the goal of mirroring some of the activist tactics used by the CSR crowd—such as advancing shareholder proposals and publicly criticizing CEOs—but for the very different purpose of keeping businesses focused on their traditional wealth creation role.

As Citigroup shareholders, the Free Enterprise Action Fund requested that the company account for the decisions it made in the Equator review. Having declined more than $200 billion worth of loans, we thought the managers might welcome the opportunity to justify their new business model. But when we advanced a shareholder proposal to ask the company why it rejected these loans and what beneficial environmental and social impacts stemmed from its Equator review, Citigroup refused to answer, stating that such disclosures are not legally required and would not be "appropriate."[8]

Why does Citigroup refuse to justify the benefits of the Equator Principles? If such benefits existed, you'd think the bank would be eager to publicize them. But if there aren't any benefits, then it becomes clear why the company keeps quiet. The hundreds of billions of dollars in lending rejected in the firm's Equator review represent potential corporate earnings denied to its shareholders. Remember that the loans had to be deemed financially viable just to make it to the review. They were denied for non-financial, supposedly green reasons that Citigroup doesn't want to discuss.

It's possible that shareholders might be willing to forego the earnings that could be generated by $200 billion in lending, but shouldn't they be informed of what they received in return? Otherwise, the Equator Principles simply look like a reason to say no to energy and infrastructure projects in the developing world that greens oppose— which seems to be virtually all of them—and to deny Citigroup shareholders increased corporate earnings.

But, wait, it gets worse.

Bank of America, JPMorgan Chase, Wachovia, and Wells Fargo have also adopted the Equator Principles.[9] That means the five largest

U.S. banks have agreed to give the greens a veto on lending to the developing world.

What's more, all these banks except for Wachovia are bringing the Equator Principles to America in the form of the so-called "Carbon Principles." Modeled after the Equator Principles and developed in conjunction with green activist groups including Environmental Defense and the Natural Resources Defense Council, the Carbon Principles are touted as a way to reduce the risks to banks of making loans to coal-fired power plants allegedly arising because of future global warming regulation. The real-world impact is that banks could essentially be giving the greens veto power over bank lending to the coal-fired electricity industry that currently provides about 50 percent of America's electricity.

And banks aren't the only companies feeling the green squeeze. Big energy companies like American Electric Power, Consumers Energy, and several others all agreed to serve as "industry advisors" to the banks that will implement the Carbon Principles. These firms are heavily dependent on coal, yet they've all signed up to a process designed to make coal more scarce and more expensive.

How the Carbon Principles will benefit their shareholders is difficult to see.

Corporate Tools of the Global Warming Industry

Reducing carbon emissions means replacing the least expensive forms of energy—coal, oil, and natural gas—with much more expensive sources like biofuels, wind, and solar power. To force this conversion, greenhouse gas regulation essentially taxes the use of fossil fuels to make them more expensive. There are two ways to levy such a tax: through a cap-and-trade scheme or through a carbon tax levied on goods and services produced with fossil fuels.

Regardless of the form, taxes on fossil fuels are widely projected to have dire economic consequences. In 1998, just after the Clinton Administration signed the Kyoto Protocol (which the Senate effectively rejected), the Department of Energy estimated that overall economic growth in the U.S. could decline by almost $400 billion (4.2 percent) if a Kyoto-style cap-and-trade system were implemented.[10] A 2000 study by the Congressional Budget Office reported that cap-and-trade was a regressive economic policy—that is, lower-income individuals faced a larger burden from the cap-and-trade regulations than higher income individuals.[11] And a September 2007 study led by Arthur Laffer determined that limiting greenhouse gas emissions would lower energy production and lead to an energy supply shock like those of 1974–75, 1979–81, and 1990–91, when the economy and stock market declined and unemployment spiked.[12]

When the Lieberman-Warner proposal for a cap-and-trade scheme was being debated in November 2007, economists testified before the Senate that the plan would cost $4–6 trillion dollars in welfare costs over forty years and up to $1 trillion per year by 2050.[13] Even the Environmental Protection Agency projected in March 2008 that the scheme would shrink U.S. GDP by up to $2.9 trillion (6.9 percent) by 2050.[14]

These projections of economic damage helped torpedo the Lieberman-Warner bill, but cap-and-trade is likely to return—not because it makes any economic or financial sense, but because a few of the largest U.S. corporations think it makes sense for them.

That's where the U.S. Climate Action Partnership (USCAP) comes into play. This is a coalition of twenty-six U.S. and foreign companies and five green activist groups that lobbies for global warming regulation.[15]

Corporations have different reasons for their seemingly inexplicable decision to join greens in this pressure group. Some industrial companies, such as Alcoa, Dow Chemical, and DuPont, are hoping for a cap-and-trade regime where the government provides free carbon emitting permits, which companies can then sell to others. These firms believe they could get a lot of free permits in recognition of their past actions to fight global warming, then sell the permits to other companies for a big profit. Fellow USCAP members FPL Group and NRG Energy, on the other hand, see global warming as a way to advance their interests in nuclear power. And then there's GE, which expects that global warming regulation will provide it with tax credits and other taxpayer subsidies to help it sell wind turbines and energy efficient products.

Additionally, some companies belong to USCAP for no discernible reason other than the feeling that "if you're not at the table, then you're going to be on the menu." These include Caterpillar, Ford, and General Motors. The membership of Caterpillar in USCAP is particularly perplexing since one of its largest customers is the coal industry, which global warming regulation targets for extinction. Imagine belonging to a group whose goal is to put your largest customer out of business.

Oil giant Chevron is not a USCAP member, but you wouldn't know it from the energy efficiency advertising campaign it launched in September 2008. One ad featured a smiling young woman with the caption, "I will leave the car at home more."[16] The ad's text notes that Chevron is "eliminating 1.85 million miles of driving and saving over 73,000 gallons of fuel each month." A related website suggests you make commitments like carpooling, biking, telecommuting, and taking public transportation—all aimed at getting cars off the road.[17] But if we do that, who will buy Chevron's gasoline? The caption at the bottom of Chevron's newspaper ads reads, "Join us in one of the most important efforts of our time—using less."

Chevron's shareholders may be surprised to learn that their CEO wants to sell less gasoline.

These companies don't seem concerned that green corporate activism could, and does, backfire. Consider USCAP member Pepsi-Co, which has come under attack from anti-bottled water activists for its production of Aquafina, the top selling bottled water. PepsiCo is trying to mollify its critics with steps like reducing the amount of plastic in its water bottles, but the greens say these measures are inadequate.[18] As noted in chapter four, the greens' attack on bottled water is having an effect. The *New York Times* reported in October 2008, "Tap water is making a comeback. That's bad news for PepsiCo's profits." It's bad for jobs, too, as the company announced it was cutting 3,300 positions and closing six plants as a result of falling sales of bottled water and soda. "Revitalizing this business is a huge priority for us," PepsiCo's CEO says.[19] But if the CEO hadn't rushed onto the global warming bandwagon to start with, perhaps no resurrection would be needed.

The agenda of the USCAP's green members, such as Environmental Defense and the Natural Resources Defense Council, is to get almost any form of global warming regulation approved. They're not particularly concerned by the details because once such legislation is enacted they'll be able to strengthen it and mold it to their liking through their influence in the EPA, which will most likely be tasked with its implementation.

Perhaps the best way to describe the USCAP's corporate members is by Lenin's old term for Western supporters of communism: "useful idiots." The firms often can't even publicly justify their actions. GE, for example, tried and failed to exclude from its annual proxy statement and annual meeting a shareholder request for the company to justify in financial terms its lobbying for global warming regulation.[20] GE, like most companies that find themselves in this situation, issued a vacuous response that clouded the issue in vague platitudes and corporate jargon.[21]

You can't really blame the GE brass. How can they possibly explain making common cause with greens who routinely proclaim that evil corporate executives—just like them—are raping the Earth?

A Question of Judgment

Green organizations don't have sufficient power on their own to bring about economy-crippling global warming regulation, but with the help of corporate lobbyists, anything is possible. So what does the USCAP phenomenon mean to you and your investments?

A lot.

Investment is largely a matter of trust and confidence. That is, do you trust the CEO's ability to grow the company and make your investment profitable? I don't know about you, but CEOs who lobby against their own company's products and earnings—without providing any sort of justification—inspire little confidence in me. For example, in response to a question from the Free Enterprise Action Fund, Caterpillar CEO James Owens admitted that his company had not conducted a cost-benefit analysis before joining USCAP to lobby for global warming regulations.[22] What are you as an investor to make of a CEO who joins a group lobbying against some of his own biggest customers without even taking the time to think the action through?

Many corporate advocates of global warming regulation have come from the financial services sector—firms like Goldman Sachs, Morgan Stanley, Lehman Brothers, Merrill Lynch, American International Group (AIG). In early 2007 Goldman issued a so-called "CEO Confidential" memo stating, "By now, the dynamics of global warming are widely known, and we find no reason to dispute the scientific assumptions."[23] *Of course* Goldman finds no reason to dispute the science—it owns a good portion of the exchange where carbon credits are going to be traded. Moreover, by the end of 2007, it had over

$2 billion invested in wind power, solar power, geothermal, and bio-fuel companies that are expected to profit from global warming regulation.[24] Likewise, Morgan Stanley announced in November 2006 that it planned to invest up to $3 billion in various global warming projects.[25] And Lehman Brothers employees have issued reports predicting hundreds of millions could be made by investing in carbon emission reduction projects.[26]

Not long ago, a lot of people thought these sophisticated Wall Street types must know what's best for their own companies. But just a few years after these firms signed on to the green agenda, they were all overtaken by the sub-prime mortgage crisis. In September 2008 Lehman Brothers filed for bankruptcy, AIG was effectively nationalized, and Goldman Sachs and Morgan Stanley were forced to convert into regular, heavily-regulated banks. All-in-all, between January 2007 and mid-September 2008, shareholders in the four firms lost in excess of $322 billion.

The lesson here isn't that the greening of the financial services sector caused its destruction—it didn't. The lesson is that these firms failed to properly assess the risks to their very survival posed by their own activities in sub-prime mortgages. Investors should then ponder, if these CEOs couldn't manage their own financial matters, why would anyone have confidence in their analysis of the impact of global warming regulations?

Jumping on the Bandwagon: Green CEOs

Sometimes the CEOs of major corporations adopt green policies for the simple reason that they're bona fide greens themselves. Take, for example, Ford CEO William Clay Ford, Jr., the great grandson of Henry Ford. Fancying himself an environmentalist who is determined to fight global warming, Ford has always seemed more concerned about being green than being profitable.[27] In the late-1990s and again in 2004, Ford—whose company's profitability depended on sales of gas-guzzling SUVs—called for *higher* gas taxes to encourage consumers to switch to hybrid vehicles.[28] Although he never got the gas tax hike, he witnessed a similar effect when high gas prices forced consumers to abandon SUVs.

So how did this work out? In September 2008, though Ford announced it was doubling production of hybrids for 2009, it had "abandoned a forecast of returning to profitability in 2009 and [couldn't] say when it will make money again."[29] Ford's stock price has now fallen from $37 a share in the late 1990s to under $2 in February 2009. *Fortune* once wrote that "Bill Ford, Jr. is idealistic, but he is not stupid."[30] Well, he may not be stupid, but Ford stockholders would be hard-pressed to argue that he's smart.

Green CEOs are more common than you would think. Another one is Henry M. Paulson, Jr. Before becoming Treasury Secretary for President George W. Bush, Paulson served as CEO of Goldman Sachs. In late 2002, Goldman Sachs gained title to 680,000 acres of forest land in Chile. It originally intended to adopt the plans of the land's previous owner, the Trillium Corporation, which had proposed a wood harvesting operation that would generate revenues of $150 million per year—even while setting aside 70 percent of the land for conservation. But under Paulson, who at the time was also a top leader of the green group Nature Conservancy, Goldman Sachs decided instead simply to take a tax write off, worth around $10 million, and turn all the land into a nature preserve. The company donated the land to a group called the Wildlife Conservation Society—for whom Paulson's son just happened to serve as a trustee. So in the end, a potential multi-billion dollar asset worth $150 million in annual revenues was given away to the greens for a one-time, $10 million tax write off.[31]

Another CEO who seems intent on wreaking green havoc on his shareholders is Duke Energy's Jim Rogers. Duke Energy is one of America's largest electric power companies, providing electricity to 4 million customers. Although more than 70 percent of its electricity relies on coal, Rogers is lobbying for global warming regulation. In fact, he's been so successful in advancing the cause that green groups view him as a major ally. According to *New York Times Magazine,* "Prominent environmentalists, thrilled, credit Rogers for clearing the way politically [for global warming regulation]; many are his friends. 'It's fair to say that we wouldn't be where we are in Congress if it weren't for him,' says Eileen Claussen, head of the Pew Center on Global Climate Change. 'He helped put carbon legislation on the map.'"[32]

Curiously, Rogers is less than thrilled about his own effectiveness. "Instead, he is very, very worried, fearful that the real-world version of his dream legislation may end up threatening the company he has spent so many years building," reports the *Times Magazine.*[33]

This fear is obviously justified, since carbon caps would penalize coal-fired electricity generators, like Duke Energy, the most. So what is Rogers thinking? He says he wants to pass "the grandchildren test"—that years from now, his grandchildren will look back and say he made "a good decision." He speaks sentimentally about his 10-year-old granddaughter telling him she wants to "protect endangered species" when she grows up.[34]

This is quite touching. The problem, however, is that Rogers' professional responsibility is not to his grandchildren, but to Duke Energy's shareholders who pay his $10 million in annual compensation.

Fear the Reaper

Even when CEOs are not actively lobbying for parts of the green agenda, companies and shareholders pay the price when their executives make decisions out of fear of the greens. Consider the Big Three auto makers: Chrysler, Ford, and General Motors. Since the 1980s, sport utility vehicles have been the cornerstone of the Big Three's profitability. SUV sales, however, had an Achilles' heel—high gas prices. As gas prices skyrocketed between 2006 and 2008, SUV sales plummeted. In 2008 all three companies reduced SUV production due to high gas prices.[35] By mid-July 2008, the investment ratings service Moody's announced that it might cut the car makers' ratings as they shifted away from high-profit SUVs and trucks.[36]

Curiously, during that time none of the Big Three CEOs called for more domestic drilling of oil or lobbied the government to ensure ample U.S. oil production and refinery capacity.[37] Similarly, airline CEOs also remained strangely silent as rising fuel costs caused billions of dollars of losses and plummeting stock prices.[38] It wasn't until September 12, 2008—two months after the peak in oil prices—when the CEOs of General Motors and Northwest Airlines finally called on Congress to expand offshore oil drilling. Inexplicably, coffee purveyor Starbucks declined to join the appeal, even though higher gasoline prices were a key factor in its July 2008 decision to close 600 stores.[39]

What explains the silence of these CEOs as their businesses took hit after hit? Well, publicly calling for drilling certainly wouldn't ingratiate them with the greens. And if you think CEOs can expect to cross the greens without suffering any consequences, then consider the fates of a few executives who thought they could get away with it.

When the Rainforest Action Network wanted Citigroup to stop lending money to energy and logging projects in the developing world, the bank at first disregarded the group's demands. Like the Glenn Close character in *Fatal Attraction*, however, RAN was not going to be ignored. RAN protested the bank at its branches and launched an Internet campaign urging Citigroup customers to destroy their bank cards. Volunteers rappelled down the side of Citigroup's Manhattan headquarters, unveiling a sixty-foot-wide banner reading, "FOREST DESTRUCTION & GLOBAL WARMING? WE'RE BANK-ING ON IT!" Activists chained themselves to the door of bank branch offices and protested CEO Sandy Weill when he gave a lecture at Cornell University. When Weill traveled to Europe on a family vacation, he opened up the *International Herald Tribune* in front of his grandson only to see a full-page ad demonizing him as a destroyer of the environment. By January 2004, Weill had had enough. He agreed to RAN's demands that Citigroup establish a policy to screen its developing world loans on an even more stringent basis than required by the Equator Principles.[40]

But RAN wasn't finished.

Following the Citigroup capitulation, RAN's campaigns director Ilyse Hogue explained that the group had deliberately sought to make an example out of Citigroup in order to intimidate other banks:

> We felt we needed to get at the private financial sector. When we started to look at potential candidates, the name Citigroup just kept coming up. There were a lot of reasons Citigroup was attractive to us as a target. First, when attempting to change a whole sector, we think it is helpful to change the leader, because if you can get concessions out of them, they set a standard to be followed by the other players.[41]

Soon after Citigroup caved in, RAN announced it would be going after Bank of America and JPMorgan Chase, the next two largest U.S. banks. Hogue vowed to unleash "a hard-hitting campaign against the banks that fail to see the writing on the wall that these policies are the way of the future."[42]

In discussions with RAN, Bank of America pleaded that it had a strong environmental record, that it already considered global warming in its loan decisions, and that it did not lend to developing countries for energy and infrastructure projects in the first place.[43] Nevertheless, in March 2004 RAN demanded that Bank of America meet or beat the Citigroup policy, including: ending all financing for logging, energy, and mining projects in endangered ecosystems; guaranteeing local activists in the developing world the right to reject projects in their areas; ending funding of all coal projects; and cracking down on illegal logging—which, to the greens, typically means any logging. Bank of America pre-empted RAN's pressure campaign by quickly capitulating.[45]

RAN then turned to JPMorgan Chase and Wells Fargo. With a protest in front of Wells Fargo's San Francisco headquarters on July 13, 2004, RAN launched its "Barbeque the Banks" campaign to "turn up the heat" on what it termed "America's most environmentally destructive banks."[46] Citing Wells Fargo's financing of oilfield service firms and offshore drillers, a RAN media release proclaimed, "From the Bay Area to Boston, we'll be turning the up the heat on banks this summer until they turn down the heat on the Earth."

Wells Fargo bought a degree of peace with the greens by announcing a ten-point plan for environmental responsibility. The plan, in which the bank adopted the Equator Principles, included a commitment to lend more than $1 billion to "environmentally friendly business opportunities." Wells Fargo announced it would implement this plan with input from environmental groups.[47]

As for JPMorgan Chase, RAN turned to its kiddie corps. This was the campaign in which teacher Paula Healy took her second-grade class out of their school in Fairfield, Connecticut—the hometown of JPMorgan Chase CEO William Harrison—to JPMorgan's headquarters, where the kids protested with handmade posters like one that read, "Be A Hero . . . Save the Rainforest. Save the World. Please protect the rainforest instead of hurting the Earth for oil." Then in March 2005, RAN went back to Harrison's neighborhood, tacking up old-fashioned wanted posters. Urging Harrison's friends and neighbors to "ask him to do the right thing," the posters harangued the bank for making "reckless investment in environmentally and socially destructive projects in dozens of countries."[48] In a later protest, RAN activists wearing white HAZMAT suits marked "BANK CRIMES UNIT" protested at JPMorgan bank branches around the country. Yale University students also returned to Harrison's hometown, tying giant green ribbons on trees "to remind him to stop lending money to projects that destroy endangered forests and cause global warming."[49] The bank put up a good fight, but on April 25, 2005, it agreed to restrict its lending along the greens' guidelines.[50]

Brave New World

The greens' success in influencing banks' lending policies bodes ill for our economy. Having already put the coal industry in their crosshairs, it's only a matter of time before the oil and gas industries, the greens' perennial whipping boys, come under attack.

What are the consequences? First, and foremost, the Equator Principles and other green restrictions on bank lending subtract from the banks' bottom lines, diminish investors' returns, and quash viable development projects. But do they even deliver the promised environmental benefits? When the Free Enterprise Action Fund asked Bank of America to report to shareholders on the environmental benefits of the Equator Principles, the bank, like others to which we made the same request, refused. Arguing that Equator only applies to a small number of loans, the bank further insisted that our requests "call for subjective conclusions and require information outside of our normal processes which we may not be able to obtain."[51]

The bank essentially claimed that the Equator Principles' effectiveness is impossible to measure. So what benefit do the principles provide to investors? Nothing. All these sorts of lending restrictions accomplish is to legitimize some very illegitimate groups, making them a key part of the decision-making process in some of the country's most influential business and financial institutions. The greens have weaseled and wedged themselves into our top banking, industrial, and energy companies. They're not shareholders, employees, or executives. They're "stakeholders" with no real stake in their companies except to ensure that they support the green agenda.

CHAPTER 10

AMERICA IN THE REARVIEW MIRROR

In addition to all the direct effects a green revolution will have on your day-to-day life, there will certainly be larger, cumulative effects on America's economy, our national security, and our system of government. As currently envisioned, green policies threaten us with hampered productivity, costly regulation, huge tax burdens, and the prospect of giving other industrialized countries a permanent competitive advantage. Green policies also undermine our military readiness, and they jeopardize our sovereignty as we slouch toward global governance.

Green Trade

In all the discussion about America signing on to an international "carbon pricing" treaty, one consequence for America often goes unmentioned: it will reduce our competitive advantage against the rest of the world. This was one reason why European Union countries favored the Kyoto Protocol—it would have given them a competitive advantage over the U.S. in energy costs. First, carbon pricing makes fossil fuel produced-energy—especially coal-fired electricity—more expensive. It would give countries like France that rely heavily on

carbon-free nuclear power a distinct advantage against the U.S.[1] Former EU Environment Minister Margot Wallstrom admitted as much,
declaring that Kyoto "is about the economy, about leveling the playing field for big businesses worldwide." Canadian prime minister
Stephen Harper put it even more bluntly, calling Kyoto "essentially a
socialist scheme designed to suck money out of wealth producing
nations."[2]

Next, even if other countries agree to limit carbon emissions,
there's no way to verify it—carbon emissions are, after all, invisible
and there is no international mechanism to inspect and enforce emissions limits. When a number of nations in the EU, which has had its
own carbon pricing scheme since 2005, arbitrarily decided in 2006
that they had excess carbon credits, they simultaneously dumped
them on the market, causing the credits' price to collapse.[3] There is
no evidence that EU CO_2 emissions commensurately declined—the
Europeans just wanted to make money by selling their credits, which
expire annually, before they became worthless.

While the Europeans can get away with such shenanigans, U.S.
businesses will face a much tougher standard under a carbon pricing
regime. As discussed in chapter seven, the greens have ensured that
every U.S. environmental statute includes provisions allowing green
groups aggressively to enforce the law through lawsuits. Supported by
America's bounty-hunting trial lawyers, the policing of greenhouse gas
emissions would be enforced in the U.S. like nowhere else.

And lastly, the EU's current carbon pricing system is already hurting our economy by allowing Europe to disguise protectionist polices.
It works along the same lines as the EU's "precautionary principle,"
which gives manufacturers the impossible task of proving that their
products are safe under any conditions and uses. American anti-
biotechnology activist Jeremy Rifkin noted the principle's implications
for U.S. exporters:

The EU hopes that by integrating the precautionary principle into international treaties and multilateral agreements, it will become the unchallenged standard by which governments oversee and regulate science and technology. . . . But the US views Europe's tightening regulatory regime as a noose around US exports. . . . America's National Foreign Trade Council warned that the EU's invocation of the precautionary principle "has effectively banned US and other non-EU exports of products deemed hazardous" and stifled scientific and industrial innovation.[4]

The EU's carbon pricing regime operates in a similar way, allowing the EU arbitrarily to exclude U.S. goods from the European market on the basis of their alleged failure to meet carbon regulations—even while similar infractions by European companies are overlooked with a wink and a nod.

This all meets with the approval of greens, who oppose free trade anyway. They don't seem to know or care that trade is vital to the U.S. economy—exports accounted for around one-quarter of America's dynamic economic growth in the 1990s. Ten percent of all U.S. jobs (around 12 million) now depend on exports, and one-fifth of our factory jobs depend on international trade.[5]

Despite these and many other benefits—including the fact that wealthier nations tend to have the highest environmental quality—the greens view international trade as a wasteful use of fossil fuels that encourages undeveloped countries to exploit their natural resources. Although they occasionally pay lip service to free trade, in practice they vociferously opposed NAFTA and just about every other major free trade agreement.

Greens, in fact, should be among the foremost supporters of free trade. As Cato Institute trade expert Dan Griswold argues, free trade is an excellent way to improve the environment in developing nations. As free trade improves developing economies and raises the standard of living of their people, their companies have more money to control emissions. Furthermore, their people have more money to spend on environmental protection which, whether we like it or not, is a luxury. An expanding, better-educated middle class tends to demand a clean environment, but a poor citizenry concerned with securing its daily sustenance does not.[6]

Moreover, trading with poorer nations will make them wealthier, which will enable their citizens to buy more American goods, creating more American jobs. But more consumption is the last thing the greens want. And to prevent it, they're willing to sacrifice all the environmental benefits that free trade creates.

Former environmental activist-turned-critic Paul Driessen coined an accurate term for the green effort to block the economic empowerment of the world's poor: "eco-imperialism."[7]

A Lean, Green War Machine

The green agenda makes no exception for national defense. This was made depressingly clear at a September 2008 press conference at which Defense Secretary Robert Gates was asked how the Department of Defense (DoD) is "addressing more amorphous threats such as climate change, water quality and availability and energy."

One may have expected an indignant response, something akin to, "With wars in Iraq and Afghanistan, the expanding Chinese military, Russian aggression in Georgia, and ongoing attempts by Iran to acquire nuclear weapons, I really have other things on my mind."

Instead Gates replied,

Well, the services actually have some very aggressive, and the department itself, some very aggressive energy conservation programs going on. The Air Force is doing a lot of interesting things, in terms of biofuels. They've test flown several aircraft using synthetic fuels, biofuels rather. So I think there are a number of green initiatives under way, both in the department and in the services that have a lot of promise.

It's important for us to do this. And the Senate and particularly Senator [John] Warner have pushed us very hard to exercise some leadership in this area, in no small part because we're probably the biggest single energy user in the country. But there is a lot going on. And frankly I was surprised at how much was going on.[8]

And indeed there is a lot of greening going on in our military—hardly any of it "promising" for our national defense.

The Energy Independence and Security Act of 2007 bars the federal government from purchasing fuels whose life-cycle greenhouse gas emissions are greater than those from fuels produced from conventional petroleum sources. This puts two of our domestic oil sources with incredible future promise, oil shale and domestic coal-to-liquid processing, off-limits to the military.

As mentioned in chapter two, the bill also excludes Canadian tar sands. This is particularly problematic, since imported Canadian oil, of which the U.S. receives more than 1 million barrels per day, mixes tar sands with conventional oil.[9] Although House and Senate Republicans tried to amend the measure in September 2008 so that DoD would not be blamed for incidental quantities of non-conventional fuels found in its purchases, congressional Democrats blocked the effort.[10]

So the military is required to expend Herculean efforts to trace the exact provenance of the fuel it purchases and then to refuse North American oil from friendly, unconventional sources, apparently in favor of conventional oil from our usual big suppliers—like Saudi Arabia and Venezuela. How this contributes to our national security is not quite clear.

This absurd regulation takes on added significance given that, as Secretary Gates indicated, the military is working on using biofuels in aircraft. Recent research indicates that many of these biofuels, such as corn-based ethanol, actually have long lifecycle greenhouse gas emissions and therefore must also be placed off limits to the military.[11]

Green policies are also going after the military's airborne radar system known as the Airborne Warning and Control System (AWACS), which has been used by the U.S. Air Force since 1977 as a state-of-the-art air battle management function for tactical and air defense forces. With its distinctive radar dome atop the fuselage of a Boeing 767, AWACS enables the detection, identification, tracking, and interception of airborne threats. It's been a key part of the enforcement of no-fly zones in Bosnia and Kosovo, and played a major role in the Gulf War and in our current military campaigns in Afghanistan and Iraq.[12]

But AWACS has been targeted by greens because of its use of sulfur hexafluoride (SF6), a greenhouse gas that is about 24,000 times more potent than carbon dioxide and has an atmospheric life of 3,200 years. Consequently, DoD in July 2008 placed SF6 on its "emerging contaminants action list," meaning that it would examine options for minimizing its environmental impacts, including consideration of substitutes.[13] Although SF6 is used for a variety of DoD purposes, its principle use is in the dome of AWACS planes to prevent the distortion of radar signals.

Regardless of the implications for our military preparedness, a source in the Environmental Protection Agency lauded the DoD's decision to consider fazing out SF6 as "visionary."[14] Another EPA source declared that the move could aid military preparedness and help the environment. The risks of not taking action now include the possibility that production of the gas will go down or disappear, or it could become extremely expensive under a cap-and-trade program given its high global warming potential, the source says. Also, DOD's work could lead it to determine that the substance is so valuable it will go to great lengths to ensure it is not emitted when used.[15]

So the EPA is applauding the DoD's foresight in recognizing that the greens intend on banning or restricting the use of SF6, including in the seventy or so airplanes used by the air forces of the U.S., UK, France, Saudi Arabia, Japan, and NATO. According to the EPA, these planes emit about 114,000 pounds of SF6 per year.[16] This is comparable to about 1.4 million tons of CO_2 annually, which translates to a miniscule one five-thousandth of a percent of the amount of CO_2 released by world energy production every year.

You would think that DoD—and even the greens—would have bigger fish to fry, particularly given the national and international security value of AWACS airplanes.

Should we really substitute untested, politically-correct materials in place of materials already proven to work? Do we really want to risk compromising airborne defense for an infinitesimal amount of perceived risk?

Green policy could put ground-based air defense radar at risk, too. According to a 2006 DoD report to Congress, windmill farms pose a risk to military readiness and national security.[17] The report concluded that wind turbines can limit the ability of air defense radars to detect and track aircraft and can adversely impact military training. The British military has noted the same problem. In February 2008, Britain's Ministry of Defense objected to four onshore wind farms as a "threat to national security" because they make it impossible to spot aircraft.[18] DoD has also warned that wind turbines could inhibit America's ability to monitor international nuclear explosions.[19]

Overall, the greens are pressing the army to operate in a more environmentally sensitive way. Remember their concern over your "carbon footprint"? Well, they've got the Army worried about its own "carbon bootprint." A recent Reuters article began like this:

> What if cutting greenhouse emissions could also save the lives of soldiers in Iraq, where fuel-laden convoys make them targets?... The goal is to bring Army emissions of climate-warming carbon dioxide down by 30 percent by 2015, said Tad Davis, deputy assistant secretary for environment, safety and occupational health. "What I'm interested in doing is finding out what the greenhouse gas emissions, this carbon bootprint, are for the Army in two to three years at the latest.... We want to emit less than that, hand in hand with reducing energy consumption from fossil fuels."[20]

While there's no doubt that fuel convoys can be targets, what's the alternative? It's hard to imagine wind or solar energy powering a tank or other armored vehicles, and even biofuels would require convoys. And do we really want the military worrying about how many miles to the gallon our tanks get? As we've seen, increased fuel efficiency comes at a price—the weight of the vehicle. In the case of military vehicles, that probably means skimping on the armor plate. As we know from early news coverage of the Iraq War, many U.S. soldiers in Humvee vehicles were killed or wounded by roadside bombs because they lacked armor.[21] Yet, when the Army recaptured Iraq's Sadr City from Shiite militias during 2008, its specially-armored tanks and

Bradley fighting vehicles struck 120 improvised explosive devices (IEDs) without incurring any casualty to crews.[22]

But making vehicles lighter is precisely what the Army is considering due to green pressure. As Reuters reported,

> Limiting greenhouse emissions from Army vehicles presents a different challenge, since making a Humvee or Bradley fighting vehicle more lightweight to save fuel would offer less protection for troops. But this could change, Davis said. "There's emerging technology that is providing lighter-weight armor, so I think at some point...you're going to see more hybrid vehicles in the tactical military fleet."[23]

Do we really want the Army sacrificing safety and combat effectiveness in order to fight global warming? Shouldn't decisions about military equipment be based on military considerations rather than green ones?

And most important, should soldiers' lives be imperiled any more than they already are for the sake of limiting inconsequential greenhouse gas emissions?

Saving the Whales

Before Paul Revere's midnight ride, he famously instructed Robert Newman to send lantern signals to indicate how the British were arriving: "one if by land, two if by sea." We've progressed pretty far technologically since then, but we'll be taking a big step backward if the greens succeed in a campaign that would impair the U.S. Navy's ability to detect the enemy.

In October 2005, the Natural Resources Defense Council sued the Navy in federal court, claiming that the use of sonar during Navy training exercises violates environmental laws. According to the group, "Whales, dolphins and other marine animals could be spared excruciating injury and death with common-sense precautions, but the Navy refuses to implement them."[24] In court, the Navy maintained that even a temporary ban would disrupt crucial training of sailors in the use of active sonar to detect hostile vessels, including quiet diesel submarines—"the most lethal enemy known," according to one Navy captain. "Today, dozens of countries—including North Korea and Iran—have extremely quiet diesel-electric submarines, and more than 180 of them operate in the Pacific," testified Vice Admiral Samuel Locklear, commander of the U.S. 3rd Fleet. "Active sonar is the best system we have to detect and track them," he added.[25]

Although the NRDC presented no evidence showing that any whales were actually harmed by sonar sound waves, a federal judge banned the Navy from using sonar in August 2007, forcing the service to appeal to the U.S. Court of Appeals for the Ninth Circuit. The Navy initially won a reprieve, then lost on a rehearing that reinstituted the original decision. As the *Los Angeles Times* reported, the decision "essentially forc[ed] the world's most powerful navy either to negotiate with environmental attorneys or unilaterally propose measures that will satisfy the [lower federal] court."[26]

President Bush exempted the Navy from these laws in January 2008, but the Navy lost two successive court challenges in the following two months.[27] Hoping to use the case to usher in a larger pressure campaign against the military, the NRDC boasted that the legal battle "is a precedent that will govern ongoing and future litigation between environmental groups and the military in California, Hawaii and elsewhere."[28] Insisting that sonar is vital to national security and poses little threat to whales, the Navy took the case to the Supreme Court, which ruled 5–4 to lift the restrictions on the Navy's use of sonar.[29]

The narrow ruling demonstrated how key elements of our national security hinge on the capricious whims of a judicial system that is increasingly sympathetic to the greens. The *Wall Street Journal* editorialized,

> Not so long ago, an opinion so obviously rational might have been unanimous—or, more to the point, superfluous in the first place.
>
> . . . Justice Ginsburg's dissent is telling about the willful cast of mind on the judicial left about war powers. She does not seem troubled that a nonexistent threat to whales impaired the readiness and effectiveness of the military, which in any case she dismisses as "an alleged risk."
>
> . . . Such thinking is an indication of where the U.S. is headed if the Supreme Court's composition swings left in the coming years. We are very close to making judges co-Secretaries of Defense—and next time they may want to do more than save the whales.[30]

In contrast, the *New York Times*'s fluorescent green editorial page lamented that "the Supreme Court showed extreme and troubling deference to the . . . professional judgments of military officers. . . . We hope the next administration requires the Navy to take environmental harms more seriously."[31]

Yes, that's exactly what we want our Navy to be focusing on—the rights of whales not to have their serenity disturbed by sonar.

America: The Real Nuclear Threat?

The greens are ideologically opposed to nuclear weapons, but they seem much more concerned with nukes being possessed by America than by anyone else. In 2001 the NRDC called on the Bush administration to scrap America's nuclear weapons program, and in 2004 it objected again when the Bush administration requested $6.8 billion for nuclear weapons research and production, calling such nuclear weapons "irrelevant to the defense and security challenges" of America.[32]

Of course, there remain eight other nations with known nuclear weapons capability including Russia, China, Pakistan, and North Korea—and Iran is feverishly working to join the club. But the greens seem unfazed by such threats, and have even worked to undermine our ability to defend ourselves against them; a number of green activist groups, including the NRDC, Physicians for Social Responsibility, and Greenpeace USA, sued the DoD—and obtained a settlement—to force new environmental impact analyses of proposed missile defense testing activities in Alaska and the northeastern Pacific.[33]

The greens' chief military concern seems to be that so-called "abrupt climate change" will cause armed conflicts and possibly even nuclear war. The scenario is described by Environmental Defense:

> Imagine eastern European countries, struggling to feed their populations with a falling supply of food, water, and energy, eyeing Russia, whose population is already in decline, for access to its grain, minerals, and energy supply. Or, picture Japan, suffering from flooding along its coastal cities and contamination of its fresh water supply, eyeing Russia's Sakhalin Island oil and gas reserves as an energy source to power desalination plants and energy-intensive agricultural processes. Envision Pakistan, India, and China—all armed with nuclear weapons—skirmishing at their borders over refugees, access to shared rivers, and arable land.[34]

Let's assume, for the sake of argument, that there's some chance that Estonia or Japan will one day decide to employ their powerhouse militaries to attack nuclear-armed Russia. How would America's preemptive abandonment of its own nuclear weapons deter such a scenario?

Consider that, through their political allies in Congress, the greens are now pressuring DoD to study the national security considerations of climate change, including the risks to military missions.[35] Now ask yourself this: wouldn't America's lack of a reliable nuclear deterrent pose a far greater risk to our national security?

National Sovereignty: It Was Nice While It Lasted

Aside from our economy and national security, a greener America also has implications for our political system. Namely, the greens aim to use the specter of a global warming catastrophe to subjugate America to global governance.

International leaders have stated this intention quite openly. In a November 2000 speech in favor of the Kyoto Protocol, then-French president Jacques Chirac declared, "For the first time, humanity is instituting a genuine instrument of global governance, one that should find a place within the World Environmental Organization which France and the European Union would like to see established."[36] Then-Dutch Prime Minister Wim Kok in the same year also advocated "global governance" for environmental issues.[37]

What exactly does "global governance" mean? The concept was spelled out in a 2007 paper by the director of climate change and energy at the International Institute for Sustainable Development. Arguing in favor of the Kyoto Protocol, John Drexhage wrote that "countries need to breathe in, seriously look at what they can do and by when, and with that information confidently go forward in joining an internationally binding regime that will literally determine the mode of societies' development over this century and beyond."[38]

Similar ambitions lay behind the November 2008 appeal of a British high court judge for a body similar to the International Court of Justice in The Hague—the forum for war crimes trials—to be created for *environmental* prosecutions. Backed by British prime minister Gordon Brown, the court would first be tasked with enforcing an international agreement on greenhouse gas limits that the international climate alarm brigade hopes to negotiate in 2009.[39]

So "global governance" means life in the U.S. being subject to the diktats of an international government that are enforced by international courts. The Hudson Institute's John Fonte explains exactly what this entails:

> Unlike the traditional international system of sovereign nation-states, this new transnational system of global governance seeks to establish supranational laws, regulations, and institutions whose authority extends beyond and within nation-states (including democratic ones). Nation states continue to exist but they are subordinate to transnational authority. This authority is exercised by new definitions ("evolving norms") of international law (really transnational law); transnational courts such as the International Criminal Court; myriad UN conventions that establish new global norms, particularly in the area of human rights; supranational institutions like the European Union; and non-government organizations (NGOs) that act as "global civil society."[40]

As Fonte notes, the "post-democratic" EU provides a good model of how global governance would work. Although it was originally intended as a collection of sovereign states, much of the EU's authority has been centralized in the hands of European Commission bureaucrats in Brussels—to the point that former European Commissioner Ralf Dahrendorf has called the EU's decision-making process "an insult to democracy."[41]

Imagine this system on a global scale, where the U.S. is simply one of many equal nations—right alongside other countries, large and small, democratic and banana. Advocates of global governance view an international global warming treaty as a key step down this road, since it would be a first step toward international control of the U.S. energy supply and, ultimately, our economy.

And the fight against global warming isn't the first cause for which greens have asked Americans to sacrifice our national sovereignty. In 1986 the U.S. signed the Montreal Protocol, which required the phase out of allegedly ozone-depleting chemicals known as chlorofluorocarbons (CFCs). Former UN secretary general Kofi Annan described the protocol as "perhaps the single most successful international agreement to date."[42] That depends on what the meaning of "success" is, though. On an environmental level, the claim that CFCs were causing "holes" in the ozone that would contribute to an epidemic of skin cancer was a half-baked idea from the get-go. Namely, there were no actual "holes" in the ozone, just a thinning of the ozone layer in certain parts of the world, especially Antarctica—where not too many people live. Eventually, it became clear to scientists that the supposed "ozone hole" over Antarctica regularly shrinks and expands with no apparent rhyme or reason. Unsurprisingly, no epidemic of skin cancer ever materialized.[43]

Yet a panicky U.S. Senate ratified the Montreal Protocol anyway, forcing the replacement of CFC substances like Freon with so-called hydrochlorofluorocarbons and hydrofluorocarbons.

So, since there were no real environmental benefits, what exactly did the Montreal Protocol accomplish for the greens? At a global warming presentation I attended in January 2006, Al Gore declared that the *real* value of the Montreal Protocol was that it demonstrated the global political power of the environmental movement and served as a model for international environmental treaties. The protocol, in other words, served as a gateway to more stringent international treaties in the future.

One of these is the pending Law of the Sea Treaty (LOST), whose ostensible purpose is to put the world's oceans and fish stocks under international regulation. This is necessary, LOST supporters claim, to stave off a so-called "tragedy of the commons" situation—where a lack of clear maritime ownership rights results in overfishing. While overfishing is a legitimate concern, it's not at all clear that LOST is the best, or even an acceptable, solution. It's just the internationalist, green solution. As the Heritage Foundation notes, LOST will undermine U.S. sovereignty by: requiring that decisions affecting U.S. territorial waters be made by international consensus; creating yet another unaccountable UN bureaucracy; barring the U.S. from collecting intelligence in territorial waters of other countries—including Iran and North Korea; and requiring that our submarines travel above the surface with flags raised at all times.[44]

LOST has been around for decades. It was rejected by President Reagan in 1982, and presidents George H. W. Bush and Bill Clinton never submitted it to the Senate for ratification. Although President George W. Bush pushed for ratification, the Senate declined to act. Its fate now lies in the hands of President Obama and the Senate's new Democratic majority.

And finally, we have the tax implications of global governance. We've already discussed how global warming regulation is going to saddle our economy with greater state, federal, sales, and other taxes. But how do you feel about paying an entirely new category of taxes—international taxes? The levying of an international tax on carbon emissions is an idea that has grown increasingly popular within the international green movement. One of its prominent advocates, Switzerland's Othmar Schwank, proposes that countries pay a tax to the UN of $2 per ton of carbon dioxide emitted.[45] This would translate to an additional $14 billion per year from U.S. taxpayers—almost tripling our annual UN contribution.[46]

The confiscation of more American wealth is a specific goal of the greens, who look at climate change as a way to level society's haves and have-nots. Friends of the Earth openly states that "a climate change response must have at its heart a redistribution of wealth and resources."[47] And it's unlikely that they're thinking of redistributing any "wealth and resources" to America. No, this redistribution will be a one-way street: *from* America, *to* unaccountable international bureaucrats pursuing a green agenda.

CHAPTER 11

THE FIRST
GREEN PRESIDENT

So what does the election of Barack Obama as president mean for the green agenda? One thing: pedal to the metal.

The greens made an early investment in Obama's political career when the Sierra Club and League of Conservation Voters (LCV) endorsed him during his 2004 campaign for the Senate in Illinois. Obama later acknowledged these endorsements were pivotal to his campaign. "I had no money, had no organization, it was unlikely that the democrats would nominate a skinny guy from the Southside with a funny name like Barack Obama," he said. But the green stamp of approval began shifting the momentum his way. Obama recalled,

> Not only did they provide us financial support, not only was [LCV head] Deb Callahan's gorgeous face on television saying I was a pretty good guy—and that sold some tickets right there—more importantly the League, along with the Sierra Club and other environmental organizations, signaled to those who are considered swing voters in the state of Illinois, Republicans and independents who may sometimes veer toward that side of the aisle.[1]

Obama was indeed a special project for the LCV, which made him the first non-incumbent member of Congress included on its list of "environmental champions."[2] Callahan said that LCV made an early decision to invest heavily in Obama's race

> largely because of his support for environmental issues during his tenure in the state Senate.... Early on, we recognized Barack's leadership on these issues, and made a substantial investment in helping him win the Democratic primary. We are now committed to ensuring his election to the U.S. Senate where he will continue to be a true champion of public health and environmental protections.[3]

In the 2008 presidential race both LVC and the Sierra Club again endorsed Obama—and they are expecting a good return on their "substantial investment." When Sierra Club president Carl Pope was asked just before the election whether expectations surrounding Obama were too high, Pope replied,

> We are not electing the Archbishop of Canterbury or a saint. We're electing an American politician. Is he susceptible to pressure? He damn well should be. This is a democratic society. Do I worry that he's going to cave massively in response to special interests? No, I don't. We're not going to go away when he's elected. We and other forces that are supporting him are going to stay organized. And as he told the environmental community when he met with us, we're going to have to keep his feet to the fire.[4]

So it's no wonder that, immediately following Obama's victory, the Sierra Club program director for global warming told the media that a federal renewable energy mandate—that is, compulsory use of expensive and unreliable wind and solar power—"is almost a certainty."[5]

Gentlemen, Start Your Payments

Obama's agenda for the greening of America is as broad and deep as can be—the president has drunk and completely metabolized the green Kool-Aid. Echoing the rhetoric of Al Gore, Obama believes that humans are causing global warming and that "we have a moral, environmental, economic and security imperative to tackle climate change in a serious and sustainable manner."[6]

Unfortunately, the most "serious" consequence of Obama's policies is that they will seriously raise the cost of electricity and gasoline. For example, the cap-and-trade scheme that Obama favors is much more severe than the failed Lieberman-Warner proposal. Lieberman-Warner would have issued tradable emissions permits to coal-fired electric utilities and carbon-emitting companies. Seventy-five percent of the permits would have been given to emitters for no charge, while 25 percent would have been auctioned. This plan was described as a "financial disaster" by the CEO of Duke Energy, Jim Rogers. Although Rogers himself favors global warming regulation, he said the 75–25 split would require Duke to raise electricity rates by 40 percent in the first year.[7] But the Obama plan is even more stringent—it would auction off *all* the permits, likely more than doubling electricity prices.[8]

Obama claims some of the revenues from the auctions will be used "to invest in energy efficiency improvements to help families reduce their energy prices, and to address transition costs, including helping American workers affected by economic transition and helping lower-income Americans with their energy costs."[9]

What this fluffy jargon really means is this: higher electricity prices will stoke inflation and raise unemployment, but Obama hopes to counteract this through some sort of energy welfare system. None of this would be necessary, of course, if Obama didn't feel compelled to take drastic action against the non-existent threat of global warming. But he really has no choice. Not only do his past voting record and public speeches indicate a long-standing belief in manmade, catastrophic global warming, but Obama owes his political rise to the greens. As he surely knows, in politics "you've got to dance with them what brung you," as the old adage goes.

Other Obama policies will also add to higher electricity prices, especially his plan to require that 10 percent and 25 percent of electricity come from renewable energy sources by 2012 and 2025, respectively.[10] This will require the creation of a massive new electricity infrastructure. Obama also says he will force stringent (and expensive) emissions limits for mercury onto coal-fired electric utilities. While the Bush administration required coal-fired utilities to reduce mercury emissions by 70 percent by 2018 at a cost of up to $5 billion per year—a cost that electricity users pay, incidentally—Obama has indicated he may require a 90 percent reduction even sooner at a much higher cost.[11]

Obama himself has made clear that these policies are specifically geared toward prohibiting the creation of new coal-fired power plants. While discussing his energy plans in January 2008, he declared, "So if somebody wants to build a coal-fired power plant, they can. It's just that it will bankrupt them because they are going to be charged a huge sum for all that greenhouse gas that's being emitted."[12] Though Obama backed off the statement amid the election-eve controversy it sparked, his plans indisputably will make coal-fired electricity much more expensive—and you will be paying that bill.

As an alternative to coal, Obama supports so-called "clean coal technology," which refers to technologies that would capture CO_2

emissions before they are emitted into the air and then store them permanently underground. Like all the renewable energy sources that Obama touts, however, clean-coal technology isn't anywhere near being ready for the sort of commercial scale usage that Obama envisions; in fact, its advocates are not even sure if vast amounts of CO_2 can be stored safely underground. Additionally, the cost of converting America's coal-fired plants to "clean coal" is staggering—at least $50 billion per year. Passing along the capital and operating costs to consumers would raise electricity prices by at least 40 percent, the Environmental Protection Agency admits. This is without even factoring in the cost—probably hundreds of billions of dollars—of building the necessary nationwide network of pipelines to pump the CO_2 away from power plants.[13]

Even if all these problems could magically be solved, Obama will face a surprising source of opposition: radical greens. Some fundamentalist greens even oppose clean coal—not because it's impractical, but because they're ideologically opposed to all coal usage. One of Obama's own supporters, Robert F. Kennedy, Jr., insists "there is no such thing as clean coal." Kennedy doesn't sound willing to compromise on this issue, warning that the "true costs" of coal include "dead forests and sterilized lakes from acid rain, poisoned fisheries in 49 states and children with damaged brains and crippled health from mercury emissions, millions of asthma attacks and lost work days and thousands dead annually from ozone and particulates."[14] An e-mail alert from Greenpeace in the last weeks of the 2008 campaign likewise called clean coal a "myth," since coal mining "destroys mountains and forests and pollutes America."[15]

Obama is also unlikely to contain electricity prices by allowing more nuclear power plants to be built. Obama says he's for "safe and secure nuclear energy." Among other things, this means finding a safe, secure place to store nuclear waste—which probably will not happen during Obama's presidency, since he opposes the nuclear waste storage repository being constructed at Nevada's Yucca Mountain in Nevada. Locating an alternative site does not seem to be a high priority for him.[16]

Perhaps even worse, President Obama is eager to micro-manage your electricity use. Under the guise of investing in a "smart grid," he advocates deploying "smart-metering [and] demand response." These are euphemisms for state-controlled thermostats like the ones the state of California tried and failed to implement. Obama even wants to control energy use on a state-by-state basis, holding states hostage to meeting "energy conservation" requirements or risk losing federal highway subsidies.[17]

It's a safe bet that the Obama administration will usher in higher gas prices as well. The president says he supports more "responsible domestic production of oil and gas," but first he insists that oil companies drill on the 68 million acres for which they have drilling rights.[18] This is a convenient way to keep new drilling off-limits while blaming the oil companies themselves.

Of course, it might seem strange that oil companies would pay millions or even billions of dollars for a land lease, and continue paying additional rents on it, just to leave the land sitting idle. That's because that's not what's happening. It can take several years to evaluate a land lease, and even if significant, high-quality reserves are found it can take up to a decade for a company to conduct all the necessary environmental studies, acquire permits, install production facilities, and create infrastructure to transport the oil. This is typically what's happening on so-called "idle" lands.[19]

So we're unlikely to see new drilling allowed in the outer continental shelf, despite the expiration of the moratorium on drilling

there. And while Obama says he supports certain smaller drilling projects, like in the Bakken Shale in Montana and North Dakota, his plans
do not include allowing drilling on much bigger sites like the Arctic
National Wildlife Refuge or the Green River Formation, nor do they
call for easing restrictions against Canadian oil tar sands. He also has
refrained from advocating measures to increase our gasoline refinery
capacity.

The public statements of Obama's transition team point to a general reluctance to allow new drilling just about anywhere. Less than a
week after Obama's election victory, *FOX News Sunday* host Chris
Wallace asked Obama transition chief John Podesta whether Obama
intends to reverse certain Bush administration policies. Podesta
responded, "[The Bush administration wants] to have oil and gas
drilling in some of the most sensitive, fragile lands in Utah that they're
going to try to do right as they're walking out the door. I think that's
a mistake."[20]

As for large-scale projects, what Obama does support is using so-
called "enhanced recovery" methods to extract as much as 85 billion
barrels of technically recoverable oil that is stranded in existing fields.
But Obama's support is contingent on the companies sequestering carbon dioxide underground during the extraction process.[21] Unfortunately, current "enhanced recovery" methods do not exist on a large
scale, nor do they currently involve carbon sequestration and it is
unclear if it ever will. Thus, Obama's support for "enhanced recovery"
is little more than lip service to a non-existent technology.

The bottom line is that by blocking expanded drilling—and the
Obama administration is clearly bent on such a course—gas will only
get more expensive and our reliance on foreign oil will continue and
probably worsen. You can also expect oil companies to pass on various new costs to consumers, including: the cost of carbon credits for

Obama's favored cap-and-trade scheme; the cost of reformulating their fuels to emit 10 percent less carbon dioxide by 2020, as Obama advocates; and the cost of a "windfall profits" tax for which Obama has periodically expressed support.

As if increased electricity and fuel costs aren't enough, President Obama also aims to make your car more expensive—and less safe. He wants to raise fuel economy standards by 4 percent per year, which will result in lighter and deadlier cars. He also wants to subsidize the purchase of "advanced technology vehicles" by $7,000 per vehicle, with the goal of putting 1 million plug-in electric vehicles on the road by 2015. This will cost you, the taxpayer, a pretty penny, as will Obama's stated goal of converting half of all federal government vehicles by 2012 into plug-in hybrid or all-electric models—cars so expensive that they are totally non-viable without government subsidies.[22]

Green, Green Everywhere, But Not a Drop to Drink

A centerpiece of Obama's campaign was his promise to create 5 million green or "green-collar" jobs funded by the money raised through global warming regulation—that is, the higher electricity prices that you will be paying. What kind of jobs will you be paying for? Jobs that will make your energy bills go even higher. Obama wants to commit $150 billion to jobs that will accelerate the commercialization of hybrid vehicles, to develop next-generation renewable fuels, and to build the national infrastructure for renewable energy. He brags that these will be jobs "that cannot be outsourced."[23]

That's because they will largely be government-funded blue-collar construction jobs. Thus, Obama's plan is akin to a Depression-era public works program. While it may keep people off the streets, it is expensive and not very productive. These workers, essentially government employees, won't be producing goods and services that expand our economy. Instead, they will be building the infrastructure that will be used to limit our development and energy use.

Obama also wants to increase federal workforce training programs for "green technologies training" for weatherization. That's right, President Obama is coming to weatherize your house—to insulate your attic, caulk your windows and doors, fix your leaky ducts, and upgrade your furnace. He wants to do this for 1 million homes annually, claiming there are 28 million homes that would qualify for this weatherization welfare. He estimates the program will reduce energy bills by 20 to 40 percent.[24] Obama doesn't say how much this will cost, but an army of federal workers doing weatherizing work, along with the purchase and installation of a bevy of new furnaces and other equipment, probably won't come cheap.

On the water front, Obama has promised to implement the very same green policies that will ensure a perpetual water shortage. He opposes exporting water from the Great Lakes and says nothing else about generating new supplies of water, say, through desalination. Instead, he simply concedes that "we do not have enough water to meet the West's fast growing needs." Water conservation is the best he can offer. As "an excellent model of conservation," Obama touts Nevada's "cash for grass" program in which people are paid to remove grass from their lawns and put in desert landscaping.[25]

In fact, when you study his past record, public statements, and campaign promises, it becomes clear that Obama is a true-blue ecophile who supports green policies across the board, often resorting to green euphemisms to describe his plans. He advocates corralling people into planned neighborhoods ("more livable and sustainable" communities), organic food and the buy-local movement ("sustainable agriculture"), and hindering commercial development ("preserving wetlands"), while advocating more stringent regulations on meat farms.[26]

America has truly elected its first green president. So get ready to live small.

Global Warming to the Forefront

Obama has already made clear his support for a cap-and-trade scheme for carbon emissions. Although approval of cap-and-trade in the Senate is not guaranteed, its prospects are better now than in 2008. Such a radical bill would probably face a filibuster, meaning supporters would need to muster sixty senators to put it to a vote. Although only forty-eight senators supported moving the Lieberman-Warner bill to a vote last year, Democrats, who are the main supporters of cap-and-trade, have expanded their control of the Senate and may still end up with sixty seats. That said, some Republicans and Democrats may cross sides on the vote, making the outcome unclear. Future events could hurt the bill, such as another spike in fuel prices, but for now the global warmists appear to have the edge.

In October 2008 Obama's then-energy adviser Jason Grumet vowed that if the Senate doesn't take action to limit greenhouse gas emissions, the Obama administration will do it through the Environmental Protection Agency's authority under the Clean Air Act.[27] This would require the EPA to make a determination that carbon dioxide is an air pollutant and thus in need of regulation. The Bush Administration was sued by a number of states and environmental groups in 2003 after the EPA refused to make this determination. The Supreme Court eventually found in 2007 that the EPA does have the legal authority to regulate carbon dioxide.[28] The court did not order the EPA to do so, but said the agency should reconsider its 2003 decision in light of the court's new ruling.

The EPA's invocation of this authority, however, would be a mere consolation prize for greens since the agency's authority to implement and enforce such a regime is much more limited than the authority of Congress, which alone has the power to set up a comprehensive cap-and-trade scheme.

In pushing for global warming regulation, Obama has a powerful ally in Congressman Henry Waxman (D-Calif.), the new chairman of the House Energy and Commerce Committee, which has jurisdiction over these issues. Waxman got the seat after Democrats ousted his predecessor, John Dingell (D-Mich.), largely due to Dingell's perceived lukewarm support for global warming regulation.[29] Waxman, in contrast, is a reliable green supporter who in March 2007 introduced the "Safe Climate Act," which aimed to reduce annual greenhouse gas emissions to 80 percent below 1990 levels—compared to a goal of just 7 percent set by the Kyoto Protocol.

While he has repeatedly spoken of the need for cap-and-trade, it's not clear if Obama would support an international global warming regime along the lines of Kyoto. His passionate advocacy on this issue indicates he would, but such a treaty would face tough odds in the Senate, where it would require sixty-seven votes for approval. Seeing as the Senate voted 95–0 against Kyoto in 1997, Obama will likely take the path of least resistance and push for an America-only solution—at least at first.

All the Green King's Men

In mid-December 2008 Obama announced his choices to implement his energy and environmental policies. Perhaps the most notable—and worrisome—is the naming of Carol Browner as White House coordinator of energy and climate policy. Browner previously worked as a staffer for then-senator Al Gore and headed the EPA during the

Clinton administration, where she earned a reputation as a committed green. Browner, in fact, is something of a radical, as evident in her
recent membership in the Socialist International's Commission for a
Sustainable World Society, a group that aims to "establish a genuine-
ly new international economic order."[30]

As EPA head, Browner proposed the most expensive air pollution
regulations ever issued to that date. Though she acknowledged that
the $100 billion regulations would not measurably improve public
health and brazenly ignored congressional requests to review the scientific data supposedly supporting the regulations, Browner finalized
the regulations in 1997 over the objections of the Clinton administration, including Al Gore.[31] She also was an early advocate of the
EPA's authority to pass new taxes and restrictions on energy by labeling carbon dioxide as a "dangerous pollutant."[32]

Browner is not particularly indicative of Obama's promise to bring
a less partisan tone to Washington. She was an unrestrained opponent
of efforts by congressional Republicans in 1995 to streamline environmental regulations, rallying green activists to her cause with her
repeated accusations that Republicans sought to "roll back 25 years
of environmental protection efforts." She also accused her critics of
trying to intimidate her when congressmen from both parties alleged
that Browner and the EPA had engaged in illegal lobbying against
Republican-backed environmental proposals.[33]

Obama's other major energy and environment appointment is Dr.
Steven Chu as Secretary of Energy. Although a Nobel prize winner in
physics, Chu spouts a brand of global warming alarmism that puts
even Obama to shame. He envisions a catastrophe of "hundreds of
millions, to billions of people being flooded out permanently," and
mused three years ago that it "may already be too late" to do anything
about global warming.[34] He worries about the waste and proliferation

issues associated with nuclear energy and calls coal his "worst night-mare"—thus he finds problematic the sources of 70 percent of our electricity supply.[35]

Perhaps he should have been nominated as Secretary of No-Energy.

To be fair, Chu does have hopes for cellulosic ethanol technology. Specifically, he anticipates that in ten to twenty years scientists will figure out how to use bacteria found in termite guts to convert wood into alcohol.[36] So we have that to look forward to. Casting further doubt on his grounding in reality, when Chu heard that his laboratory would share in $500 million of funding from oil giant BP to work on alternative energy technology, he exclaimed, "Partnering with BP, we will have the resources to actually carry out some of the things we want to do in order *to help save the world*" (emphasis added).[37]

There's nothing like having a level-headed, sober-minded leader in charge of our energy policy.

Bailout Nirvana

Finally, there is the Troubled Asset Relief Program (TARP)—the $700 billion Wall Street bailout that was passed in early October 2008 in response to the financial crisis. The greens fought hard to get their piece of the bailout action. "Environmentalists and some Democrats are seizing upon the financial sector crisis to call for major federal investments in energy efficiency and improvements in the electricity grid as a way to address climate change and spur a lagging economy," reported *Carbon Control News* shortly before TARP's approval.[38]

Since TARP envisioned the federal government taking big stakes in either financial services companies or their assets, the activist group Friends of the Earth began lobbying the Treasury Department to conduct global-warming impact reviews of the government's new

acquisitions under the National Environmental Policy Act (NEPA)—
the federal law requiring federal agencies to conduct environmental-
impact studies of their own actions. "Subjecting entities that receive
financial backing from taxpayers to NEPA could provide a hook for
environmentalists to force greater scrutiny of actions by those entities
that increase greenhouse gas emissions, including the underwriting
of fossil fuel projects," the group declared.[39]

TARP funds can also be used by the Treasury Department to purchase debt securities that are secured by real property either coveted
by greens or targeted for energy or natural resource development projects that the greens oppose. Once the government owns the securities
(and, thereby, the property), the Treasury Department could essentially take the land out of circulation by "preserving" it as public land
and blocking development. It's not at all far-fetched, since TARP is the
brainchild of a bright green powerbroker—former Goldman Sachs
and Nature Conservancy chairman and Bush administration Treasury
Secretary Henry Paulson.

Paulson also gave $125 billion in TARP money to nine of the
largest U.S. banks with no strings attached. Instead of using the
money to ease the ongoing credit crunch, the banks hung onto it, and
some began mulling options for acquiring smaller banks. In light of
most of the big banks' adherence to green lending policies like the
Equator Principles and the Carbon Principles, consolidation of the
banking industry could constrict commercial lending and give the
greens an even greater say in lending practices.

Since further bailouts as big or even bigger than TARP seem likely,
we must assume that buried in these mammoth bills will be various
proposals inspired by demands from *New York Times* columnist
Thomas Friedman and others to "green the bailout."[40] What they're
looking for is massive, direct investment in green energy infrastruc-

ture and the creation of millions of government-funded "green-collar" jobs. What we are witnessing is a demand for action similar to the appeal of UK Green Party head Caroline Lucas, who urged a "Green New Deal" that would "re-regulate the national and international finance systems, encourage fair and green taxation, close down tax havens, and generate a transformational economic programme to substantially decarbonise our economy."[41]

In November 2008 Paulson indicated he would leave $350 billion of TARP funds for allocation by the Obama administration. We'll have to wait and see how much of this largesse, along with Obama's own gigantic proposed bailout, is redirected to further the greens' anti-development agenda.

Concerns about our first green president were well summed up by the UK's Christopher Booker in a *Daily Telegraph* column with the arresting title, "President-elect Barack Obama proposes economic suicide for US." In spotlighting Obama's video address to a December 2008 meeting of UN climate alarmists, Booker wrote,

If the holder of the most powerful office in the world proposed a policy guaranteed to inflict untold damage on his own country and many others, on the basis of claims so demonstrably fallacious that they amount to a string of self-deluding lies, we might well be concerned. The relevance of this is not to President Bush, as some might imagine, but to a recent policy statement by President-elect Obama.

. . . Delegates from 190 countries will meet in Poznan, Poland, to pave the way for next year's UN conference in Copenhagen at which the world will agree to a successor to the Kyoto Protocol on climate change. They will see a video of Mr. Obama, in only his second major policy commitment, pledging that America is now about to play the leading role in the fight to "save the planet" from global warming.

... For 300 years science helped to turn Western civilisation into the richest and most comfortable the world has ever seen. Now it seems we have suddenly been plunged into a new age of superstition, where scientific evidence no longer counts for anything. The fact that America will soon be ruled by a man wholly under the spell of this post-scientific hysteria may leave us in wondering despair.[42]

President Obama can believe, of course, in whatever he wants to believe, and he can even sign us up to participate in an international global warming treaty—just as President Bill Clinton did in 1997. But Clinton never submitted the treaty to the Senate (which rejected Kyoto in a "sense of the Senate" vote, not a vote on Kyoto's actual ratification). That's because Clinton knew he didn't have enough votes for ratification. Our—your—job is to help make sure that Obama finds himself in the same position. The next chapter will explain how to do that.

CHAPTER 12

FIGHTING BACK

There's no question that the greens have us out-funded and out-organized on every front. They have scores of advocates in the Obama administration and Democrat-controlled Congress; they command activist groups, NGOs, charities, universities, and professional societies; and they're a powerful force in big business, venture capital firms, and pension funds. But they don't necessarily have us out-*manned.* When the American *people* get a chance to speak out—which is all too rarely these days—they usually give the greens a big red raspberry.

In the 2008 elections, five major energy and environmental initiatives were put to a vote in California, Colorado, and Missouri. Despite all the green hype, four of the five were defeated, including initiatives to require California utilities to ramp up use of renewable energy; to authorize California to issue $5 billion in bonds as cash payments to purchasers of alternative fuel vehicles; to require the city of San Francisco to purchase most of its electricity from renewable energy sources; and to raise taxes on oil and gas companies operating in Colorado to fund various green projects.[1] The only measure to pass was a mild Missouri initiative to increase gradually the use of renewable energy and to limit associated rate increases to 1 percent per year.

Whenever Americans are polled about expanded domestic oil and gas drilling they express overwhelming support for it—even in coastal states like Florida, where an August 2008 poll reported that 73 percent of Floridians favor offshore drilling.[2] Eighty-four percent of Florida Republicans and 63 percent of Florida Democrats expressed support. There are very few political issues that enjoy such resounding public consensus to act.

Moreover, people around the world are increasingly skeptical of the kind of massive overhauls and expenditures that the greens advocate to "stop" global warming—even according to the greens' own polls. In November 2008 the Earthwatch Institute asked 12,000 people in eleven countries if they were willing to make personal lifestyle changes to reduce carbon emissions. Only 47 percent said they favored such changes, down from 58 percent the year before.[3] Only 20 percent said they would spend extra money to reduce climate change, down from 28 percent in 2007. American polls show a similar lack of support. The failed ballot initiatives and dismal polling results show there is no broad support for "green" legislative measures—yet politicians continue endlessly trying to out-green one another as though the populace had marched on Washington demanding a green constitutional amendment.

What is going on? Why is there such a disconnect between what the American people want and the clueless behavior of so many of our elected representatives? It is, in my opinion, partially a testament to the power of the demonizing tactics that the greens have used to attack anyone who questions them or their claims. Dare to do so and you're labeled a "flat-Earther" or likened to someone who "believes the moon landing was staged," to recall Al Gore's comparison. Scientists, politicians, and corporate executives who publicly question global warming alarmism are threatened with an appearance in front of some future "Climate Nuremburg" court. A very telling illustration of this fear factor was seen during the December 13, 2007, Republican presidential debate, when the moderator asked the candidates—many of whom had previously expressed reservations about global warming alarmism in one form or another—for a show of hands as to "how many of you believe that global climate change is a serious threat and caused by human activity?" Only one, Fred Thompson, had the courage of his convictions to leave his hand at his side.

Another contributing factor is the tendency of timid and lazy politicians to get caught up in the Washington, D.C. echo chamber. Whenever a political force like the greens is so thoroughly over-represented and outspoken in the nation's capital, you end up with a closed-circuit environment where messages get amplified far out of proportion to their actual popular constituency and repeated *ad infinitum*. A politician is only as good as the bubble he's kept in. Unfortunately for us, the result is government at its most sheepish—in the fullest sense of that word—and the creation of a herd mentality that is exquisitely sensitive to fear.

Quick—what is the organized political opposition to green public policies called?

Struggling for the right phrase? There isn't one, which brings us to yet another factor contributing to the greens' success—a lack of political identity among their opponents. While there are many individuals in Congress who have taken on green special interests and have been willing to endure the backlash enabled by the greens' rich financial backing, there has not been any coherent coalition that stands in defiance of the green steamrolling of Capitol Hill. It's hard for a following to find its leadership when that leadership has no name and no clear identity.

While some will no doubt try to claim that the election of Barack Obama and the expansion of Democratic majorities in the House and Senate imply strong public support for green policies—since virtually all Democratic politicians try to append the green label to themselves in one fashion or another—that's simply not the case. First, there was virtually no daylight between Obama and John McCain on environmental and energy issues, so voters who prioritize their opposition to green policies had no meaningful choice. Next, Obama's election largely stemmed from other factors like McCain's poor candidacy and mismanaged campaign, the September-October 2008 economic meltdown, and Bush fatigue. Finally, even plummeting oil and gas prices toward the end of the campaign came to Obama's aid, as they defused the urgency of the domestic drilling issue.

Lacking anything near the popular mandate they claim, greens often have to circumvent democracy to get their policies approved. We have already seen how this works in the context of the so-called corporate social responsibility movement, the importation of European Union regulation to America, and many other examples.

Green Changes Everything

It's important to keep in mind that the sweeping governmental reforms the greens propose do not simply represent an isolated political island that touches nothing else of any importance. No matter what your particular political outlook—whether you are conservative, liberal, independent, or something else—there are ways in which your own concerns will be pushed aside by the green juggernaut.

Worried about federal spending and the deficit? How about the looming bankruptcy of Social Security and Medicare? What about spiraling health care and education costs? Perhaps you are worried about the economy? Green policies will not only add to the government's already-onerous financial burdens but, more important, will raise prices, severely damage the economy, and destroy the tax base that feeds the government.

Want to see the U.S. stand up to OPEC? You can forget about energy independence, as the greens won't let us develop any of our own natural resources. No expansion of domestic oil and gas drilling. No more coal mining and no nuclear power. Even if the greens permitted the mass development of wind, solar power, and biofuels, these expensive, unreliable sources would not even come close to satisfying the nation's energy needs.

Even traditional political opponents can find common ground in their opposition to green policies. Whether you are pro-life or pro-choice on abortion, the ultra-greens' demands for a say in the number of babies you can have should offend you greatly. Civil libertarians should be particularly concerned by these aspects of the green agenda, which entails the severe diminishing of personal privacy under an intrusive regulatory regime.

If you are a big proponent of school choice, even if you succeed in getting a voucher system, what have you gained if the greens have overrun your child's school and put the curriculum in eco-lockdown? Perhaps you're interested in schools turning out more scientists and engineers? That can't happen if academic inquisitiveness is displaced by unquestioning, politicized dogma. How can a budding scientist learn to solve problems if he is not encouraged to consider *all* the possible solutions?

Oppose big government? All you need do is look at any green "solution" to any real or invented environmental problem—it invariably involves a larger, more powerful, and more intrusive government, preferably on an international level. There is no shortage of examples: the Montreal Protocol regulating CFC use, the Kyoto Protocol regulating energy use, the Law of the Sea Treaty regulating use of the oceans, and so on. Moreover, the cleaner our environment gets, the shriller the green insistence becomes for *more* government regulation. It seems they won't be satisfied until there's a green global secretariat governing every move we make.

Fighting back against the oppressive public policies being promoted by the greens will require grassroots political participation. Voting is a start, but it's not enough. As the greens have demonstrated to great effect, activism is the key to getting your message out. However you formulate your personal opposition to green public policies, remember to highlight how they adversely impact all the other issues we care about.

The War of Words

Your first challenge is to overcome and counteract green rhetoric. One of the most effective weapons in the greens' arsenal has been their ingenious manipulation of language and, in turn, the framing of ideas. While green opponents have yet to even *name* their cause, the greens for a long time have shaped the debate through the use of loaded buzzwords and hard-to-argue modifiers. These virtually guarantee that the greens begin every discussion with a distinct advantage. Their terminology invariably aims to capture the moral high ground so that anyone who opposes them automatically assumes a morally inferior position.

Take the terms "smart growth" and "optimum population," for example. It's hard to argue against anything "smart" or "optimum," isn't it? Most people are totally stymied by such terms. Don't be. Remember what these euphemisms really mean. As discussed earlier, smart growth means a return to the days of yore when villagers lived in isolated, self-contained communities and rarely left them. Optimum population is government-enforced population control—like China's one-child policy.

And what about that most ubiquitous of green terms, "sustainability"? What does it mean? Does it mean we can't use a natural resource unless there is an endless supply of it? Does it mean we can't use a resource if getting at it or using it alters the environment, however transiently, in some way, shape, or form? For the greens, the answer to both questions is yes. But of course being *for* "sustainable development" is much more positive sounding and socially acceptable than the greens' real position, which is being *against* all economic activity and development. When the greens wield the battle axe of "sustainable development," opponents automatically start on the defensive, practically from a position of would-be Earth pillagers.

If you actually dissect green arguments, however, their notions of sustainability tend to fall apart upon close examination. To the greens, oil, coal, and natural gas are not sustainable forms of energy because they involve Earth-harming drilling and mining, and supposedly contribute to global warming. Nuclear power is not sustainable because it involves mining and disposal of radioactive waste. Yet they also find ways to oppose wind farms, solar power, and biofuels, citing various "adverse environmental impacts." It seems that all energy use is unsustainable to the greens.

Logging is another allegedly unsustainable activity because, even if a timber company replants trees, they won't be the same as the "old-growth" that was just cut down. And the greens oppose modern agricultural technologies even though they allow farmers to grow *more* food with *less* land and water use. They ignore the dramatic conservation benefits of biotechnology, declaring it "unsustainable." Instead they hail organic farming, which requires *more* fossil fuel, land, and water use. By any level-headed reckoning of environmental impacts, organic agriculture is wasteful and therefore less "sustainable" than conventional agriculture.

Then there are terms like "carbon footprint" and "carbon neutrality"—which supposedly bring "sustainability" to a personal level.

These terms are designed to engender a "smaller is always better" mentality. Both are simply marketing concepts aimed at giving people the sense that their mere existence is an ecological problem and that their every action is a violation. Pardon is, of course, available in the form of cash or a check made out to the greens in exchange for "carbon offsets."

And what exactly does a carbon offset accomplish? Not much, seeing as carbon emissions are supposedly a global problem and thus must be tackled globally. But not all the rest of the globe is going along with the program. As observed by Gregg Easterbrook in the *New York Times*,

> Since 1990, according to the World Resources Institute, American greenhouse emissions rose 18 percent while Chinese emissions rose 77 percent. China may pass America as the No. 1 emitter of greenhouse gases as soon as 2010. If current trends hold, by 2050 emerging nations led by China and India will emit twice as much carbon as the United States and Western Europe combined.
>
> China's emissions are soaring because the Chinese economy is nearly three times as "carbon intensive" as America's, burning far more fossil fuel per unit of gross domestic product. Chinese coal-fired power plants are notoriously inefficient, consuming twice as much coal per kilowatt produced as American generating stations. They also run without the elaborate anti-pollution "stack scrubbers" found in Western power plants. And China opens a new coal-fired generating station every week to 10 days.[4]

And the Chinese don't seem intent on buying a lot of carbon offsets. The *Financial Times* reports that "both Beijing and New Delhi fear that binding [greenhouse gas] emission caps that limit energy use could threaten future economic development—and condemn many of their people to perpetual poverty."[5]

A final proof of the vapidity of the terms "carbon footprint" and "carbon neutral" is that the U.S. has been reducing its carbon output for decades without the help of the greens, just by virtue of the fact that, through technology, we are continually becoming more energy efficient. From 1949 to 2007, the amount of energy it took to produce one dollar of gross domestic product declined by about 50 percent.[6] This trend will certainly stretch into the future as technology continues to improve.

Then there's the term "green" itself. It seems that everything and everyone is going green and if you're not, you must be opposed to progress, anti-Earth, and unhip to how the world is changing. "Green" is used as a synonym for "cool," "progressive," "modern," "futuristic," "conscientious," "efficient"—and generally, the right way to be, if not the only way. In reality, however, "green" is simply a soothing symbol disguising an oppressive lifestyle full of unnecessary burdens and hardships.

Don't let green buzzwords catch you off-guard and put you on the defensive. They're meant to convey a sense of urgency, to end debate and to rush to a solution—one that invariably expands green power at your expense.

If you want to stop the green wave, you need to take a page from the greens' playbook. The Friends of the Earth slogan, "Think Globally, Act Locally," would work just as well for you as it does for them. You may feel too tired to attend the meetings of your local community planning board, but the greens will be there. You may simply turn up your nose at a grossly biased or factually inaccurate newspaper article, but the greens will overwhelm a media outlet with carefully-orchestrated outrage if it questions one of their sacred cows. Politicians and lobbying may turn you off, but rest assured that greens go to bed every night knowing they are well represented in your local community, state capital, and in Washington, D.C. Whatever kind of visible political action you can name—marches, protests, lawsuits, boycotts, lobbying, corporate shareholder activism, TV and newspaper advertising, Internet campaigns—the greens already engage in it to advance their ideas. Now it's your turn.

If You Can't Out-gun Them, Out-smart Them

Once you've versed yourself in the facts, take a look around you. You are surrounded by "green" campaigns, editorials, and events everywhere you look. The prevalence of all this hype and misinformation opens up a multitude of opportunities for grassroots activism. Figure out whether there's any mindless green-ness going on in your workplace or your community that you could counteract in some way. It could be a town council meeting, a neighborhood planning meeting, a zoning hearing, a workplace meeting, a community organization event, or a charity event. Take advantage of any opportunities to participate or comment. Get your facts straight and make a nuisance of yourself. Ask questions. How much will it cost? What are the supposed benefits? Is there really a problem to start with or is one being manufactured for some reason?

And demand answers. You'll be surprised at how off-guard you'll catch the greens, how they can't defend their demands, and how they'll try to ignore you or shout you down. Get on the Internet and share your experience with the world. If you have a good story that makes a good point, others will spread it around for you. Introduce yourself to some free-market and anti-green bloggers. Be on the lookout for green grandstanding; it makes an especially juicy target.

I'll give you a personal example. In the summer of 2000, I was enjoying some ice cream at a scoop shop of Ben & Jerry's, a company known for supporting green causes. At the shop I noticed a Ben & Jerry's marketing brochure entitled "Our Thoughts on Dioxin." Curious as to what ice cream makers knew about dioxin, I read in the brochure that "dioxin is known to cause cancer, genetic and reproductive defects and learning disabilities. . . . The only safe level of dioxin exposure is no exposure at all."

What the brochure *didn't* say was that dioxin occurs naturally in the environment since, any time organic matter is burned, dioxin is produced as a by-product. Knowing that dioxin is present in virtually all food, my friend Dr. Michael Gough and I put Ben & Jerry's ice cream to the test. We measured the level of dioxin in a sample of Ben & Jerry's "World's Best Vanilla" ice cream and presented the results at the Dioxin 2000 scientific conference in Monterey, California. We found that a single serving of the ice cream contained about 200 times the level of dioxin the EPA considered to be "safe" for an adult and about 740 times what the agency considered to be safe for a child. We then posed the following questions: "If dioxin is as dangerous as Ben & Jerry's, Greenpeace—Ben & Jerry's science advisor—and the EPA claim, then how can Ben & Jerry's be permitted to sell its ice cream? Doesn't the company care about 'the children?'" Our dioxin study was a huge hit. It throttled Ben & Jerry's ill-conceived anti-dioxin campaign—an embarrassment the company is still trying to explain away on its website.[7]

Another example of grassroots anti-green activism is the debunking of the infamous "hockey stick" graph, which showed average global temperature over the past 1,000 years with a huge spike upward during the twentieth century, giving the graph a dramatic hockey stick-shaped appearance. The graph had become a persuasive icon of the manmade global warming crisis and was prominently featured in the 2001 report by the United Nations Intergovernmental Panel on Climate Change (IPCC). But you don't see the hockey stick anymore, largely because of the work of a semi-retired Toronto minerals consultant named Steve McIntyre, who spent two years and $5,000 of his own money trying to validate the hockey stick graph. McIntyre eventually discovered that the mathematical technique used to generate the graph is prone to generate a hockey stick shape no matter what data are used. Thus, he showed that the hockey stick graph proved nothing.

When McIntyre probed the issue with the hockey stick's creator, Dr. Michael Mann of the University of Virginia, Mann at first cooperated and then cut McIntyre off, telling the *Wall Street Journal* that he didn't have time to respond to "every frivolous note" from nonscientists.[8] But McIntyre's work was anything but frivolous. It resulted in congressional hearings, the discrediting of the hockey stick graph, and the graph's omission from the most recent IPCC report on climate change.

You don't have to be a scientist or a mathematician to do your part. One week before Earth Day in 2007, professors who taught the course "Core 101: Science, Technology and Society" at Roger William's University pronounced Al Gore's movie *An Inconvenient Truth* to be mandatory viewing. The students were not presented with any other view on the global warming controversy. That unfortunate situation came to an end when junior Dana Peloso complained to the school administration. He asked simply, "With the issue of global warming being such a highly politicized topic, with the scientific community unsure if global warming is man-induced or part of the natural cycle of the earth, do you think that it is intellectually honest to only show the alarmist viewpoint?"[9]

The school initially defended the requirement with a statement arrogantly asserting that the debate on global warming is over:

There is no doubt that we're warming the Earth and that a continuation of activities will lead to profound changes. Penguins, polar bears and your unborn children have no vote in this. They must live with decisions we make today. As educators, we're charged to encourage your intellectual growth.

That can (actually, will) be uncomfortable at times, and we're also here to help you deal with that discomfort. It's truly what makes being a human such a joy, privilege and challenge.[10]

But if anyone learned how "uncomfortable" learning can be it was the school administrators, who became the focus of unflattering attention. A university spokesman told me that the backlash against the required viewing had prompted the school to "explore alternatives" to teaching global warming.[11]

Then there's Nathan Zohner, a 14-year old boy who won first prize in the Great Idaho Fall Science Fair with a project titled "How Gullible Are We?" in which he polled his classmates about the dangers of "dihydrogen monoxide." Zohner reported that forty-three of the fifty-nine students surveyed favored banning the substance, six were undecided, and only one recognized "dihydrogen monoxide" by its common name—water. Zohner wasn't the first to explore our irrational fears of dihydrogen monoxide, but he sure has been one of the most successful, garnering coverage around the world such as in Ontario's *Hamilton Spectator*, whose article about Zohner was captioned, "Scientific ignorance is no laughing matter."[12] Nathan's brilliantly simple experiment showed how ignorance and a herd mentality—combined with flawed perceptions—can lead us down an incredibly foolish path.

Don't be afraid to draw attention to your point of view. When Al Gore spoke at the Live Earth concert event on July 7, 2007, I hired aerial advertisers to fly over the Meadowlands stadium with a banner that read "DON'T BELIEVE AL GORE." One of the pilots, who eaves-dropped on the concert via his cockpit radio, took the initiative to dive down and buzz the stadium right as Al Gore was speaking to the crowd. As I like to say, it was the first pro-free market air raid in history.

There was a ground assault, too. In the parking lot before the concert, we had a group of college students from the libertarian group BureauCrash hand out dozens of blue and green Earth-themed beach balls emblazoned with the motto, "I'm more worried about the intellectual climate." Millions who watched the concert live on TV that afternoon saw the beach balls bouncing all over the place—some were even thrown right up on stage with the performers. After the show, Live Earth performer John Mayer spent most of his press conference angrily complaining about our antics.[13] Nevertheless, we made our point in front of the Live Earth crowd. Did we turn the tide of public opinion? No—nor did we expect to. But we did reach our goal of harnessing some priceless exposure of our message for just a couple hundred dollars—in the case of the beach balls—and a few thousand dollars—in the case of the aerial advertising.

But you don't even have to leave your house to be heard. You can star in your own well-thought-out rant and upload it to on YouTube. Al Gore has famously ducked every effort to get him to debate global warming. So I produced and posted a YouTube video entitled "Al Gore Debates Global Warming."[14] I juxtaposed clips from Gore's movie *An Inconvenient Truth* with counter-arguments taken from the excellent British documentary *The Great Global Warming Swindle*. It was Al Gore versus seven climate experts. The video became one of the most commented upon YouTube videos on global warming.

Once you decide to get involved, send us an e-mail at JunkScience.com so we can spotlight your activism.

Let Your Shareholder Status Do the Talking

Perhaps the most important action that most of us can undertake is to help recapture American business from the greens. When I began working on environmental issues in 1990, you could count on most businesses and their trade associations to oppose nonsensical green initiatives. Almost twenty years later, the situation has reversed. Now, many businesses support and promote green initiatives regardless of whether they make any scientific or economic sense.

The reason that businesses are so important—especially the biggest corporations—is that they have tremendous amounts of money, manpower, and influence to use on public policy issues. They are so valuable in public policy debates that their shift from anti-green to pro-green is the primary reason that the rest of us are so perilously close to being permanently placed under the green thumb.

Consider the all-important issue of global warming. When the Clinton administration signed the Kyoto Protocol in 1997, the greens, Europeans, and the UN were already bent on imposing greenhouse gas regulation on the U.S. But American business largely opposed the effort, even lobbying successfully for the Senate to spike the treaty.[15] Jumping ahead more than a decade, the government now appears hellbent on imposing a domestic version of Kyoto on America.

So what's changed over the last ten years? Certainly, the science has not changed—except that even more flaws have come to light in the scientific claims underlying global warming orthodoxy. What has most dramatically changed, in fact, is the position of big business, which is increasingly lobbying *for* greenhouse gas regulation. It is this change that is actually driving legislators forward. The powerful green political lobby now has the added resources and influence of some of the largest U.S. and even foreign corporations.

But there's still hope. The good news is that most of the big businesses lobbying for greenhouse gas regulation are publicly-owned, meaning they have publicly-traded stocks. Here's where you can really do your part to help stop the Big Green Machine. As an investor you have federally-protected rights you can exercise to influence managers against the great green assault.

First, you need to figure out what companies you own common stock in and what the companies' positions are concerning greenhouse gas regulation and other green-related issues. As discussed throughout this book, the fact that global warming regulation is likely to harm the entire economy means that every business should be concerned about the negative impacts of mandatory greenhouse gas regulation. Higher energy prices will hurt *everyone*. Even alternative energy companies will find that reduced economic growth also reduces political interest and public resources for high-priced energy. If you don't manage your own investments, call your broker and find out what you own.

Next, it's time to act. Start with a letter to the CEO in order to establish a dialogue with the company, to inform the CEO where you stand, and to learn the CEO's position. Don't be intimidated. Not only do CEOs put their pants on one leg at a time just like you and me, many of them actually read the correspondence sent to them. To prioritize your letter, send it by overnight or registered delivery. Your letter should be firm but polite, short (no more than one page) and to the point. Ask the CEO to explain to you the company's position on greenhouse gas regulation and what actions management is taking in that regard. Allow ten days for a response.

This is a common tactic of the greens, and they employ it for a reason: it sometimes works. Consider this July 1999 report in the *Wall Street Journal*:

The letter scrolling out of a fax machine at the Gerber baby-food company in Michigan on May 28 was just one of many arriving that day and didn't even name the person it was meant for, but it sure got attention. Within days, it had found its way to Gerber's parent company in Switzerland, Novartis AG, and come to the attention of its CEO. There, executives soon were taking steps to overhaul a decades-old product that generates $1 billion in annual sales.

The letter came from Charles Margulis, a New York man who addressed it simply "to the CEO" because he didn't know the chief executive's name. The return address was his small apartment on the Upper West Side of Manhattan. But the letter also carried the logo of his employer, Greenpeace, the activist European environmental group.

"As you know, there is growing concern around the world about genetically engineered food," it said. Greenpeace is "concerned that the release of genetically engineered organisms into the environment and food supply may have irreversible consequences." Does Gerber use genetically engineered products in its baby food, the letter wanted to know. If so, which products? And "what steps have you taken (if any) to ensure you are not using" genetically modified ingredients?

Mr. Margulis asked for a reply within five business days

... But this summer... at some cost and considerable inconvenience, Gerber is dropping some of its existing corn and soybean suppliers in favor of ones that can produce crops that aren't genetically altered.[16]

So don't think a CEO will reflexively disregard your concerns. Your chances of success will depend on what you have to say and what problems the CEO thinks you can cause for him.

So you may get a meaningful response—but it's more likely that you won't. If you don't get a response at all, you can follow up with another letter, a fax, or a phone call, but you should probably just consider that box checked and escalate your campaign. If you do get a response, it will probably be some missive issued by a corporate flunky that thanks you for your interest and points you to the corporate website for more information—in the hope that you will simply go away and not pester the CEO any further. But don't let yourself be dismissed—it's time to turn up the pressure.

As a shareholder—even of just one share of stock—you have the right to attend a company's annual shareholder meeting. If you can, go to the meeting, where there's a good chance you will get the opportunity to press your case directly to the CEO in front of other shareholders. Take some friends who are shareholders with you. The CEO has to listen to you, so make him earn his multimillion dollar pay. It's also a good opportunity for other shareholders and the media to hear about your issue.

Shareholders usually have a chance to speak during the portion of the meeting when the board of directors is elected, and again at the end during a general questions-and-answers session. Be short and to the point, polite but firm. Remind the CEO that he previously blew you off, if that's the case. Put him on the defensive. Insist on a substantive answer to your specific question. Remember that the CEO is proscribed by law from making materially false and misleading statements. That doesn't require him actually to answer your question but, if you're asking about a significant corporate matter, it does mean the CEO can't lie. Get a commitment for some sort of follow-up. Be a nuisance. The squeaky wheel gets the grease—this is what green activists have been doing to CEOs for years and it's gotten them incredibly far.

If you've owned enough shares of stock for a long enough period—the current requirements are owning $2,000 worth of stock continuously for at least one year—you can file a shareholder proposal with a company. That's a request or command to corporate management to take action on your issue, and it gives shareholders a chance to vote for or against your position.

Shareholder proposals can be submitted in two ways: either under the provisions of state corporate laws or under the federal securities laws. If you file a proposal pursuant to state law, your fellow shareholders are unlikely to find out about the proposal until the annual meeting, since the company is not required to publicize it. You could do your own publicity campaign, but that takes a lot of work and can be expensive. Filing proposals pursuant to the federal securities laws, then, is preferred since the law essentially compels companies to include such proposals in corporate proxy statements that are sent to all shareholders. Your proposal—which includes your request and a supporting statement, all in 500 words—will then have a wide audience, including large institutional shareholders, Wall Street analysts, and the media.

If your proposal makes the company uncomfortable, the firm may ask the Securities and Exchange Commission for permission to exclude it. While the SEC process for reviewing such requests is pretty opaque and appears quite arbitrary, you'll have one advantage at this stage—thanks, oddly enough, to the greens. Under pressure from the greens, the SEC staff has special provisions for shareholder proposals that pertain to the environment. If your proposal requests information about the company's environmental impacts, you can almost be assured that the SEC will deny the company's request to exclude it.

Here's another personal example: the SEC repeatedly allowed companies to exclude a proposal from the mutual fund I co-manage, The

Free Enterprise Action Fund, which requested a company to report to shareholders about the potential risks and liabilities of global warming regulation. The SEC considered this a request for information about ordinary business operations, which they often frown upon. So we retooled the proposal to request a report on the environmental impacts of the company's global warming-related actions. The proposal, which PepsiCo tried to exclude from its 2008 proxy statement, essentially looked like this:

Global Warming Report

Resolved: The shareholders request that the Board of Directors prepare by October 2008, at reasonable expense and omitting proprietary information, a Global Warming Report. The report may describe and discuss how action taken to date by PepsiCo to reduce its impact on global climate change has affected global climate in terms of any changes in mean global temperature and any undesirable climatic and weather-related events and disasters avoided.

Supporting Statement: PepsiCo says on its web site that it supports action on global warming. PepsiCo is a member of the U.S. Climate Action Partnership (USCAP), a group that lobbies for global warming regulation.

But scientific data show that atmospheric levels of carbon dioxide, the greenhouse gas of primary concern in global warming, do not drive global temperature.

Even assuming for the sake of argument that atmospheric carbon dioxide levels affect global temperatures, the U.S. Environmental Protection Agency recently projected that U.S. regulation of manmade greenhouse gas emissions would have a trivial impact on atmospheric concentrations of carbon dioxide over the next 90 years.

So U.S. greenhouse gas regulation is not likely to discernibly affect global climate in the foreseeable future.

Global warming regulation is expected to harm the economy. The Congressional Budget Office, U.S. Department of Energy and prominent economists such as Alan Greenspan, Arthur Laffer and Greg Mankiw all say that cap-and-trade—a type of greenhouse gas regulation promoted by USCAP—would reduce economic growth.

Shareholders want to know how PepsiCo's actions relating to global warming may be improving global climate.

In light of this new emphasis on environmental impacts, the SEC refused PepsiCo's effort to exclude the proposal.

If your shareholder proposal makes it into the proxy statement, oftentimes the company will contact you in an effort to negotiate it away. The greens use these opportunities to get companies to adopt green policies and to support green projects, lobbying efforts, and organizations. And it's quite remarkable how easily CEO's can be intimidated.

If you refuse to give up on your proposal, bear in mind that management will issue voting recommendations to all shareholders in advance of the annual meeting—and that virtually all resolutions that management opposes will fail. This is true whether the resolutions are pro-green or pro-free market. This happens, in large part, because management can cast votes on behalf of all shareholders who either did not send in their voting ballot or did not attend the annual meeting—which is the vast majority of shareholders. You'll likely only receive a few percentage points of the vote total, but that's not nearly as important as the fact that you had the opportunity to thrust your issue into a public dialogue with the CEO and the board in front of the media and fellow shareholders.

You don't even have to own stock directly to play the shareholder game. If you are a state or local government employee or retiree, or have a pension or investment plan that is managed by someone else, contact the organization responsible for managing the plan and find out what they're doing about the green problem. The people that manage state and local government pension funds have a legal responsibility to act in your best interest—it's their fiduciary duty. How much sense does it make for a pension fund system to lobby for global warming regulation that is going to hurt its own investment portfolio—and drive up energy costs for the very people who depend on the fixed incomes that the pension fund manages?

Pension funds that aren't lobbying on global warming shouldn't be let off the hook. Demand to know why they aren't lobbying *against* global warming regulation. Energy rationing is going to hurt them too, even if they didn't expressly support it. Remind them that ignoring global warming regulation is a form of negligence—meaning that they are also breaching their legal duty to you.

The greens long ago grasped the value and ease of harnessing corporate power. People often take it for granted that business will be on the side of individual liberty, limited government, and free markets. This assumption is outdated—especially when it comes to big business. Many corporations promote expensive or otherwise burdensome regulation in an effort to hurt existing and would-be competitors, while others view regulation as a business opportunity. Think, for example, of how the alternative energy industry would like nothing better than to see fossil fuel-based electricity made less competitive—or banned outright—through global warming regulation.

Traditional grassroots activism focuses on pressuring and persuading politicians. There's also a place for that in our efforts. But if you can stop corporate lobbyists from championing green policies in the first place, our job will be that much easier.

Looking Forward

While we're all in favor of protecting the environment and controlling pollution, the greens portray themselves as inhabiting a higher moral plane. Their underlying message is that if you don't sign on to what they want, it means you don't love the planet, or worse, you're out to destroy it. And they have fingered their primary villain, or at least the villain of the moment: carbon dioxide—a colorless and odorless gas that exists naturally in the atmosphere at trace levels. Humans exhale it. Plants need it to grow. Both industrial and personal "manmade" emissions of carbon dioxide *combined* are vanishingly small when compared to natural CO_2 emissions. There's no scientific data indicating that controlling human emissions of carbon dioxide will change, much less "improve," global climate in any predictable or even detectable way.

Yet, according to the greens, *your* responsibility for carbon dioxide necessitates *you* sacrificing *your* standard of living. And not only you—think of all the people around the world denied the ability to use their own natural resources to better their lives, denied the ability to climb out of crushing poverty through economic development and free trade, and denied even the ability to use pesticides like DDT to protect themselves and their children against deadly Malaria-bearing mosquitoes. Now contrast their situation to how the green elites live—Al Gore and his prodigious personal consumption of electricity; Richard Branson and his private island getaways and space travel for VIPs only; the Google guys and their personal sky pig; and the World

Wildlife Fund and its private jet expedition around the world, to name just a few examples.

Aside from providing perks and exemptions to be enjoyed by these folks and other special interests, green is a political movement that seeks to put a happy face on an otherwise oppressive and regressive social and political agenda. Green is not "green" as some eco-profiteers would have you believe. As many free-market thinkers have warned us, green is the new red—both financially and politically.

It's crucial that we fight the misinformation they promote. So much of the greens' rationale for forcing us to adopt new behaviors is based on their claims of scarcity for nearly all of life's essentials. But let's look at the facts.

Are we in danger of running out of food? Hardly—we have so much corn we can afford to turn it into ethanol and burn it as fuel. We have so much farmland that the federal government actually pays farmers $1.8 billion per year *not* to grow crops on 34 million acres in order to prop up prices.[17] What about water? Well, it is the most abundant substance on Earth. We can't run out, although green-inspired government policies are making it harder to export water from regions with ample supplies to those with scarcity.

What about energy? Are we running out of conventional forms of energy? As far as conventional energy goes, the U.S. is the Saudi Arabia of coal. We have so much coal that we could also convert it to liquid fuel—if the greens would just let us. The only way that coal is not a major part of our energy future is if the greens regulate it out of existence. How about natural gas? We have plenty of it from our domestic and nearby Canadian supplies as long as free markets, rather than government mandates, drive supply and demand. While any future supply shortcomings could be met by importing liquefied natural gas, the greens are doing their best to block the construction of the necessary terminals and port facilities.

We also have plenty of oil—if you include what's offshore and on public lands like the Arctic National Wildlife Refuge. Past that there are the oil tar sands in Canada and oil shale in the western U.S.—both of Saudi Arabian proportions. These vast oil resources are the solutions to our energy needs and to our vexing dependence on Mideast oil. It's true that oil from tar sands and oil shale will be more expensive than conventionally produced oil, but cost is not the main hurdle we face in developing these resources—the greens are.

If you throw nuclear power into the energy mix, then we really are an energy powerhouse—or to be precise, a potential powerhouse. For the mere existence of these resources doesn't mean anything if we prohibit ourselves from extracting and using them.

At the center of the greens' agenda is their opposition to economic growth, which is ironic given that economic growth and prosperity has proven to be the most effective and most humane way both to protect the environment and to prevent over-population—two crucial goals for the greens. But they don't seem to have noticed that the chief population concern in the Western world—where the greens are primarily active—is not over-population but the opposite: that birth rates in many countries have dropped below the replacement level of around 2.1 children per woman. So greens really should welcome economic development as a natural and coercion-free form of family planning. But they've chosen to go down a different road, hoping to ram through their agenda via intimidation, demonization, and government diktats.

While there's no "vast green conspiracy" that meets regularly to plot and plan, the disparate groups that comprise the green movement are all working toward a common goal—increased government control of your life.

Our goal is to make sure that day never comes—and we have our work cut out for us.

ACKNOWLEDGMENTS

I would like to thank everyone at Regnery who helped bring this book to fruition, especially Jack Langer for his expert guidance and editing. Heartfelt thanks go to Francis Collins for his unflagging irreverence and inspiration, and to his lovely wife, Erin, for putting up with both of us. My trusty trench-mates Barry Hearn and Tom Borelli deserve special appreciation as do Red, Deneen Borelli, Peter Farrell, Audrey Mullen and her staff at Advocacy Ink, Fred Smith and the Competitive Enterprise Institute, and Amy Ridenour and the National Center for Public Policy Research. Finally, I am much indebted to all the JunkScience.com fans around the world who have supported our work over the last thirteen years.

SUGGESTED READING AND VIEWING

Reading

Brian Fagan, *The Great Warming: Climate Change and the Rise and Fall of Civilizations* (Bloomsbury, 2008).

Christopher Booker and Richard North, *Scared to Death: From BSE to Global Warming: Why Scares are Costing Us the Earth* (Continuum, 2008).

Christopher Horner, *Red Hot Lies: How Global Warming Alarmists Use Threats, Fraud, and Deception to Keep You Misinformed* (Regnery, 2008).

Christopher C. Horner, *The Politically Incorrect Guide to Global Warming (and Environmentalism)* (Regnery, 2007).

Henrik Svensmark and Nigeler Calder, *The Chilling Stars: A New Theory of Climate Change* (Totem, 2007).

Howard C. Hayden, *Solar Fraud: Why Solar Energy Won't Run the World* (Vales Lake, 2005).

Iain Murray, *The Really Inconvenient Truths: Seven Environmental Catastrophes Liberals Don't Want You to Know About—Because They Helped Cause Them* (Regnery, 2008).

John Berlau, *Eco-Freaks: Environmentalism Is Hazardous to Your Health* (Thomas Nelson, 2006).

Julian Lincoln Simon, *The Ultimate Resource 2* (Princeton University Press, 2008).

Lawrence Solomon, *The Deniers: The World Renowned Scientists Who Stood Up Against Global Warming Hysteria, Political Persecution, and Fraud—And those who are too fearful to do so* (Richard Vigilante Books, 2008).

Michael Crichton, *State of Fear* (HarperCollins, 2004).

Patrick J. Michaels, *Shattered Consensus: The True State of Global Warming* (Rowman and Littlefield, 2005).

Robert Bryce, *Gusher of Lies: The Dangerous Delusions of Energy Independence* (PublicAffairs, 2008).

Roy Spencer, *Climate Confusion: How Global Warming Hysteria Leads to Bad Science, Pandering Politicians and Misguided Policies that Hurt the Poor* (Encounter, 2008).

S. Fred Singer and Dennis Avery, *Unstoppable Global Warming: Every 1,500 Years* (Rowman and Littlefield, 2008).

Steven J. Milloy, *Junk Science Judo: Self-defense Against Health Scares and Scams* (Cato Institute, 2001).

William Tucker, *Terrestrial Energy: How Nuclear Energy Will Lead the Green Revolution and End America's Energy Odyssey* (Bartleby, 2008).

Vaclav Klaus, *Blue Planet in Green Shackles: What is Endangered: Climate or Freedom?* (Competitive Enterprise Institute, 2007).

Viewing

Apocalypse? NO! Why 'global warming' is not a global crisis, featuring Christopher Monckton of Brenchley, Robert Ferguson SPPI (2008).

Carbon Dioxide and the 'Climate Crisis': Reality of Illusion? CO_2 Science (2008).

The Great Global Warming Swindle, by Martin Durkin (Writer and Director), WAGTV (2007).

Little Ice Age: Big Chill, History Channel (2008).

Mine Your Own Business: The Dark Side of Environmentalism, New Bera Media (2006).

NOTES

Introduction

1. See William P. Barrett, "America's 200 Largest Charities," *Forbes*, November 19, 2008.
2. See e.g., Steven Milloy, "Al Gore Debates Global Warming," October 2007, http://www.youtube.com/ watch?v=XDI2NVTYRXU.
3. Steven Milloy, "Will Al Gore Make Peace With Reality," JunkScience.com, December 13, 2007,
   http://www.junkscience.com/ByTheJunkman/20071213.html.
4. See www.petitionproject.org.
5. See e.g., Antonio Regalado, "Global Warring: In Climate Debate, The 'Hockey Stick' Leads to a Face-Off—Nonscientist Assails a Graph Environmentalists Use, And He Gets a Hearing—Defenders Call Attack Political," *Wall Street Journal*, February 14, 2005.
6. See Steven Milloy, "Hey Al Gore, We Want A Refund!" JunkScience.com, October 19, 2007.

Chapter 1

1. "Why our economy is killing the planet and what we can do about it," *New Scientist*, October 18, 2008.
2. Tim Jackson, "What politicians dare not say," *New Scientist*, October 18, 2008.
3. Jo Marchant, "We should act like the animals we are," *New Scientist*, October 18, 2008.
4. Herman Daly, "On a road to disaster," *New Scientist*, October 18, 2008.
5. James Gustave Speth, "Swimming upstream," *New Scientist*, October 18, 2008.
6. Andrew Simms, "Trickle-down myth," *New Scientist*, October 18, 2008.

7.   Susan George, "We must think big," *New Scientist*, October 18, 2008.

8.   Paul R. Ehrlich and Anne H. Ehrlich, "Too Many People, Too Much Consumption," Yale Environment 360, Yale School of Forestry and Environmental Studies, Yale University, August 4, 2008, http://e360.yale.edu/content/feature.msp?id=2041.

9.   Ibid.

10. See e.g, Ehrlich's bio at http://www.stanford.edu/group/CCB/Staff/Ehrlich.html.

11. Nature Conservancy, "Carbon Footprint Calculator: What's My Carbon Footprint?" http://www.lastgreatplaces.net/initiatives/climatechange/calculator/?src=f1.

12. General Accounting Office, "Carbon Offsets: The U.S. Voluntary Market Is Growing, but Quality Assurance Poses Challenges for Market Participants" (GAO-08-1048), August 2008.

13. Ibid.

14. See Steven Milloy, "Carbon Offsets: Buyer Beware," FoxNews.com, July 19, 2007, http://www.foxnews.com/story/0,2933,290066,00.html.

15. Joseph Romm, "Is the Chicago Climate Exchange selling 'rip-offsets'?" ClimateProgress.org, October 6, 2008, http://climateprogress.org/2008/10/06/is-the-chicago-climate-exchange-selling-rip-offsets/#more-3947.

16. Environmental Audit Committee, "Personal carbon Trading," House of commons, The United Kingdom Parliament, May 13, 2008, http://www.publications.parliament.uk/pa/cm200708/cmselect/cmenvaud/565/565.pdf.

17. Ibid.

18. Ibid.

19. H.R. 3220, "New Direction for Energy Independence, National Security, and Consumer Protection Act (Introduced in House)," July 30, 2007.

20. Kenneth R. Harney, "Tax Deduction Under Fire for McMainsion," *Washington Post*, August 25, 2007, http://www.washingtonpost.com/wp-dyn/content/article/2007/08/24/AR2007082400897.html.

21. California Energy Commission, "2008 Building Energy Efficiency standards for Residential and Nonresidential Buildings" (CEC-400-2007-017-45DAY), November 2007; and Chelsea Schilling, "California Schemin'," WorldNetDaily.com, January 11, 2008, http://www.wnd.com/news/ article.asp?ARTICLE_ID=59639.

22. See e.g., Felicity Barringer, "California Seeks Thermostat Control," *New York Times*, January 11, 2008, http://www.nytimes.com/2008/01/11/us/11control.html.

23. Charles Burress, "Critics cool to 'smart thermostat' proposal," *San Francisco Chronicle*, January 12, 2008, http://www.sfgate.com/cgi-bin/article.cgi?f=/c/a/2008/01/12/MNHDUDAQ3.DTL.

24. Walter Williams, "California Energy Rules Latest Burst of Government Tyranny," *Human Events*, January 23, 2008.

25. Michael T. Burr, "California learns painful lessons from its proposal to mandate demand response," *Public Utilities Fortnightly*, April 2008.
26. Ibid.
27. Elisabeth Rosenthal, "Trying to Build a Greener Britain, Home by Home," *New York Times*, July 20, 2008, http://www.nytimes.com/2008/07/20/world/europe/20greenhouse.html.
28. Marc Levy, "Pennsylvania law tries to cut electricity usage," Associated Press, October 16, 2008.
29. Randal O'Toole, "The Folly of 'Smart Growth'," *Regulation* Fall 2001, http://www.cato.org/pubs/regulation/regv24n3/otoole.pdf.
30. Ibid.
31. Smart Growth Network, "This is Smart Growth," http://www.smartgrowthonlineaudio.org/pdf/TISG_2006_8-5x11.pdf.
32. Ibid.
33. Randal O'Toole, "The Folly of 'Smart Growth'," *Regulation* Fall 2001, http://www.cato.org/pubs/regulation/regv24n3/otoole.pdf.
34. Albert Gore, *Earth in the Balance: Ecology and the Human Spirit* (NY: Houghton Mifflin, 1992), 325–326.
35. Smart Growth Network, "This is Smart Growth," http://www.smartgrowthonlineaudio.org/pdf/TISG_2006_8-5x11.pdf, 12.
36. Ibid.
37. Ibid.
38. Ibid.
39. Ibid.
40. Randal O'Toole, "The Folly of 'Smart Growth'," *Regulation* Fall 2001, http://www.cato.org/pubs/regulation/regv24n3/otoole.pdf, 21.
41. Smart Growth Network, "This is Smart Growth," http://www.smartgrowthonlineaudio.org/pdf/TISG_2006_8-5x11.pdf, 18.
42. Paul R. Ehrlich, *The Population Bomb* (NY: Ballantine Books, 1970), 131.
43. Ibid., 136.
44. Ibid., 137.
45. Ibid., 139.
46. Ibid., 175.
47. Ibid., 172.
48. Ibid., 173.
49. Food and Agriculture Organization of the United Nations, *The State of Food insecurity in the world 2004* (FAO, 2004), ftp://ftp.fao.org/docrep/fao/007/ y5650e/y5650e00.pdf.
50. Ibid., 5.
51. John P. Holdren, "Science and Technology for Sustainable Well-Being," AAAS presidential address, http://www.sciencemag.org/cgi/ content/full/319/ 5862/424
52. David Nicholson-Lord, "A Population-based Climate Strategy—An Optimum Trust Briefing," Optimum Population Trust, May 2007,

http://www.optimumpopulation.org/opt.sub.briefing.climate.population.May07.pdf.

53. Ibid.

54. John Guillebaud, "Population growth and climate change: Universal access to family planning should be the priority," *British Medical Journal* Vol. 337:247–248, August 2, 2008.

55. Anne and Paul Ehrlich, "Zero Population Growth 40 Years On," *The Reporter*, Population Connection, June 2008, Vol 40, Issue 2, http://www.populationconnection.org/media/upload/June2008.pdf?referral id=571&download=June2008.pdf.

56. Hill Heat, "Al Gore and IPCC Win Nobel Peace Prize," October 12, 2007, http://www.hillheat.com/articles/2007/10/page/2.

57. Population Connection, "Bush Withholds Funds for Family Planning... Again!" http://capwiz.com/zpg/issues/alert/?alertid=11234911.

58. Population Connection, "House Bill Increases Funding for Title X Family Planning Program, No New Money for Abstinence-Only," http://capwiz.com/zpg/issues/alert/?alertid=11516016.

59. Gregory Dicum, "Maybe None; Is having a child—even one—environmentally destructive," *San Francisco Chronicle*, November 16, 2005.

60. "One Last Chance to Save Mankind," *New Scientist*, January 23, 2009, http://www.newscientist.com/article/mg20126921.500-one-last-chance-to-save-mankind.html?full=true&print=true.

61. Carter J. Dillard, "Rethinking the Procreative Right," *Yale Human Rights and Development Law Journal* 10 (2007), 1. Http://papers.ssrn.com /sol3/papers.cfm?abstract_id=1089552).

62. Ibid., 11–12.

63. Ibid., 61.

64. Therese Hesketh, Li Lu, and Zhu Wei Xing, "The Effect of China's One-Child Family Policy after 25 Years," *New England Journal of Medicine* 353 (September 15, 2005) 1171–1176.

65. Ibid.

66. Pascal Rocha da Silva, "La politique de l'enfant unique en République Populaire de Chine," Université de Genève, August 2006, http://www.sinoptic.ch/textes/recherche/2006/200608_Rocha.Pascal_mem oire.pdf.

67. Therese Hesketh, Li Lu, and Zhu Wei Xing, "The Effect of China's One-Child Family Policy after 25 Years," *New England Journal of Medicine* 353 (September 25, 2005): 1173.

68. Ibid.

69. Carter J. Dillard, "Rethinking the Procreative Right," *Yale Human Rights and Development Law Journal* 10 (2007), 61. Http://papers.ssrn.com/sol3/papers.cfm?abstract_id=1089552).

Chapter 2

1. John Shadegg, "Democrats Still Aren't Serious About Drilling," *Wall Street Journal*, September 17, 2008, http://online.wsj.com/article/SB122161650517646313.html.
2. Andrew Cline, "Environmentalists Say Yes to Offshore Drilling," *Wall Street Journal*, July 12–13, 2008, http://online.wsj.com/article/SB121581714417147413.html.
3. Ibid.
4. Linda Krop, "Santa Barabara Deal Stops Drilling," *Wall Street Journal*, July 18, 2008, http://online.wsj.com/article/SB121634556264664385.html.
5. Anthony Andrews, "Oil Shale: History, Incentives and Policy," *Congressional Research Service*, April 13, 2006, http://www.fas.org/sgp/crs/misc/RL33359.pdf.
6. See e.g., "Critics charge energy, water needs of oil shale could harm environment," U.S. Water News Online, July 2007, http://www.uswaternews.com/archives/arcsupply/7critchar7.html.
7. Ken Salazar, "Heedless Rush to Oil Shale," *Washington Post*, July 15, 2008, http://www.washingtonpost.com/wp-dyn/content/article/2008/07/14/AR2008071401846.html.
8. Tony Blankley, *American Grit* (Washington, D.C.: Regnery Publishing, 2009), 67.
9. See e.g., Bernard Simon, "Alberta plans to capture CO2 with surplus oil sands revenue," *Financial Times*, July 9, 2008, http://www.ft.com/cms/s/0/edcda7b8-4d4e-11dd-b527-000077b07658.html.
10. Editorial, "Plugging up the Pipeline," *Investor's Business Daily*, July 10, 2008, http://www.ibdeditorials.com/IBDArticles.aspx?id=300582577325477.
11. See e.g., Jessica Resnick-Ault and Susan Daker, "Conoco Refinery Expansion Is Set Back," *Wall Street Journal*, June 9, 2008, http://online.wsj.com/article/SB121297027456055851.html.
12. See e.g., "California Attorney General Seeks climate Deal on Refinery Project," *Energy Washington Week* June 11, 2008.
13. *Chicago Tribune*, "Environmental group files suit over BP expansion permit in Indiana," July 10, 2008, and Tom Coyne, "Group Challenges BP's Ind. refinery expansion plan," Associated Press, July 10, 2008.
14. Editorial, "Refining Incapacity," *Wall Street Journal*, September 28, 2005.
15. According to the Department of Energy, the generation of electricity by sources is as follows: coal (50.7 percent); nuclear (19.7 percent); natural gas (19.2 percent); hydroelectric (6.2 percent); other energy sources (3.1 percent); and petroleum (1.2 percent). Electric Power Monthly, U.S. Department of Energy, Energy Information Administration, July 10, 2008, http://www.eia.doe.gov/cneaf/electricity/epm/epm_sum.html.

16. "Coal Plants Cancelled in 2007," Center for Media and Democracy, http://www.sourcewatch.org/index.php?title=Coal_plants_cancelled_in_2007 (accessed, July 13, 2008).
17. "Move Beyond Coal," Sierra Club, http://www.sierraclub.org/coal/.
18. Heather Green, "How Green Green-lighted the TXU Deal," *BusinessWeek*, February 27, 2007.
19. Everglades Earth First! "Earth First! Blockades Power Plant Construction Site in Florida, 27 Arrested," Media Release, February 19, 2008, http://www.climateimc.org/en/climate-actions/2008/02/19/earth-first-blockades-power-plant-construction-site-florida-27-arrested.
20. Review and Outlook, "Mr. Frank's Wild River," *Wall Street Journal*, July 9, 2008.
21. Ibid.
22. Lisa Rein and Christy Goodman, "Little outcry on Nuclear Reactor proposal," *Washington Post*, August 4, 2008, http://www.washingtonpost.com/wp-dyn/content/article/2008/08/03/AR2008080301642.html.
23. Matthew L. Wald, "After 35-Year Lull, Nuclear Power May Be in early Stages of a Revival," *New York Times*, October 24, 2008.
24. Ibid.
25. "Environmentalists Make New Economic Case Against Nuclear's Climate Benefits," Carbon Control News, July 1, 2008.
26. Amory Lovins and Imran Sheikh, "The Nuclear Illusion," Ambio, November 2008, http://www.rmi.org/images/PDFs/Energy/E08-01_AmbioNucIllusion.pdf.
27. Robert F. Kennedy, Jr., "An Ill Wind of Cape Cod," *New York Times*, December 16, 2005, http://www.nytimes.com/2005/12/16/opinion/16kennedy.html.
28. This quote was previously available at http://www.martinomalley.com/leadership/524.
29. "Gov. confirms wind turbine ban," *Baltimore Sun*, April 13, 2008.
30. Mark Hume, "Lack of will, lack of funds, wiping out migratory birds," Globe and Mail, July 14, 2008, http://www.theglobeandmail.com/servlet/story/LAC.20080714.BCHUME14/TPStory/Sports.
31. Jennifer Bowles, "Hearings to debate impact of solar farms on threatened species," Press-Enterprise, June 14, 2008, http://www.pe.com/localnews/inland/stories/PE_News_Local_S_solar15.48dbdb9.html.
32. Catherine Elsworth, "US halts solar energy projects over environment fears," *Daily Telegraph*, June 27, 2008, http://www.telegraph.co.uk/earth/main.jhtml?xml=/earth/2008/06/27/easolar127.xml.
33. Jeffrey Brainard, "Patton tank marks suggest long recovery," *Science News*, August 8, 1998, http://findarticles.com/p/articles/mi_m1200/is_n6_v154/ai_21064046.
34. See e.g., Natural Resources Defense Council, "Move Over Gasoline: Here Come Biofuels," http://nrdc.org/air/transportation/biofuels.asp (accessed July 15, 2008).

35. Martha G. Roberts, Timothy D. Male, and Theodore P. Toombs, "Potential Impacts of Biofuels Expansion on Natural Resources: A Case Study of the Ogallala Aquifer region," Environmental Defense, 2007, http://www.edf.org/documents/7011_Potential%20Impacts%20of%20Biofuels%20Expansion.pdf.

36. Sarah Laitner, "Target vote delivers blow to biofuel expansion," *Financial Times*, July 9, 2008, http://www.ft.com/cms/s/0/72a6ee4a-4d4f-11dd-b527-000077b07658.html.

37. Beth Novey, "Environmentalists Weigh In on Ethanol," National Public Radio, February 15, 2007, http://www.npr.org/templates/story/story.php?storyId=9647424.

38. Elisabeth Rosenthal, "Biofuels Deemed a Greenhouse Threat," *New York Times*, February 8, 2008, http://www.nytimes.com/2008/02/08/science/earth/08wbiofuels.html.

39. George F. Will, "Our Fake Drilling Debate," *Washington Post*, December 15, 2005, http://www.washingtonpost.com/wp-dyn/content/article/2005/12/14/AR2005121401933.html.

Chapter 3

1. U.S. Department of Transportation, "FHWA Fun Facts: Traffic Congestion," January 2008, http://www.fhwa.dot.gov/pressroom/ fhwatraffic-facts.htm.

2. Natural Resources Defense Council, "Drive Less and Drive Smarter," The Green Gate, http://www.nrdc.org/greengate/guides/driving.asp (accessed August 26, 2008).

3. World Carfree Network, "Global Member Organisations," http://www.worldcarfree.net/about_us/global/memberorgs.php.

4. World Carfree Network, "Global Charter," http://www.worldcarfree.net/about_us/global/charter.php.

5. Patrick J. McMahon, "Greening the Old City: Baltimore's Sustainability Program," Car Free Portland, June 2008, http://www.slideshare.net/TCC08/thurs1415greymcmahon.com.

6. "Road closed Ahead: Why Only Second-Generation Car Sharing Can Move the Car-Free Cities Agenda," Car Free Portland, June 2008, http://www.slideshare.net/TCC08/thurs1415buildfriendlybradshaw/; Eric Anderson, "Berkeley Bicycle Boulevards," Car Free Portland, June 2008, http://www.slideshare.net/TCC08/thurs1015bikewaysanderson; and Eric Doherty, "Better Transit, Not Freeways," Car Free Portland, June 2008, http://www.slideshare.net/TCC08/thurs0900alternativesdoherty.

7. Lynn Thompson, "Weather puts damper on car-free Sunday," *Seattle Times*, August 25, 2008, http://seattletimes.nwsource.com/html/localnews/2008136287_carfree25m.html.

8. Ibid.

9. Magee Hickey, "Bicycle Activists propose 'Car-Free' Prospect Park," WCBS TV, August 26, 2008, http://wcbstv.com/local/car.free. brooklyn.2.803198.html.

10. Eric M. Weiss, "Drivers Feeling Shunned by D.C.," *Washington Post*, July 6, 2008, http://www.washingtonpost.com/wp-dyn/content/article/2008/07/05/AR2008070500564_pf.html.

11. Mike Ivey, "Should Madison ban the drive-through?" *The Capital Times*, June 25, 2008, http://www.madison.com/tct/news/stories/293046.

12. Thomas L. Friedman, "No, No, No, Don't Follow Us," *New York Times*, November 4, 2007, http://www.nytimes.com/2007/11/04/opinion/04friedman.html.

13. Emily Wax, "Fuel Prices Boost Cause of S. Asia's Maligned Rickshaw," *Washington Post*, June 28, 2008, http://www.washingtonpost.com/wp-dyn/content/article/2008/06/27/AR2008062703786.html?nav=rss_world/asia.

14. Ibid.

15. Institute for Transportation and Development Policy, "Who We Are," http://www.itdp.org/index.php?/who_we_are/ (accessed August 28, 2008).

16. Andy Mukherjee, "Don't miss the larger point of Tata Nano," Mint, January 11, 2008, http://www.livemint.com/2008/01/10235018/Don8217t-miss-the-larger-po.html.

17. Editorial, "Paying for Roads," *Washington Post*, September 15, 2008, http://www.washingtonpost.com/wp-dyn/content/article/2008/09/14/AR2008091401657.html.

18. Editorial,"Raise the Gas Tax," *Washington Post*, November 16, 2008, http://www.washingtonpost.com/wp-dyn/content/article/2008/11/15/AR2008111502145.html.

19. "Taming Traffic in London," Environmental Defense Fund, April 5, 2007, http://www.edf.org/article.cfm?contentID=6159 (accessed August 26, 2008).

20. Appleseed Inc., "Congestion pricing in the Manhattan Central Business District: Let's Look Hard before We Leap," Keep NYC Congestion Tax Free, May 2007, http://www.keepnycfree.com/reports/files/Congestion%20Tax%20Report.pdf.

21. Queens chamber of Commerce, "A Cure Worse than the Disease? How London's 'Congestion Pricing' System Could Hurt New York City's Economy," February 2006, http://www.nytimes.com/packages/pdf/ nyregion/empire_zone/20070425_congestion.pdf

22. Ibid.

23. Joe Mahoney and Michael Saul, "Bloomberg's congestion fee on skids in Albany," *New York Daily News*, April 24, 2007, http://www.nydailynews.com/news/2007/04/24/2007-04-24_bloombergs_congestion_fee_on_skids_in_al.html.

24. See Deron Lovaas, "Future Federal Role for Surface Transportation," Testimony before the U.S. Senate Environment and Public Works Committee, June 25, 2008, http://epw.senate.gov/public/index.cfm?FuseAction=Files.View&FileStore_id=13b6eb8c-a6f0-43e5-9069-e52d113f731d.

25. Environmental Defense, "Drive Less, Pay Less for Insurance," November 12, 2008, http://www.edf.org/page.cfm?tagID=31651.

26. Ibid. And Jason E. Bordoff and Pascal J. Noel, "Pay-As-You-Drive Auto Insurance: A Simple Way to Reduce Driving-Related Harms and Increase Equity," can be accessed at http://www.brookings.edu/~/media/Files/rc/papers/2008/07_payd_bordoffnoel/07_payd_bordoffnoel.pdf.

27. Progressive Casualty Insurance Company, "MyRate Privacy Statement," http://www.progressive.com/myrate/myrate-privacy-statement.aspx.

28. Natural Resources Defense Council, "Gas Price Pain Relievers," Move Beyond Oil, http://beyondoil.nrdc.org/fuel/gasprices (accessed August 21, 2009).

29. Edmunds.com, 2009 Toyota Camry, http://www.edmunds.com/ toyota/camry/2009/index.html, and 2009 Toyota Camry Hybrid, http://www.edmunds.com/toyota/camryhybrid/2009/index.html.

30. Press Release, "Most Hybrid Vehicles Not as cost-Effective as They seem, Reports Edmunds.com," June 1, 2005, http://www.edmunds.com/help/about/press/105827/article.html.

31. See e.g., Thomas J. Borelli and Steven J. Milloy, "Environmentalists Force Use of Hybrid Trucks" Letter to *Wall Street Journal*, October 9, 2006, http://online.wsj.com/article/SB116034887039686283.html.

32. Bill Visnic, "Fuel-Cell Experiment Misses the Bus," *Auto Observer*, February 28, 2008, http://www.autoobserver.com/2008/02/fuel-cell-experiment-misses-the-bus.html, and L. Eudy, K. Chandler, and C. Gikakis, "Fuel Cell Buses in U.S. Transit Fleets: Summary of Experiences and Current Status," Technical Report NREL/TP-560-41967, September 2007, http://www.nrel.gov/docs/fy07osti/41967.pdf.

33. See e.g., U.S. Environmental Protection Agency, "New Energy Tax Credits for Hybrids," http://www.fueleconomy.gov/feg/tax_hybrid.shtml (accessed September 17, 2008).

34. Jerry Taylor, "Get Toyota's Hands Out of Your Wallet!" Cato Institute, December 1, 2006, http://www.cato-at-liberty.org/2006/12/01/get-toyotas-hands-out-of-your-wallet/.

35. Toyota Motor Corp North America, "Environment," article used to be available at http://www.toyota.com/about/whynot/#/Environment_Hybrid/ (accessed August 21, 2008).

36. U.S. Department of Energy, "Where Does My Gasoline Come From?" Energy Information Administration Brochures, April 2008, http://www.eia.doe.gov/bookshelf/brochures/gasoline/index.html (accessed August 21, 2008).

37. See e.g., U.S. Global Change Research Information Office, "How Do We Know That Atmospheric Build-up of Greenhouse Gases Is Due to Human Activity?" http://www.gcrio.org/ipcc/qa/05.html (accessed August 21, 2008).

38. See e.g., Fred Sissine, Energy Independence and Security Act of 2007: A Summary of Major Provisions, P.L. 110-140, H.R. 6. Prepared for Members and Committees of Congress by Congressional Research Service, December 21, 2007, http://energy.senate.gov/public/_files/RL342941.pdf.

39. Natural Resources Defense Council, "Comparing the Oil Savings and Global Warming Pollution Reductions of Senate and House CAFE Proposals," October 2007, http://www.nrdc.org/legislation/ factsheets/leg_07101801A.pdf.

40. Press Release, "Automakers Respond to New Nationwide Fuel Economy Proposal," Auto Alliance, April 22, 2008, http://www.autoalliance.org/index.cfm?objectid=7724C605-1D09-317F-BB29B57A30F2D182, and Natural Resources Defense Council, "Clean Getaway: Toward Safe and Efficient Vehicles," http://www.nrdc.org/air/transportation/cafe/execsum.asp (accessed August 21, 2008).

41. National Research Council, "Effectiveness and Impact of Corporate Average Fuel Economy (CAFé) Standards," National Academy Press: Washington DC, 2002, http://www.nap.edu/openbook.php?isbn=0309076013.

42. Charles J. Kahane, Ph.D., "Vehicle Weight, Fatality Risk and Crash Compatibility of Model Year 1991-99 Passenger Cars and Light Trucks," National Highway Traffic Safety Administration, Department of Transportation, Washington, D.C., October 2003, http://www.nhtsa.dot.gov/cars/rules/regrev/evaluate/809662.html.

43. James R. Healey, "Death by the Gallon," *USA Today*, July 2, 1999, http://www.suvoa.com/assets/PDFs/DeathByTheGallon.pdf.

44. Editorial, "Automakers have fair beef with new federal mpg requirements," *Detroit News*, July 11, 2008, http://www.detnews.com/apps/pbcs.dll/article?AID=/20080711/OPINION01/807110318/1008.

45. Federal Highway Administration, "Public Road Length – 2006," October 2007, http://www.fhwa.dot.gov/policy/ohim/hs06/pdf/hm10.pdf.

46. Federal Highway Administration, "Focus on Congestion Relief," http://www.fhwa.dot.gov/congestion/ (accessed August 22, 2008).

47. Cambridge Systematics, Inc., "Traffic Congestion and Reliability: Trends and Advanced Strategies for Congestion Mitigation," September 1, 2005, http://www.ops.fhwa.dot.gov/congestion_report/congestion_report_05.pdf.

48. Ibid.

49. Deron Lovaas, "Future Federal Role for Surface Transportation," Testimony before the U.S. Senate Environment and Public Works Committee, June 25, 2008, http://epw.senate.gov/public/index.cfm? FuseAction=Files.View&FileStore_id=13b6eb8c-a6f0-43e5-9069-e52d113f731d.

50. Ibid.

51. Randy Dotinga, "Mass transit plan makes waves in Seattle ecotopia," *Christian Science Monitor*, November 5, 2007, http://www.csmonitor.com/2007/1105/p01s05-usgn.htm.

52. Ibid.

53. E.J. Schultz, "Environmental groups undecided on high-speed rail plan," *Sacramento Bee*, August 4, 2008, http://www.sacbee.com/111/story/1130046.html.

54. Natural Resources Defense Council, "The Foothill-South Toll road: Fact vs. Fiction," http://docs.nrdc.org/land/lan_07011001a.pdf.

55. Press Release, "Sierra Club and Its Allies Challenge Fish and Wildlife Service," Sierra Club, August 15, 2008, http://www.surfline.com/surf-news/environmental-news/sierra-club-and-its-allies-challenge-fish-and-wildlife-service_17696/.

56. Glenda March, "My View: A wider U.S. 50 would only worsen matters," *Sacramento Bee*, August 22, 2008, http://www.sacbee.com/110/story/1176517.html.

57. Tom McClintock, "Ending California's 25-Year Hate Affair with the Car," March 17, 1999,
http://republican.sen.ca.gov/web/mcclintock/article_detail.asp?PID=30.

58. Ibid.

Chapter 4

1. FoxNews.com, "Experts Fear Much of U.S. Could Face Water Shortage," Associated Press, October 26, http://www.foxnews.com/story/0,2933,305578,00.html.

2. Marty Toohey, "Armstrong tops list of city's largest water users," Austin-American Statesman, August 15, 2008.

3. Veronica Lorraine and Brian Flynn, "The great drain robbery," *The Sun*, October 6, 2008.

4. Ann Hayden, "Where Will Southern California Get Its Water?" Environmental Defense: On the Water Front, August 5, 2008,
http://environmentaldefenseblogs.org/waterfront/2008/08/05/where-will-southern-california-get-its-water/.

5. Letter to Don Perata, Mike Machado, and Darrell Steinberg from Gov. Arnold Schwarzenegger, February 28, 2008,
http://environmentaldefenseblogs.org/waterfront/files/2008/03/governors-letter-to-senators-2-28-08.pdf; and Spreck Rosekrans, "The Governor's 20 Percent," Environmental Defense: On the Water Front, March 4, 2008,
http://environmentaldefenseblogs.org/waterfront/2008/03/04/the-governors-20-percent/.

6. Sierra Club, "Sierra Club Conservation Policies: Water,"
http://www.sierraclub.org/policy/conservation/water.asp (accessed August 31, 2008).

7. Heather Hacking, "Several groups file suit over federal water," Chico Enterprise-Record, August 10, 2005, http://www.watershedportal.org/news/news_html?ID=421; and Eric Bailey and James Ricci, "Smelt ruling may cut into water supply," *Los Angeles Times*, September 1, 2007,
http://articles.latimes.com/2007/sep/01/local/me-delta1.

8. Eric Bailey and James Ricci, "Smelt ruling may cut into water supply," *Los Angeles Times*, September 1, 2007, http://articles.latimes.com/2007/sep/01/local/me-deltal.

9. Rebecca Wodder, "Damming the Flint River is so old-school; Smarter water management strategies could cost less, do more," Atlanta Journal-Constitution, August 13, 2008, http://www.ajc.com/opinion/content/ opinion/stories/2008/08/13/flint_river_dam.html.

10. Associated Press, "Carter Takes Up new Fight Railing Against Georgia Dams," Fox News.com, July 27, 2008, http://www.foxnews.com/story/0,2933,391821,00.html.

11. Ibid.

12. "Desalination," Las Vegas Valley Water District, http://www.lvvwd.com/html/wq_water_facts_desalination.html (accessed September 1, 2008).

13. Editorial, "Desalination plant should be first of many," *North County Times*, Augsut 27, 2008, http://www.nctimes.com/articles/2008/08/27/opinion/editorials/doc48b5841a99098674917789.txt.

14. See e.g., San Diego Coastkeeper, "The Water Factory: Impacts of Poseidon's Carlsbad Desalination Plant," http://www.sdbaykeeper.org/assets/pdf/campaigns/waterSupply/factsheet_%20impacts.pdf (accessed September 1, 2008).

15. Bradley J. Fikes, "Carlsbad, Calif., Desalination Plant Nears End of Regulatory Process," *North County Times*, August 8, 2008, http://www.istockanalyst.com/article/viewiStockNews + articleid_2494855 &title=Carlsbad_Calif.html.

16. David Kracman, "International Water marketing - Canada," Water-Bank.com, July 5, 2001, http://www.waterbank.com/Newsletters/nws37.html.

17. Sierra Club, "Sierra Club Conservation Policies: Water Commodification and Corporate Privatization of Municipal Water/Sewer Services Policy," November 14–15, 2003, http://www.sierraclub.org/policy/ conservation/commodification.asp (accessed September 1, 2008).

18. U.S. Environmental Protection Agency, "Great Lakes: Basic Information," http://www.epa.gov/glnpo/basicinfo.html (accessed September 1, 2008).

19. Jerry Zremski, "Loophole feared in Great Lakes accord," *Buffalo News*, September 1, 2008, http://www.buffalonews.com/ cityregion/story/428047.html.

20. Ibid.

21. See e.g., Elizabeth Royte, "A tall, cool Drink of... Sewage?" *New York Times*, August 10, 2008, http://www.nytimes.com/2008/08/10/ magazine/10wastewater-t.html?ref=science.

22. Editorial, "Yuck! San Diego should flush 'toilet to tap' plan," *San Diego Union-Tribune*, July 24, 2006, http://www.signonsandiego.com/uniontrib/20060724/news_mz1ed24top.html.

23. Rich Connell, "Turning Los Angeles wastewater to tap water," *Los Angeles Times*, June 7, 2008, http://articles.latimes.com/2008/jun/07/local/me-water7.

24. Cynthia Koehler, Spreck Rosekrans, Laura Harnish, Tom Graff, and Ann Hayden, "Finding the Balance: A Vision for Water Supply and Environmental Reliability in California," Environmental Defense Fund, July 2008, http://www.edf.org/documents/8093_CA_Finding_Balance_2008.pdf.

25. U.S. Environmental Protection Agency, "The History of Drinking Water Treatment" (EPA-816-F-00-006), Office of Water, February 2000, http://www.epa.gov/OGWDW/consumer/pdf/hist.pdf.

26. American Chemistry Council, U.S. Typhoid fever Rates (1920–1960), http://www.americanchemistry.com/100years/typhoid-graph.pdf (accessed September 8, 2008).

27. Rachel Carson, *Silent Spring* (NY: Houghton Mifflin, 1962), 15–37.

28. Harold M. Schmeck, Jr., "E.P.A. Orders a National Study of Chemical Contaminants in Drinking Water," *New York Times*, November 9, 1974.

29. See e.g., Michelle Malkin and Michael Fumento, "Rachel's Folly: the End of Chlorine," Competitive Enterprise Institute, March 1996, http://cei.org/pdf/1518.pdf.

30. "High Lead Levels Found in D.C. Kids," *Washington Post*, January 27, 2009, http://www.washingtonpost.com/wp-dyn/content/article/2009/01/26/AR2009012602402.html?hpid=moreheadlines.

31. Natural Resources Defense Council, "Report Finds Deteriorating Infrastructure, Pollution Threaten Municipal Drinking Water Supplies" (Media release), June 11, 2003, http://www.nrdc.org/media/ pressReleases/030611.asp.

32. U.S. Environmental Protection Agency, "Drinking Water and Health: What You Need to Know," http://www.epa.gov/safewater/dwh/index.html (accessed September 8, 2008).

33. Erik Olson, "What's on Tap? Grading Drinking Water in U.S. Cities," Natural Resources Defense Council, June 2003, p.78, http://www.nrdc.org/water/drinking/uscities/pdf/whatsontap.pdf.

34. Douglas A. Levy, "Widespread drinking water contamination," United Press International, September 27, 1993.

35. Robert C. Frederiksen, "Report highlights public drinking water violations; Watchdog groups are trying to bolster support for extending the 1974 Safe Drinking Water Act," Providence Journal-Bulletin, August 10, 1994.

36. Erik D. Olson, "Bottled Water: Pure Drink or Pure Hype," Natural Resources Defense Council, March 1999, http://www.nrdc.org/water/drinking/bw/bwinx.asp.

37. See, e.g., Natural Resources Defense Council, "Issues: Water: Bottled Water," http://www.nrdc.org/water/drinking/qbw.asp (accessed, September 9, 2008), and Sierra Club, "Bottled Water: Learning the Facts and Taking Action," April 2008, http://www.sierraclub.org/committees/cac/water/bottled_water/bottled_water.pdf.

38. Jared Blumenfeld and Susan Leal, "The real cost of bottled water," *San Francisco Chronicle*, February 18, 2007, http://www.sfgate.com/cgi-bin/article.cgi?file=/chronicle/archive/2007/02/18/EDG56N6OA41.DTL.

39. Nick Welsh, "Bottled Water Ban: Santa Barbara beats S.F. to the Punch," *Santa Barbara Independent*, June 28, 2007, http://www.independent.com/news/2007/jun/28/bottled-water-ban/.

40. Cecilia M. Vega, "Mayor to cut off flow of city money for bottled water," *San Francisco Chronicle*, June 22, 2007, http://www.sfgate.com/cgi-bin/article.cgi?f=/c/a/2007/06/22/BAGE8QJVIL1.DTL.

41. Erik Olson, "What's on Tap? Grading Drinking Water in U.S. Cities: San Francisco," October 2002, http://www.nrdc.org/water/drinking/uscities/pdf/sf.pdf.

42. U.S. Conference of Mayors, "Mayors Vote to End Taxpayer Spending on Bottled Water" (Media Release), PR Newswire, June 23, 2008.

43. Ibid.

44. American Beverage Association, "American Beverage Association Says Small Group of Mayors Led U.S. Conference of Mayors to Choose Sound-Bite Environmentalism Over Substantive Concerns of Families," PR Newswire, June 23, 2008.

45. Stacy St. Clair, "Chicago braces for bottled-water tax," *Chicago Tribune*, December 30, 2007.

46. "Water fountains making comeback as bottles banned," *Agence France Presse*, August 20, 2008, http://www.terradaily.com/reports/Water_fountains_making_comeback_as_bottles_banned_999.html.

47. IndependentTraveler.com "Drinking Water Safety," August 22, 2008, http://www.independenttraveler.com/resources/article.cfm?AID=55&category=5.

48. Centers for Disease Control and Prevention, "Emergency Preparedness & Response: Gather Emergency Supplies; Water Supplies," http://emergency.cdc.gov/preparedness/kit/water/ (accessed September 9, 2008).

49. Jennifer Gitlitz and Pat Franklin, "Water, Water Everywhere: The Growth of Non-carbonated Beverages in the United States," Container Recycling Institute, February 1, 2007, http://www.container-recy-cling.org/assets/pdfs/reports/2007-waterwater.pdf.

50. Sierra Club, "Bottled Water: Learning the Facts and Taking Action," April 2008, http://www.sierraclub.org/committees/cac/water/bottled_water/bottled_water.pdf.

Chapter 5

1. See Lori Wedle-Shott, "Cattle don't have much to do with global warming," Hutchison Leader, August 9, 2008, http://www.hutchinson leader.com/cattle-don-t-have-much-do-global-warming-9308; citing U.S. Environmental Protection Agency, "Inventory of U.S. Greenhouse Emis-

sions and Sinks 1990-2006" (EPA-430-R-08-005), April 15, 2008, http://www.epa.gov/climatechange/ emissions/downloads/08_CR.pdf.

2. Mark Bittman, "Rethinking the Meat-Guzzler," *New York Times*, January 27, 2008, http://www.nytimes.com/2008/01/27/weekinreview/27bittman.html.

3. Mark Bittman, "Rethinking the Meat-Guzzler," *New York Times*, January 27, 2008, http://www.nytimes.com/2008/01/27/ weekinreview/27bittman.html.

4. Sheryl Eisenberg, "Another Reason to Eat Less Meat," Natural Resources Defense Council: This Green Life," November 2007, http://www.nrdc.org/thisgreenlife/0711.asp.

5. ScienceDaily, " 'Burpless' Grass cuts methane Gas from cattle, May Help Reduce Global Warming," May 8, 2008, http://www.sciencedaily.com/releases/2008/05/080506120859.htm.

6. See e.g., David biello, "Can Bovine Growth Hormone Heal Slow Global Warming?" Scientific American, July 2, 2008, http://www.sciam.com/article.cfm?id=can-bovine-growth-hormone-slow-global-warming.

7. See e.g., James Kirkup, "Meat and milk prices will rise to reflect environmental costs," *Daily Telegraph*, July 8, 2008, http://www.telegraph.co.uk/news/uknews/2265116/Meat-and-milk-prices-will-rise-to-reflect-environmental-costs.html.

8. "Drink rats' milk," says Heather Mills, *Daily Telegraph*, November 21, 2007, http://www.telegraph.co.uk/news/uknews/1569871/Drink-rats'-milk,-says-Heather-Mills.html.

9. Natural Resources Defense Council, "Food miles: How far your food travels has serious consequences for your health and the climate," November 2007, http://www.nrdc.org/health/effects/camiles/foodmiles.pdf.

10. Ibid.

11. Ibid.

12. Ibid.

13. This report, "Issues: Water: Alfalfa: The Thirstiest Crop," has been removed from the Natural Resources Defense Council's website. It was previously available at http://www.nrdc.org/water/conservation/fcawater.asp.

14. Ronnie Cohen, Barry Nelson, and Gary Wolff, "Energy Down the Drain: The Hidden Costs of California's Water Supply," August 2004, http://www.nrdc.org/water/conservation/edrain/edrain.pdf.

15. Ibid.

16. Mark Bittman, "What's wrong with what we eat," TED Conferences LLC, December 2007, http://www.ted.com/index.php/talks/ mark_bittman_on_what_s_wrong_with_what_we_eat.html.

17. Ibid.

18. Slow Food USA, "Our Mission," http://www.slowfoodusa.org/index.php/slow_food/good_clean_fair/ (accessed September 4, 2008).

19. Slow Food USA, "The Slow Food USA Blog: Even though EVERY day is earth day," April 10, 2008, http://www.slowfoodusa.org/index.php/slow_food/blog_post/even_though_every_day_is_earth_day/.

20. Slow Food USA, "The Slow Food USA Blog: Help Save the New Mexican Chile," February 12, 2008, http://www.slowfoodusa.org/index.php/slow_food/blog_post/help_save_the_new_mexican_chile/.

21. Renewing America's Food Traditions, "The How of Raft," http://www.environment.nau.edu/raft/how.htm (accessed September 5, 2008).

22. Slow Food USA, "New Analysis of At-Risk Foods in North America," April 20, 2008, http://www.slowfoodusa.org/index.php/about_us/news_post/new_analysis_of_at_risk_foods_in_north_america/

23. Ibid.

24. Brian Halweil, "Are you going to San Francisco? The First Continental culinary congress wants you," Edible Nation, July 20, 2008, http://www.ediblecommunities.com/ediblenation/?cat=29.

25. Bobby White, "The Challenges of Eating 'Slow'," *Wall Street Journal*, September 2, 2008, http://online.wsj.com/article/SB122022613854086965.html.

26. Ibid.

27. Commission of the European Communities, "PROPOSAL FOR A REGULATION OF THE EUROPEAN PARLIAMENT AND OF THE COUNCIL concerning the placing of plant protection products on the market," July 12, 2006, http://ec.europa.eu/food/plant/protection/ evaluation/com2006_0388en01.pdf.

28. Paul Eccleston, "EU pesticide rules 'would decimate crop yields'," *Daily Telegraph*, June 22, 2008, http://www.telegraph.co.uk/earth/main.jhtml?xml=/earth/2008/06/22/eapest122.xml.

29. Ibid.

30. Ibid.

31. Jeremy Watson, "Food costs 'to soar' after pesticide ban," Scotsman, August 17, 2008, http://news.scotsman.com/environment/Food-costs-39to-soar39-after.4398728.jp.

32. Farmers Weekly Interactive, "Scots MEPs demand rethink on EU pesticides plan," September 11, 2008, http://www.fwi.co.uk/Articles/2008/09/11/112118/scots-meps-demand-rethink-on-eu-pesticides-plan.html.

33. Lyndsey Layton, "Chemical Law Has Global Impact," *Washington Post*, June 12, 2008, http://www.washingtonpost.com/wp-dyn/content/article/2008/06/11/AR2008061103569_pf.html.

34. See e.g., Steven Milloy, "Congress Working Hard to Make Schools Safe for Roaches and Rodents," FoxNews.com, June 25, 2001, http://www.foxnews.com/story/0,2933,27842,00.html.

35. U.S. Environmental Protection Agency, "Accomplishments under the Food Quality protection Act (FQPA)," August 3, 2006, http://www.epa.gov/opp00001/regulating/laws/fqpa/fqpa_accomplishments.htm.

36. FDCH Political Transcripts, "Dan Glickman Holds News Conference Regarding Organic Food Labeling," December 20, 2000.

37. Whole Foods Market IP, LP, "Organic Farming Principles," http://www.wholefoodsmarket.com/values/organic-principles.php (accessed September 12, 2008).

38. Horizon Organic Dairy, "Farming Practices," http://www.horizonorganic.com/health/farmprac.html (accessed September 12, 2008).

39. Natural Resources Defense Council, "Organic Foods 101," http://www.nrdc.org/health/farming/forg101.asp (accessed September 12, 2008).

40. Organic Trade Association, "2006 Manufacturer Survey," http://www.ota.com/pics/documents/short%20overview%20MMS.pdf (accessed, September 12, 2008); and Organic Trade Association, "Industry Statistics and Projected Growth," http://www.ota.com/organic/mt/business.html (accessed September 12, 2008).

41. "Good food?" *The Economist*, December 7, 2006.

42. Department for Environment, Food and Rural Affairs, "The environment, social and economic impacts associated with liquid milk consumption in the UK and its production: A review of literature and evidence," December 2007, http://www.defra.gov.uk/science/Project_Data/ DocumentLibrary/EV02067/EV02067_6897_FRP.pdf.

43. Economic Research Service, "Adoption of Genetically Engineered Crops in the U.S.," U.S. Department of Agriculture, July 2, 2008, http://www.ers.usda.gov/Data/BiotechCrops/.

44. See e.g., Steven J. Milloy, "Monsanto Caves to Activists on Biotech Wheat," FoxNews.com, May 14, 2004, http://www.foxnews.com/story/0,2933,119884,00.html.

45. Greenpeace, "Victory: Monsanto Drops GE Wheat," May 11, 2004, http://www.greenpeace.org/international/news/victory-monsanto-drops-ge-whe.

46. "Prince Charles warns GM crops risk causing the biggest-ever environmental disaster," *Daily Telegraph*, August 12, 2008, http://www.telegraph.co.uk/earth/main.jhtml?xml=/earth/2008/08/12/eacharles112.xml.

47. Emily Hill, "The prince and the paupers," *The Guardian*, August 15, 2008, http://www.guardian.co.uk/commentisfree/2008/aug/15/monarchy.gmcrop.

48. Mark Henderson, "Analysis: is the Prince of Wales right about GM crops?" *The Times*, August 13, 2008, http://www.timesonline.co.uk/tol/news/uk/science/article4523786.ece.

49. See, e.g., Meredith Niles, "A prince's dream: far-fetched fairytale or a real future of food," grist.org, August 15, 2008, http://gristmill.grist.org/story/2008/8/14/135938/816.

50. See Energy Policy Act of 2005, P.L. 110-58 and Energy Independence and Security Act of 2007, P.L. 110-140, H.R. 6.
51. See U.S. Department of Agriculture, "USDA Increases Corn Crop and Ethanol Production" August 12, 2008, http://domesticfuel.com/2008/08/12/usda-increases-corn-crop-and-ethanol-use/.
52. See e.g., Ben Lieberman and Nicolas Loris, "Time to Repeal the Ethanol Mandate," Heritage Foundation, WebMemo No. 1925, May 15, 2008, http://www.heritage.org/research/energyandenvironment/wm1925.cfm.
53. William Tucker, "Food Riots Made in the USA," *The Weekly Standard*, April 28, 2008, http://weeklystandard.com/Content/Public/Articles/000/000/015/007jlljc.asp?pg=1.
54. Lester R. Brown, "Why Ethanol production Will drive World Food Prices Even Higher in 2008," Earth Policy Institute, January 24, 2008, http://www.earth-policy.org/Updates/2008/Update69.htm.
55. American coalition for ethanol, "Higher Food Prices, Higher gas Prices: What's the Real Impact?" July 2, 2008, http://www.ethanol.org/pdf/contentmgmt/ACE_Fuel_Food_Fact_Sheet_7_2_08.pdf.
56. Robert Bonnie, "Corn Ethanol: Importance of Performance Standards," Environmental Defense Fund: Climate 411 blog, April 29, 2008, http://blogs.edf.org/climate411/2008/04/29/corn_ethanol_standards/.
57. Environmental Defense Fund, "new Report Outlines Potential Environmental Pitfalls of Some Ethanol" (Media Release), September 20, 2007, http://www2.environmentaldefense.org/pressrelease.cfm?contentID=7492.
58. Christopher D. Cook, "Corn Rush—'Ethanol Fever' needs a Reality Check," New American Media, July 13, 2006, http://www.organicconsumers.org/articles/article_1120.cfm.
59. John Laumer, "Move to Ethanol Expected to Fuel Trend to More Vegetarianism," http://www.treehugger.com/files/2007/03/move_to_ethanol_1.php?dcitc=prev_post.

Chapter 6

1. See e.g., Malcolm Ross, "Did risk reduction backfire in space," *Washington Times*, January 28, 1996.
2. Steven Milloy, "Did PC Science Cause Shuttle Disaster?" FoxNews.com, February 7, 2003, http://www.foxnews.com/story/0,2933,77832,00.html.
3. See e.g., Steven Milloy, "Asbestos fireproofing Might Have Prevented World trade Center Collapse," FoxNews.com, January 18, 2007, http://www.foxnews.com/story/0,2933,244698,00.html.
4. See e.g., National Academy of Sciences, Committee on Research in the Life Sciences of the Committee on Science and Public Policy, 1970. The Life Sciences; Recent Progress and Application to Human Affairs; The World of Biological Research; Requirements for the Future.
5. Natalie Garcia, "Bicyclists become spokesman for greener commute," Providence Journal-Bulletin, May 17, 2008.

6. Jesse Tinsley, "Professor hit fatally while biking," Plain Dealer (Cleveland), August 18, 2008.

7. Erin McCormick, "Dangerous roads for bicyclists; Highways, city thoroughfares, rural lanes all on the list of Bay Area's deadliest for riders," *San Francisco Chronicle*, March 16, 2008.

8. Susan Kelleher, "Seattle refuses to use salt; roads 'snow-packed' by design," *Seattle Times*, December 23, 2008.

9. See "Seattle's no-salt policy for snowy roads has even plows spinning wheels," *Seattle Times*, December 23, 2008.

10. CNN, "Snow Storm Hitting Part of the Midwest and Northeast causing Delays in Airports and on the Roads," December 20, 2008, http://transcripts.cnn.com/TRANSCRIPTS/0812/20/smn.01.html.

11. Terry Macalister, "Bedbugs make a return via low-cost flights," *The Guardian*, September 22, 2008.

12. "Itch to travel? Insects ride on Italian trains," Associated Press, October 8, 2005.

13. "Itchy Travel: Bedbugs Now in Planes, Trains and Automobiles Too," Jaunted.com, September 23, 2008.

14. See e.g., Jennifer 8. Lee, "Where Bedbugs Ride Around, Beside Just Beds," *New York Times*, May 9, 2008, http://cityroom.blogs.nytimes.com/2008/05/09/where-bedbugs-ride-around-besides-just-beds/?hp.

15. Centers for Disease Control and Prevention, "2008 West Nile Virus Activity in the United States (Reported to CDC as of October 14, 2008)," http://www.cdc.gov/ncidod/dvbid/westnile/surv&controlCaseCount08_detailed.htm (accessed October 16, 2008).

16. Center for Disease Control and Prevention, "West Nile Virus: What You Need to Know: CDC fact Sheet," http://www.cdc.gov/ncidod/dvbid/westnile/wnv_factsheet.htm (accessed January 26, 2009).

17. See e.g, Pesticide Action Network North America, "Keeping Perspective on West Nile Virus," August 22, 2005, http://www.panna.org/legacy/panups/panup_20050822.dv.html.

18. Beyond Pesticides, "Fight Asthma, Ask Your Child's School to Say No to Pesticides," http://www.beyondpesticides.org/schools/alerts/asthma.htm (accessed October 16, 2008).

19. See Steven Milloy, "Unwarranted Warning," *Washington Times*, April 21, 2000.

20. See Steven Milloy, "Congress working Hard to makes Schools Safe for Roaches and Rodents," FoxNews.com, June 25, 2001, http://www.foxnews.com/story/0,2933,27842,00.html.

21. See Jesse Tarbert, "Weeding out pesticides," *Seattle Times*, November 26, 2003.

22. For example, two studies, conducted by different researchers at different institutions, examined whether the spraying of insecticides like malathion in New York City in 1999 and 2000 to control the mosquitoes that carried West Nile virus were linked with emergency room visits for asthma-related

symptoms. Neither study could find any link. See B.C. O'Sullivan, J. Lafleur, K. Fridal, S. Hormozdi, S. Schwartz, M. Belt, and M. Finkel, "The effect of pesticide spraying on the rate and severity of ED asthma," American Journal of Emergency Medicine 23(4): 463-7, July 2005; and A.M. Karpati, M.C. Perrin, T. Matte, J. Leighton, J. Schwartz, and R.G. Barr, "Pesticide spraying for West Nile virus control and emergency department asthma visits in New York City, 2000," Environmental Health Perspectives 113(3):A150, March 2005.

23. See e.g., G.L. Chew, E.J. Carlton, D. Kass, M. Hernandez, B. Clarke, J. Tiven, R.Garfinckel, S. Nagle, and D. Evans, "Determinants of cockroach and mouse exposure and associations with asthma in families and elderly individuals living in New York City public housing," Annals of Allergy and Asthma Immunology 97(4):502-13, October 2006.

24. See e.g., Sylvia Perez, "Inhalers go green," ABC-7 Chicago, October 20, 2008, http://abclocal.go.com/wls/story?section=news/health&id=6454384.

25. Ibid.

26. See Steven Milloy, "Light Bulb Lunacy," JunkScience.com, April 26, 2007, http://www.junkscience.com/ByTheJunkman/20070426.html.

27. Bureau of Remediation and Waste Management, "What if I accidentally break a fluorescent lamp in my house?" Maine Department of Environmental Protection, http://www.state.me.us/dep/rwm/homeowner/cflbreakcleanup.htm (accessed October 16, 2008).

28. See Linda S. Birnbaum and Daniele F. Staskal, "Brominated flame retardants: cause for concern?" Environmental Health Perspectives 112(1): 9-17, January 2004.

29. Agency for Toxic Substances and Disease Registry, "Public Health Statement: Polybrominated Diphenyl Ethers," September 2004, http://www.atsdr.cdc.gov/toxprofiles/tp68-pbde-c1-b.pdf.

30. Nicholas K. Geranios, "Congressman says cut trees to stop wildfires," Associated Press, August 30, 1994.

31. Larry Mitchell, "Conservationists: Fire protection not easily obtained," Oroville Mercury Register, August 13, 2008.

32. See "US Fires Release Large Amounts of Carbon Dioxide," Science Daily, November 1, 2007, http://www.sciencedaily.com/releases/2007/11/071101085029.htm.

33. Natural Resources Defense Council, "Mercury in medical and Dental Products," http://www.nrdc.org/health/effects/mercury/everyday.asp (accessed October 17, 2008).

34. Robert F. Kennedy, Jr., "Deadly Immunity," Rolling Stone, June 20, 2005, http://www.rollingstone.com/politics/story/7395411/deadly_immunity/.

35. Robert F. Kennedy, Jr., "Attack on Mothers," HuffingtonPost.com, June 19, 2007, http://www.huffingtonpost.com/robert-f-kennedy-jr/attack-on-mothers_b_52894.html.

36. Ibid.

37. See Steven Milloy, "Vaccine Vindication," FoxNews.com, January 10, 2008, http://www.foxnews.com/story/0,2933,321887,00.html.

38. Centers for Disease Control and Prevention, "Update: Measles - January to July 2008," MMWR 57(33);893-896, August 22, 2008, http://www.cdc.gov/mmwr/preview/mmwrhtml/mm5733a1.htm.

39. Ibid.

40. Hillary Copsey, "Florida parents weight vaccinations against perceived autism risk," TCPalm, October 3, 2008, http://www.tcpalm.com/news/2008/oct/04/parents-weigh-vaccinations-perceived-risk-of/.

41. Thomas Homer-Dixon and David Keith, "Blocking the Sky to Save the Earth," *New York Times*, September 20, 2008.

42. "A changing climate of opinion?" *The Economist*, September 6, 2008.

43. "A changing climate of opinion?" *The Economist*, September 6, 2008.

Chapter 7

1. See http://www.ucsusa.org/news/press_release/nobel-peace-prize-should-spur-0068.html.

2. William P. Barrett, "America's 200 Largest Charities," Forbes, November 19, 2008.

3. David B. Ottoway and Joe Stephens, "Nonprofit Land Bank Amasses Billions," *Washington Post*, May 4, 2003.

4. General Motors, "The nature Conservancy and General Motors," http://www.gm.com/corporate/responsibili ty/reports/05/images/300_company/tnc.pdf (accessed January 29, 2009).

5. David Roberts, "The denial industry," *Grist*, September 19, 2006, http://gristmill.grist.org/story/2006/9/19/11408/1106.

6. David Robers, "On climate denialists and Nuremberg," *Grist*, October 12, 2006, http://gristmill.grist.org/story/2006/10/12/115734/52.

7. James Hansen, "Global Warming Twenty Years Later," Presentation at the National Press Club, June 23, 2008, http://www.columbia.edu/~jeh1/2008/TwentyYearsLater_20080623.pdf.

8. Cristine Russell, "Climate change: Now What?" Columbia Journalism Review, July/August 2008, http://www.cjr.org/feature/climate_change_now_what.php?page=1.

9. Andrew Bolt, "License to dissent," Andrew Bolt Blog, October 28, 2008, http://blogs.news.com.au/heraldsun/andrewbolt/index.php/heraldsun/com ments/licence_to_dissent/; Alex Lockwood, "Seeding doubt: how skeptics use new media to delay action on climate change," Paper delivered to the Association for Journalism Education (AJE) annual conference; and "New Media, New Democracy?" Sheffield University, September 12, 2008, http://www.ajeuk.org/papers/2008_09_12%20AJE%20Alex%20Lockwood.pdf.

10. Marie Woolf, "Blow to image of 'green' reusable nappy," *Sunday Times* (UK), October 19, 2008.

11. Brendan O'Neill, "Global warming: the chilling effect on free speech," Spiked-Online.com, October 6, 2006, http://www.spiked-online.com/index.php?/site/article/1782/.

12. Ibid.

13. Sharon Jayson, "Psychologists determine what it means to think 'green'," *USA Today*, August 14, 2008, http://www.usatoday.com/news/nation/environment/2008-08-13-green-psychology_N.htm

14. American Psychological Association, "Shaping Pro-Environment Behaviors: Certain Messages Work, Don't Work," http://www.psychologymatters.org/environment.html (accessed October 31, 2008).

15. Ibid.

16. Rainforest Action Network, "Rainforests in the Classroom," http://ran.org/campaigns/rainforests_in_the_classroom/; Rainforest Action Network, "Rainforest heroes: Heroes Corner," http://ran.org/index.php?id=956 (accessed October 4, 2008).

17. See e.g., Steven Milloy, "Turning Children Against Business," *New York Sun*, January 27, 2005.

18. Terence Corcoran, "CSR Backlash," *National Post*, January 15, 2005.

19. Rainforest Action Network, "Factsheets: Facts About Oil," http://www.ran.org/new/kidscorner/about_rainforests/factsheets/facts_about_oil/ (accessed October 4, 2008).

20. Rainforest Action Network, "Facts About Beef," http://ran.org/fileadmin/materials/education/factsheets/fs_beef.pdf.

21. Natural Resources Defense Council, "The Green Squad: Kids Taking Action for Greener, Healthier Schools," http://www.nrdc.org/greensquad/ (accessed October 4, 2008); Defenders of Wildlife, "Kids Planet," http://www.kidsplanet.org/ (accessed October 4, 2008); National Wildlife Federation, "Kids and Families," http://www.nwf.org/kids/ (accessed October 4, 2008); World Wildlife Fund, "Local Students Learn to 'Buy Different' at Local Scavenger Hunt" (Media release), November 15, 2003, http://www.worldwildlife.org/who/media/press/2003/WWFPresitem665.html; Environmental Defense Fund, "Low-Carbon Diet Kit," http://www.fightglobalwarming.com/documents/5129_BrochureFull.pdf (accessed October 4, 2008); Greenpeace, "Kids for Whales Toolkit," http://www.greenpeace.org/usa/assets/binaries/kidstoolkit (accessed October 4, 2008); and Lisa W. Foderaro, "Pint-Sized Eco-Police, Making Parents Proud and Sometimes Crazy," *New York Times*, October 10, 2008.

22. Darragh Johnson, "Climate Change scenarios Scare, Moivate Kids," Washington Post, April 16, 2007, http://www.washingtonpost.com/wp-dyn/content/article/2007/04/15/AR2007041501164.html.

23. Ibid.

24. Ibid.

25. Brian Balchaak, "Taking a Journey with Arctic Tale," MovieWeb.com, June 25, 2007, http://www.movieweb.com/news/85/20685.php

26. Sheigh Crabtree and Gina Piccalo, "It's not-a-doc - and the truth is inconvenient," *Los Angeles Times*, July 22, 2007.

27. Kyle Smith, "Narration is Unbearable," *New York Post*, July 25, 2007.

28. Lisa W. Foderaro, "Pint-Sized Eco-Police, Making Parents Proud and Sometimes Crazy," *New York Times*, October 10, 2008.

29. Ibid.

30. Ibid.

31. ClimateCops.com, "Download Your 'Climate Crime' Cards," http://www.climatecops.com/downloads/climate_cops_crime_cards.pdf (accessed October 4, 2008).

32. Ibid.

33. Eunice Yu and Jianguo Liu, "Environmental impacts of divorce," Proceedings of the National Academy of Sciences 104:51;20629-20634, December 18, 2007.

34. See Sarah Lyall, "Take Out the Rubbish Just So. It's British Law," *New York Times*, June 27, 2008, http://www.nytimes.com/2008/06/27/world/europe/27garbage.html.

35. Ibid.

36. See John Coté, "S.F. mayor proposes fines for unsorted trash," *San Francisco Chronicle*, August 1, 2008, http://www.sfgate.com/cgi-bin/article.cgi?f=/c/a/2008/08/01/MN47122A98.DTL.

37. Ibid.

38. Nicholas Kulish, "German City Wonders How Green Is Too Green," *New York Times*, August 7, 2008, http://www.nytimes.com/2008/08/07/world/europe/07solar.html.

39. Environmental Law institute, "A Citizen's Guide to Using Federal Environmental Laws to Secure Environmental Justice," 2002, http://yosemite.epa.gov/R10/ocrej.nsf/eb1daa9965e73fdf88256b800071a40b/280e766a6452517e882570ad00833d22/$FILE/citizen_guide_ej.pdf.

40. Bruce L. Benson, "Environmental Bounty-Hunting," OpinionJournal.com, August 9, 2006, http://www.opinionjournal.com/federation/feature/?id=110008731.

41. R.J. Smith, "Clean Water Act Sanity on the Horizon?" *Human Events*, June 30, 2006.

42. See "Wetlands first; people second," Washington Times, December 20, 1989; and R.J. Smith, "Clean Water Act Sanity on the Horizon?" *Human Events*, June 30, 2006.

43. U.S. Environmental Protection Agency, "Clean Water Act Violator Is Sentenced in Federal Court," July 14, 1989.

44. See Thomas Harvey Holt, "Running wild on wetlands," *Washington Times*, October 20, 1992.

45. R.J. Smith, "Clean Water Act Sanity on the Horizon?" *Human Events*, June 30, 2006.
46. See David Armstrong, "Environmental Injustice/ Troubled Investigations," *Boston Globe*, November 17, 1999.
47. See David Armstrong, "US Judge Rules EPA Harassed Mill Owner," *Boston Globe*, August 1, 2000.
48. Joseph Farah, "Gun control? Let's Start With the Feds," *Los Angeles Times*, August 19, 1997.
49. "Greenpeace protesters take over power plant," *The Guardian*, October 8, 2007.
50. "We caused £30,000 damage to save the planet," *Western Daily Press*, September 3, 2008.
51. Tom Pugh, "Goldsmith Takes Witness Stand in Power Station Protest Trial," Press Association Newsfile, September 4, 2008.
52. Michael McCarthy, "NASA scientist in court to demand urgent review of coal power stations," *The Independent*, September 4, 2008; and Christopher Booker, "A Pythonesque Week for the Warmists," *The Sunday Telegraph*, September 14, 2008.
53. Michael McCarthy, "Cleared: Jury decides that threat of global warming justifies breaking the law," *The Independent*, September 11, 2008.
54. Michelle Nichols, "Gore urges civil disobedience to stop coal plants," Reuters, September 24, 2008.
55. Gautam Naik, "Switzerland's Green Power Revolution: Ethicists Ponder Plant's Rights," *Wall Street Journal*, October 10, 2008, http://online.wsj.com/article/SB122359549477921201.html.
56. Ibid.

Chapter 8

1. Joanne Kaufman, "Completely Unplugged, Fully Green," *New York Times*, October 19, 2008.
2. Ibid.
3. Phuong Le, "Sparse plug-ins for electric cars spark creativity," Associated Press, October 19, 2008; John-Paul Flintoff, "Save wrapping paper—or use cloth," Green Central blog, October 20, 2008, http://timesonline.typepad.com/environment/2008/10/save-wrapping-p.html; and Tumbleweed Tiny House Company, http://www.tumbleweedhouses.com/jay/ (accessed November 17, 2008), and Carol Lloyd, "It's a small world for occupants of tiny houses," *San Francisco Chronicle*, April 29, 2007.
4. See Ian Rakowski, "Experts call for end of flushing toilets on World Toilet Day," November 19, 2008, http://www.news.com.au/story/0,27574,24670784-2,00.html.
5. See Moonbattery.com, "Moonbats Campaign Against Hygiene," September 27, 2007, http://www.moonbattery.com/archives/2007/09/moonbats_campai_1.html.

6. World Wildlife Fund, "Stopping Global Warming," http://www.worldwildlifefund.org/how/goodstuff/item8179.html (accessed October 8, 2008).

7. World Wildlife Fund, "Around the World: A Private Jet Expedition," http://www.worldwildlife.org/travel/2009/Africa/WWFTripitem7467.html (accessed October 8, 2008).

8. World Wildlife Fund, "Around the World: A Private Jet Expedition," http://www.worldwildlife.org/travel/2009/Africa/WWFTripitem7467.html (accessed October 8, 2008).

9. World Wildlife Fund, "Around the World: A Private Jet Expedition," (Brochure), http://www.worldwildlife.org/travel/2009/PDF's/WWFBinaryitem7982.pdf (accessed October 8, 2008).

10. Joe Stephens and David B. Ottaway, "Nonprofit Sells Scenic Acreage to Allies at a Loss; Buyers Gain Tax Breaks With Few Curbs on Land Use," *Washington Post*, May 6, 2003.

11. Ibid.

12. David B. Ottaway and Joe Stephens, "Landing a Big One: Preservation, Private Development," *Washington Post*, May 6, 2003.

13. David B. Ottaway and Joe Stephens, "Nonprofit Land Bank Amasses Billions; Charity Builds Assets on Corporate Partnerships," *Washington Post*, May 4, 2003.

14. Ellen McGirt, "Al Gore's $100 Million Makeover," *Fast Company*, December 19, 2007.

15. Tennessee Center for Policy Research, "Al Gore's Personal Energy Use Is His Own 'Inconvenient Truth'," February 26, 2007, http://www.tennesseepolicy.org/main/article.php?article_id=367&cat=10.

16. See Steven Milloy, "Al Gore's Inconvenient Electric Bill," FoxNews.com, March 12, 2007.

17. See Steven Milloy, "Al Gore's Congressional Lovefest," FoxNews.com, March 25, 2007, http://www.foxnews.com/story/0,2933,260485,00.html.

18. Jon Gertner, "Capitalism to the Rescue," *New York Times Magazine*, October 5, 2008.

19. Ibid.

20. Ibid.

21. Robert F. Kennedy, Jr., "Coal's True Cost," HuffingtonPost.com, November 29, 2007, http://www.huffingtonpost.com/robert-f-kennedy-jr/coals-true-cost_b_74738.html.

22. Robert F. Kennedy, Jr., "The Next President's First Task [A Manifesto]," *Vanity Fair*, May 2008, http://www.vanityfair.com/politics/features/2008/05/rfk_manifesto200805.

23. Ibid.

24. "White House Unbuttons Formal Dress Code," *New York Times*, January 28, 2009.

25. The O Interview, "Oprah Talks to Richard Branson," *O, The Oprah Magazine*, December 1, 2007.

26. See Andrew Ross Sorkin, "On an Island Paradise, Seeking Global Warming's Silver Lining," *New York Times*, March 22, 2008.

27. Ibid.

28. Jane Memmler, "Virgin territory for green tycoon," *The Express*, February 24, 2007.

29. Ibid.

30. Ibid.

31. Paul Oswell, "An eco-protagonist—Virgin Limited edition's managing director believes strongly in sustainable luxury eco-tourism," Luxury Travel, January 17, 2008.

32. Steven Price, "Branson pledges $3B to fight global warming," CNN-Money.com, September 21, 2006.

33. "Branson's bogus eco-drive," *Sunday Business Post* (Ireland), August 3, 2008.

34. Richard Branson, "Branson: pledge is the real thing," *Sunday Business Post*, August 10, 2008.

35. Steven Price, "Branson pledges $3B to fight global warming," CNN-Money.com, September 21, 2006.

36. Google, "Google Announces Investments in Clean Energy and Green Technology," June 19, 2007,
http://www.google.com/intl/en/press/pressrel/cleanenergy_20070619.html.

37. See, Kevin J. Delaney, J. Lunn Lunsford, and Mark Maremont, "Wide-Flying Moguls: Google duo's New Jet Is a Boeing 767-200," *Wall Street Journal*, November 4, 2005; and Jordan Golson, "Bill Clinton flies to Africa on Google founder's party plane—until it breaks down," *The Industry Standard*, August 1, 2008, http://www.thestandard.com/news/ 2008/08/01/president-flies-africa-google-founders-party-plane-until-it-breaks-down; and Nick Denton, "Sergey's Icy Bachelor Party," ValleyWag.com, May 7, 2007, http://valleywag.com/tech/top/sergeys-icy-bachelor-party-258336.php.

38. Eric Kane, "How Green is Google?" TreeHugger.com, October 10, 2006, http://www.treehugger.com/files/2006/10/how_green_is_go.php.

39. See Evan Halper, "This puts your commute to shame," *Los Angeles Times*, March 7, 2008.

40. "Arnold Targets Global Warming," Associated Press, June 2, 2005, http://www.cbsnews.com/stories/2005/06/02/tech/main699281.shtml.

41. California Assembly Bill 32, "California "Global Warming Solutions Act of 2006," see fact sheet at
http://www.arb.ca.gov/cc/factsheets/ab32factsheet.pdf, and California Senate Bill 375, available at http://info.sen.ca.gov/pub/07-08/bill/sen/sb_0351-0400/sb_375_bill_20080930_chaptered.pdf.

42. University of Exeter, "Bleeding-heart jetsetters spell bad news for climate," October 29, 2008, http://www.exeter.ac.uk/news/newsjetsetters.shtml.

43. See T. Boone Pickens, "My Plan to Escape the Grip of Foreign Oil," *Wall Street Journal*, July 9, 2008.

44. Steven Milloy, "Pickens Gives to Meaning to 'Self-Government'," July 31, 2008, http://www.foxnews.com/story/0,2933,395304,00.html.

45. Ibid.

46. Ibid.

47. Susan Berfield, "There will be water," *Businessweek*, June 12, 2008, http://www.businessweek.com/magazine/content/08_25/b4089040017753.htm.

48. Janet M. Eaton and Ruth Caplan, "Water for People and Nature: The Story of corporate Water Privatization," Sierra Club, April 2004, http://www.sierraclub.org/committees/cac/water/ppt/Sierra_Web_4-1-04.pdf.

49. Energy Information Administration, "How much does the Federal Government spend on energy-specific subsidies and support?" U.S. Department of Energy, September 8, 2008, http://tonto.eia.doe.gov/energy_in_brief/energy_subsidies.cfm.

50. James Kanter, "Europe Is Forcing Airlines To Buy Emissions Permits," *New York Times*, October 25, 2008.

Chapter 9

1. See e.g, Sourcewatch Encyclopedia, "Corporate Social Responsibility," http://www.sourcewatch.org/index.php?title=Corporate_Social_Responsibility (accessed September 22, 2008).

2. See Steven J. Milloy and Thomas J. Borelli, "Pensions in Peril: Are State Officials Risking Public Employee Retirement Benefits by Playing Global Warming Politics?" September 2008, http://www.nationalcenter.org/NPA575.html.

3. General Electric Company, "GE 2006 citizenship Report: Solving Big Needs," http://www.ge.com/citizenship/downloads/GE_2006_citizen_06rep.pdf, and Ceres, "About us," http://www.ceres.org/NETCOMMUNITY/Page.aspx?pid=415&srcid=705 (accessed September 22, 2008).

4. Center for Global Sustainability, "Research on Sustainability Practices by the Fortune 500," University of Dallas, April 25, 2008, http://www.udallas.edu/gsm/cr/resources/Apr25ReportonSustain.pdf.

5. General Electric Company, "GE 2006 citizenship Report: Solving Big Needs," http://www.ge.com/citizenship/downloads/GE_2006_citizen_06rep.pdf.

6. Arthur B. Laffer, Andrew Coors, and Wayne Winegarden, "Does corporate Social Responsibility Enhance Business Profitability," Laffer Associates, January 2005.

7. Citigroup, "Citizenship Report 2005," http://www.citigroup.com/citi/citizen/data/citizen05_en.pdf; Citigroup, "Citizenship Report 2006,"

http://www.citigroup.com/citi/citizen/data/citizen06_en.pdf; and Citigroup, "Citizenship Report 2007," http://www.citigroup.com/citi/ citi-zen/data/citizen07_en.pdf.

8. Citigroup, "2008 Proxy Statement," March 13, 2008, http://www.citigroup.com/citi/fin/data/ar08cp.pdf?ieNocache=343.

9. Equator Principles Financial Institutions, "The Equator Principles," http://www.equator-principles.com/index.shtml (accessed September 23, 2008).

10. Energy Information Administration, "Impacts of the Kyoto Protocol on U.S. Energy Markets and Economic Activity," SR/OIAF/98-03, October 1998, http://www.eia.doe.gov/emeu/plugs/plkyoto.html.

11. Terry Dinan and Diane Lim, "Who Gains and Who Pays Under Carbon-Allowance Trading? The Distributional Effects of Alternative Policy Designs," Congressional Budget Office, June 2000.

12. Arthur Laffer and Wayne Winegarden, "The Adverse Impacts of Cap-and-Trade Regulations," Arduin, Laffer & Moore Econometrics, September 2007.

13. Prepared Statement of Anne E. Smith, Ph.D., at the Legislative Hearing on America's Climate Security Act of 2007, S.2191 of the Committee on Environment and Public Works United States Senate, Washington, DC, November 8, 2007, http://epw.senate.gov/public/index.cfm? FuseAction=Files.View&FileStore_id=80bc79be-c338-4a76-b438-205eb79da3d5.

14. U.S. Environmental Protection Agency, "The United States Environmental Protection Agency's Analysis of Senate Bill S.2191 in the 110th Congress, the Lieberman-Warner Climate Security Act of 2008," March 2008, available at http://www.epa.gov/climatechange/economics/ economicanaly-ses.html as of September 2, 2008.

15. The companies include Alcoa, American International Group, Boston Scientific Corporation, BP America, Caterpillar, Chrysler, ConocoPhillips, Deere & Company, The Dow Chemical Company, Duke Energy, DuPont, Exelon Corporation, Ford Motor Company, FPL Group, Inc., General Electric, General Motors Corp., Johnson & Johnson, Marsh, Inc., NRG Energy, PepsiCo, PG&E Corporation, PNM Resources, Rio Tinto, Shell, Siemens Corporation, and Xerox Corporation. The green groups are Environmental Defense, National Wildlife Federation, Natural Resources Defense Council, Nature Conservancy, and World Resources Institute. See U.S. Climate Action Partnership, http://www.us-cap.org (accessed September 20, 2008).

16. See willyoujoinus.com.

17. See willyoujoinus.com/takeaction/EnergyGenerator/.

18. See e.g., Betsy McKay, "Pepsi to Cut Plastic Use in Bottles," *Wall Street Journal*, May 6, 2008, http://online.wsj.com/article/SB121004395479169979.html.

19. Andrew Martin, "Tap Water's Popularity Forces Pepsi To Cut Jobs," *New York Times*, October 15, 2008.

20. "SEC denies General Electric bid to block global warming shareholder proposal; Amid economic downturn, GE should justify lobbying for economy-harming legislation, says Free Enterprise Action Fund" (Ticker: FEAOX), Free Enterprise Action Fund, January 24, 2008, http://www.freeenterpriseactionfund.com/release012408.htm.

21. General Electric Company, "Notice of Annual Meeting and 2008 Proxy Statement," March 10, 2008, http://www.ge.com/files/usa/en/ar2007/pdfs/ge_proxy2008.pdf.

22. See Thomas J. Borelli, "Serving Caterpillar at the Global Warming Table," Townhall.com, July 28, 2007, http://townhall.com/Columnists/TomBorelli/2007/07/28/serving_caterpillar _at_the_global_warming_table?page=full&comments=true.

23. Goldman Sachs, "Things Are Heating Up: Economic Issue and Opportunities From Global warming," February 8, 2007.

24. Goldman Sachs, "Environment: Principal Investments," http://www2.goldmansachs.com/citizenship/environment/business-initiatives.html (accessed September 23, 2008).

25. Morgan Stanley, "Morgan Stanley to Invest in $3bn of Emissions Reduction Credits and Other related Initiatives" (Media Relase), October 26, 2006, http://www.newswire.ca/en/releases/archive/October2006/26/c4798.html.

26. See Lehman Brothers, "The Business of Climate Change," February 2007, http://www.lehman.com/who/intellectual_capital/climate_change_i.htm; Lehman Brothers, "The Business of Climate Change II," September 20, 2007, http://www.lehman.com/who/intellectual_capital/climate_ change_ii.htm; Michael Szabo, "Lehman Brothers Shuts carbon trading desk," Reuters, September 16, 2008; Lehman Brothers, "Lehman Brothers Announces CDM Purchase Agreement with China Guodian Corporation," July 2, 2008, http://www.lehman.com/press/news/070208_china_guodion.htm.

27. Betsy Morris, "Idealist on Board," *Fortune*, April 3, 2000, and Ford Motors Co., "Sustainability," http://www.ford.com/about-ford/company-information/corporate-sustainability/sustainability-reports (accessed September 26, 2008).

28. Jamie Butters, "Ford: Hybrids Need a Boost from U.S.; CEO Says He's Willing to Accept Higher Gas Taxes," *Detroit Free Press*, April 8, 2004.

29. Ken Thomas, "Ford CEO Alan Mulally says effort to regain profits going well," September 8, 2008.

30. Betsy Morris, "Idealist on Board," *Fortune*, April 3, 2000.

31. See e.g., Kate Kelly and Ann Davis, "Goldman's Green Streak Is Questioned As Two Investors Seek Focus on Profit," *Wall Street Journal*, March 27, 2007.

32. Clive Thompson, "A Green Coal Baron?" *New York Times Magazine*, June 22, 2008, http://www.nytimes.com/2008/06/22/magazine/22Rogers-t.html.
33. Ibid.
34. Ibid.
35. Nick Bunkley, "With Demand Slipping for Its Pickups and S.U.V.'s, G.M. Will Lay Off 3,550," *New York Times*, April 29, 2008, http://www.nytimes.com/2008/04/29/business/29auto.html, and Ageence France Presse, "Ford cuts truck, SUV production, lowers profit outlook," May 22, 2008, http://afp.google.com/article/ALeqM5jSe8dOn H0PC3LZOc9QgJA8Pbur7Q.
36. "Moody's may cut GM, Chrysler on falling SUV demand," Reuters, July 16, 2008, http://in.reuters.com/article/ governmentFil-ingsNews/idINN1535076820080715.
37. Danny Hakim, "S.U.V. and Pickup Sales Are Likely to Grow," *New York Times*, February 3, 2003, http://query.nytimes.com/gst/ full-page.html?res=9907E5D61238F930A35751C0A9659C8B63, and Energy Information Administration, "Monthly U.S. All Grades All Formulations Retail Gasoline Prices," September 22, 2008, http://tonto.eia.doe.gov/dnav/pet/hist/mg_tt_usM.htm.
38. Matthew Bandyk, "Rising fuel Prices Squeeze U.S. Airlines," *U.S. News & World Report*, April 23, 2008, http://www.usnews.com/articles/business/economy/2008/04/23/rising-fuel-prices-squeeze-us-airlines.html.
39. Starbucks Corp., "Starbucks Increases Number of U.S. company-Operated Store Closures as Part of Transformation Strategy" (Media Release), July 1, 2008, http://www.starbucks.com/aboutus/pressdesc.asp?id=877; and Star-bucks corp., "Starbucks Reports Preliminary Q2 Results and Revises Fiscal 2008 Outlook," (Media Release), April 23, 2008, http://www.starbucks.com/aboutus/pressdesc.asp?id=860.
40. Marc Gunther, "The Mosquito in the Tent," *Fortune*, May 31, 2004, and *Wall Street Journal*, "Citigroup, Environmental Group Reach Pact," January 24, 2004.
41. "Running Over Citi; Banking Goliath Citigroup Agrees to Environmental Screens for Project Financing in the Developing World," *Multinational Monitor*, February 29, 2004.
42. Robert Julavits, "Group gets Citi Pact, Targeting Others," *American Banker*, January 23, 2004.
43. Ibid.
44. Greg Morcroft, "Environmental group prods banks on lending standards," CBS MarketWatch, March 11, 2004; and Associated Press, "Bank of America pledges to cut emissions, protect rainforests," May 18, 2004.
45. Rainforest Action Network, "Environmental Activists 'grill' Wells Fargo for Not Getting on the Wagon" (Media Release), Ascribe Newswire, July 13, 2004.
46. Wells Fargo, "Wells Fargo & Company Announces 10-Point environmen-

tal commitment, $1 Billion Lending Target," PR Newswire, July 11, 2005.

47. Alison Leigh Cowan, "Taking Protest to a Corporate Chief's Street, 3 Activists Face Charges in Greenwich," *New York Times*, March 13, 2005.

48. Rainforest Action Network, "Investment Inspectors Visit JP Morgan Chase's New York Headquarters, U.S. Branches Today; Yale Students Tie Giant Green Ribbons on Greenwich, Conn., Trees to Remind CEO Bill Harrison to keep His Environmental promises," Ascribe Newswire, April 11, 2005.

49. JPMorgan Chase, "JPMorgan Chase Announces Environmental Policy," Business Wire, April 25, 2005.

50. Bank of America, Form 14A DEF, March 19, 2008.

Chapter 10

1. International Atomic Energy Agency, "Nuclear Power Worldwide: Status and Outlook," October 23, 2007, http://www.iaea.org/NewsCenter/PressReleases/2007/prn200719.html.

2. CBC News, "Harper's letter dismisses Kyoto as 'socialist scheme'," January 30, 2007, http://www.cbc.ca/canada/story/2007/01/30/harper-kyoto.html.

3. See e.g., Mark Milner, "Carbon trading market fluctuates wildly after figures released early," *The Guardian*, May 1, 2006, http://www.guardian.co.uk/business/2006/may/01/europeanunion.

4. Jeremy Rifkin, "A precautionary tale," *The Guardian*, May 12, 2004.

5. Business Roundtable, "The Benefits of Trade Liberalization," http://trade.businessroundtable.org/trade_basics/trade_liberalization.html (accessed October , 12, 2008).

6. Daniel T. Griswold, "Trade, Labor and the environment: How Blue and Green Sanctions Threaten Higher Standards," Cato Institute, August 2, 2001, http://www.freetrade.org/pubs/pas/tpa-015b.pdf.

7. See Paul K. Driessen, Eco-Imperialism, http://www.eco-imperialism.com/main.php (accessed October 12, 2008).

8. U.S. Department of Defense, "Question and Answer Session with Secretary gates following remarks at National Defense University's Distinguished Lecture program at Ft. Leslie J. McNair," September 29, 2008, http://www.defenselink.mil/transcripts/transcript.aspx?transcriptid=4295.

9. "Liquid coal industry Seeks New DOD Contracts Amid GHG Concerns," *Carbon Control News*, September 22, 2008.

10. "Defense Bill Agreement Omits Clarification on Lifecycle GHGs from Fuels," *Carbon Control News*, September 24, 2008.

11. See e.g., Robert Bonnie, "Corn Ethanol: The Importance of Performance-based Standards," Climate 411 Blog (Environmental Defense), April 29, 2008, http://blogs.edf.org/climate411/2008/04/29/corn_ethanol_standards/.

12. See Boeing, "E-3 Airborne Warning and Control System (AWACS) Back-grounder," http://www.boeing.com/defense-space/ic/awacs/docs/E-

3AWACS_overview.pdf (accessed October 12, 2008).

13. "DOD Takes Unprecedented Step in Listing GFHG As "Emerging Contaminant," *Carbon Control News,* July 30, 2008.

14. Ibid.

15. Ibid.

16. Deborah Ottinger Shaeffer, Ravi Kantamaneni, and Marian Van Pelt, "Global Emissions of SF6 and the Cost of Reducing Them: EPA's Global Emissions and Mitigation Reports," U.S. Environmental Protection Agency, December 28, 2006, http://www.epa.gov/electricpower-sf6/documents/conf06_ottinger_schaefer.pdf (accessed October 12, 2008).

17. Office of the Director of Defense Research and Engineering, "The Effect of Windmill Farms on Military Readiness," 2006, http://www1.eere.energy.gov/windandhydro/federalwindsiting/pdfs/dod_windfarms.pdf.

18. Magnus Linklater and Dominic Kennedy, "Wind farms 'a threat to national security," *Times* (UK), February 4, 2008.

19. "Axis of rejection? U.S., Iran, North Korea snub nuclear test ban pact," Reuters, September 25, 2008.

20. Deborah Zabarenko, "US Army Works to Cut Its Carbon 'Bootprint'," Reuters, July 26, 2008, http://www.reuters.com/article/environment News/idUSN2641421220080727.

21. See e.g., Michael Mann, "Frantically, the Army tries to armor humvees," April 15, 2004, http://www.msnbc.msn.com/id/4731185/.

22. Ibid.; and *60 Minutes*, "Battle of Sadr City," October 12, 2008.

23. Deborah Zabarenko, "US Army Works to Cut Its Carbon 'Bootprint'," Reuters, July 26, 2008, http://www.reuters.com/article/environment News/idUSN2641421220080727.

24. Natural Resources Defense Council, "Navy Sued Over Harm to Whales From Mid-Frequency Sonar" (Media Release), October 19, 2005, http://www.nrdc.org/media/pressreleases/051019.asp.

25. Kenneth R. Weiss, "Judge Curbs Navy sonar - use of sonic blasts in exercises, which fleet officials argue are crucial for training, is ruled harmful to whales," *Los Angeles Times*, August 7 2007.

26. Kenneth R. Weiss, "Navy given choice: new safeguards or no sonar," *Los Angeles Times*, November 14, 2007, http://articles.latimes.com/2007/nov/14/local/me-sonar14.

27. Deena Beasley, "Appeals court rejects sonar waiver for Navy," Reuters, March 1, 2008, http://www.reuters.com/article/environment News/idUSN0135713620080301.

28. Ibid.

29. *Winter v.Natural Resources Defense Council*, No.-07-1239, November 12, 2008.

30. "The Greens Get Harpooned," *Wall Street Journal,* November 13, 2008.

31. "Sonar Over Whales," *New York Times,* November 15, 2008.

32. Natural Resources Defense Council, "NRDC Report Finds Current U.S. Nuclear War Plan Main Barrier to Reducing Stockpiles" (Media Release), June 18, 2001; and Natural Resources Defense Council, "Bush Administration Wasting Billions on Nuclear Weapons Stockpile Research and Production, Report Charges" (Media Release), April 13, 2004, https://www.nrdc.org/media/pressReleases/040413.asp.

33. Natural Resources Defense Council, "Environmental Groups settle Missile Defense Lawsuit Against Defense Department" (Media Release), March 18, 2002, https://www.nrdc.org/media/pressreleases/020318.asp.

34. Peter Schwartz and Doug Randall, "An Abrupt Climate Change Scenario and Its Implications for United States National Security," Environmental Defense, October 2003, http://www.edf.org/documents/3566_AbruptClimateChange.pdf.

35. "Bush Opposition To Defense Bill Snags Landmark Climate Change Review," *Carbon Control News,* January 3, 2008.

36. "Speech by Mr. Jacques Chirac, French President, to the VIth Conference of the Parties to the United Nations Framework convention on Climate Change," November 20, 2000, accessed at http://www.sovereignty.net/center/chirac.html.

37. "Address by Prime Minister Wim Kok at the sixth Conference of the Parties to the UN Framework Convention on Climate Change," November 20, 2000, accessed at http://www.minaz.nl/dsc?c=getobject&s=obj&objectid=4488.

38. John Drexhage, "Climate Change and Global Governance: Which Way Ahead?" International Institute for Sustainable Development, 2007, http://www.iisd.org/pdf/2007/geg_which_way_ahead.pdf.

39. See Louise Gray, "Lawyers call for international court for the environment," *Daily Telegraph* (UK), November 28, 2008.

40. John Fonte, "Global Governance vs. the Liberal democratic Nation-State: What is the Best Regime?" *The 2008 Bradley Symposium,* June 4, 2008, http://pcr.hudson.org/files/publications/2008_Bradley_Symposium_Fonte_Essay.pdf.

41. Ibid.

42. See e.g., United Nations Environment Programme, "First Workshop for Environmental Journalists," November 26-28, 2002, http://www.unep.org/roa/DOCS/Ms_word/First%20Workshop%20for%20Environmental%20Journalists-Report.doc.

43. See e.g, Steven Milloy, "FDA may make Breathing difficult for Asthmatics," FoxNews.com, January 26, 2006, http://www.foxnews.com/story/0,2933,182944,00.html.

44. Baker Spring, Steven Groves, and Brett D. Schafer, "The Top Five reasons Why conservatives Should Oppose the U.N. Convention on the Law of the Sea," Heritage Foundation (Web Memo #1638), September 25, 2007, http://www.heritage.org/Research/InternationalOrganizations/wm1638.cfm.

45. International Institute for Sustainable Development Reporting Services, "A Special Report on Selected Side Events at the UNFCCC SB28," June 2, 2008, http://www.iisd.ca/climate/sb28/enbots/2.html.

46. Energy Information Administration, "Emissions of Greenhouse Gases Report," U.S. Department of Energy, November 28, 2007, http://www.eia.doe.gov/oiaf/1605/ggrpt/carbon.html; and Bureau of Public Affairs, "U.S. Financial Contributions to the United Nations System," September 20, 2007, http://www.state.gov/r/pa/scp/92625.htm.

47. "Tax and Wane," *Investors Business Daily*, December 14, 2007.

Chapter 11

1. Scott Fornek, "Green day: Obama gets Sierra Club backing," *Chicago Sun-Times*, February 6, 2004.

2. John Stanton, "Environmental Groups Hitch Wagon To Obama's Rising Star," *CongressDaily* August 4, 2004.

3. Ibid.

4. "We're not robbing food from people's mouths," The Real News Network, November 2, 2008.

5. "Under Obama, Dark Days Seen Ahead for Fossil Fuels," CNNMoney.com, November 5, 2008.

6. "Barack Obama and Joe Biden: Promoting a Healthy Environment," http://www.barackobama.com/pdf/issues/EnvironmentFactSheet.pdf (accessed November 5, 2008).

7. Clive Thompson, "A Green Coal Baron?" *New York Times Magazine*, June 22, 2008, http://www.nytimes.com/2008/06/22/magazine/22Rogers-t.html.

8. This estimate is based on a straight line extrapolation of Rogers' cost estimate for the Lieberman-Warner bill.

9. "Barack Obama and Joe Biden: Promoting a Healthy Environment," http://www.barackobama.com/pdf/issues/EnvironmentFactSheet.pdf (accessed November 5, 2008).

10. See e.g., "The Obama-Biden Plan," http://change.gov/agenda/energy_and_environment_agenda/ (accessed February 5, 2009).

11. See Steven Milloy, "Senate Barely Squelches Mercury Panic," FoxNews.com, September 15, 2005, http://www.foxnews.com story/0,2933,169513,00.html.

12. See e.g., "Obama: Tax Coal Plants," *Wheeling News-Register*, November 4, 2008.

13. See Steven Milloy, "Candidates Don't Come Clean on Coal," FoxNews.com, October 16, 2008, http://www.foxnews.com/story/0,2933,439321,00.html.

14. Robert F. Kennedy, Jr., "Coal's True Cost," The Huffington Post, http://www.huffingtonpost.com/robert-f-kennedy-jr/coals-true-cost_b_74738.html?page=3&show_comment_id=10551178#comment_10551178.

15. Greenpeace, "Mine, Baby, Mine: Pre-Debate Facts on Coal, Oil, Nuclear and Clean Energy" (Media Release), October 15, 2008.
16. See e.g., "Barack Obama on Yucca Mountain," *Las Vegas Sun*, http://www.lasvegassun.com/politics/voterguide/2008/barack-obama/issues/yucca/ (accessed February 5, 2009).
17. See e.g., "Barack Obama and Joe Biden: Promoting a Healthy Environment," http://www.barackobama.com/pdf/issues/ EnvironmentFact-Sheet.pdf (accessed February 5, 2009).
18. See e.g., Christopher Hass, "A Serious Energy Policy for Our Future," http://my.barackobama.com/page/community/post/stateupdates/gG5RCv (accessed February 5, 2009).
19. American Petroleum Institute, "Facts About Non-producing Leases," http://www.energytomorrow.com/energy/Facts_about_Non_Producing_Lea ses.aspx (accessed November 5, 2008).
20. *FOX News Sunday*, November 9, 2008.
21. "Barack Obama and Joe Biden: New Energy for America," http://www.barackobama.com/pdf/factsheet_energy_speech_080308.pdf (accessed February 5, 2009).
22. Ibid.
23. Ibid.
24. Ibid.
25. See e.g., "Barack Obama and Joe Biden: Promoting a Healthy Environment," http://www.barackobama.com/pdf/issues/ EnvironmentFact-Sheet.pdf (accessed February 5, 2009).
26. Ibid.
27. Jim Efstathiou, Jr., "Obama to Declare Carbon Dioxide Dangerous Pollutant," Bloomberg.com, October 16, 2008.
28. See *Massachusetts* v. *Environmental Protection Agency,* 549 U.S. 497 (2007).
29. "Waxman chairmanship Sets Stage for More Aggressive Climate Action," *Carbon Control News*, November 20, 2008.
30. See Socialist International, "Commission for a Sustainable World Society: The members of the Commission," http://www.socialistinternational.org/viewArticle.cfm?ArticleID=1845&&ModuleID=34 (accessed January 2, 2009).
31. Joyce Price, "EPA broke law, panel charges; Bipartisan letter cites 'prohibited grass-roots lobbying'," *Washington Times*, March 22, 1995.
32. "Obama's Carbon Busters," *Wall Street Journal*, December 12, 2008.
33. See e.g., "'I will not be silenced,' EPA Administrator Insists," *St. Louis-Post Dispatch*, March 5, 1995.
34. See e.g., "Termite Guts Can Save the Planet, Says Nobel Laureate," April 13, 2005, http://www.physorg.com/news3700.html, and http://wonkroom.thinkprogress.org/2008/12/06/steven-chu-beautiful-planet/.
35. "Steven Chu: 'Coal is My Worst Nightmare'," Environmental Capital blog, December 11, 2008, http://blogs.wsj.com/environmentalcapital/

2008/12/11/steven-chu-coal-is-my-worst-nightmare/.

36. Daryl Lease, "Invest in pests, not politicians," *Sarasota Herald-Tribune*, December 17, 2007; and "Termite guts can save the planet," Physorg.com, April 13, 2005, http://www.physorg.com/news3700.html.

37. Jennifer Washburn, "An unholy alliance? UC Berkeley's $500-million deal with BP challenges traditional public-private partnerships," *Sacramento Bee*, April 8, 2007.

38. As quoted in Steven Milloy, "Greens Exploit Wall Street Bailout," JunkScience.com, October 2, 2008, http://junkscience.com/ ByThe-Junkman/20081002.html.

39. "Activists for NEPA Climate Reviews by Bailed Out Companies," *Carbon Control News*, September 26, 2008.

40. See e.g., Thomas Friedman, "Green the Bailout," New York Times, September 28, 2008.

41. Caroline Lucas, "Chasing economic growth doesn't add up in the long term," New Scientist, October 26, 2008, http://www.greenparty.org.uk/news/2008-10-26-newscientist.html.

42. Christopher Booker, "President-elect Barack Obama proposes economic suicide for US," *Daily Telegraph*, November 29, 2008, http://www.telegraph.co.uk/opinion/main.jhtml?xml=/opinion/2008/11/30/do3010.xml.

Chapter 12

1. See Keith Johnson, "Not So Green: Voters Nix Most Environmental State Ballot Measures," Environmental Capital blog, November 5, 2008, http://blogs.wsj.com/environmentalcapital/2008/11/05/not-so-green-vot-ers-nix-most-environmental-state-ballot-measures/.

2. See "AIF Poll Shows Support for Drilling," *St. Petersburg Times*, August 27, 2008.

3. Peter O'Neil, "Efforts to support global climate-change falls: Poll," *Windsor Star*, November 27, 2008.

4. Greg Easterbook, "Al Gore's Outsourcing Solution," *New York Times*, March 9, 2007.

5. Mure Dicke and Jo Johnson, "Beijing and Dehli resist calls to cap their CO_2," *Financial Times*, December 5, 2007.

6. Energy Information Administration, "Trend in U.S. Carbon Intensity and Total Greenhouse Gas Intensity," Department of Energy, December 2004, http://www.eia.doe.gov/oiaf/1605/archive/gg04rpt/trends.html.

7. Ben & Jerry's, "What does dioxin have to do with ice cream?" http://benjerry.custhelp.com/cgi-bin/benjerry.cfg/php/enduser /std_adp.php?p_faqid=362&p_created=1191594013&p_sid=VArvWWgj& p_accessibility=0&p_redirect=&p_lva=&p_sp=cF9zcmNoPTEmcF9zb3J0 X2J5PSZwX2dyaWRzb3J0PSZwX3Jvd19jbnQ9MSwxJnBfcHJvHM9JnBfY 2F0cz0wJnBfcHY9JnBfY3Y9JnBfc2VhcmNoX3R5cGU9YW5zd2Vycy5zZW

FyY2hfZXgmcF9wYWdlPTEmcF9zZWFyY2hfdGV4dD1qdW5rc2NpZW5j
ZS5jb20*&p_li=&p_topview=1 (accessed October 21, 2008).

8. Antonio Regalado, "Global Warring: In Climate Debate, The 'Hockey Stick' Leads to a Face-Off—Nonscientist Assails a Graph Environmentalists Use, And He Gets a Hearing—Defenders Call Attack Political," *Wall Street Journal*, February 14, 2005.

9. See Randy Hall, "University: Watch Al Gore Movie or Don't Graduate," May 9, 2007, http://archive.newsmax.com/archives/ic/2007/5/9/101302.shtml.

10. Ibid.

11. See Steven Milloy, "Climate-Controlled Classroom," FoxNews.com, May 10, 2007, http://www.foxnews.com/story/0,2933,271256,00.html.

12. Joel Schwarcz, "Scientific ignorance is no laughing matter," *Hamilton Spectator* (Ontario, Canada), February 21, 2998.

13. Mike Kerwick, "Live Earth rocks New Jersey with a global movement," *The Record* (Bergen, NJ), July 8, 2007.

14. See http://www.youtube.com/watch?v=XDI2NVTYRXU.

15. See Library of Congress, "1997 Byrd-Hagel Resolution," http://thomas.loc.gov/cgi-bin/bdquery/z?d105:s.res.00098:.

16. Lucette Lagnado, "Strained Peace," *Wall Street Journal*, July 30, 1999.
17 See Natural Resources Conservation Service, "Conservation Reserve Program," U.S. Department of Agriculture, http://www.nrcs.usda.gov /programs/CRP/ (accessed October 24, 2008).

INDEX